THE MAN
WHO DISOBEYED

THE MAN WHO DISOBEYED

SIR HORACE SMITH-DORRIEN
AND HIS ENEMIES

by
A. J. SMITHERS

LEO COOPER · LONDON

© 1970 A. J. SMITHERS
First published in 1970 by
LEO COOPER LIMITED
196 Shaftesbury Avenue WC2

ISBN 085052 030 4

Printed in Great Britain by
Clarke, Doble and Brendon Limited
at Plymouth

ILLUSTRATIONS

1	Lieutenant H. L. Smith-Dorrien, 95th Foot, 1878	*facing page* 16
2	*Right:* Survivors from Isandhlwana, 1879 *Left:* Egypt, 1885	17
3	Isandhlwana	32
4	Queen Victoria's last General, 1901	33
5	The Smith-Dorrien—Apthorpe Gough team, Lucknow 1895	64
6	Civic reception at Berkhampstead, 1901	64
7	Boer War General	65
8	Lady Smith-Dorrien	80
9	With Sir Evelyn Wood, about 1908	81
10	With General Nogi, 1911	128
11	With his mother, 1901	129
12	GOC-in-C, Aldershot, 1911	144
13	Royal visit to Aldershot	145
14	Presentation of the Army Cup to the 2nd Bn Sherwood Foresters	145
15	In attendance on President Poincaré and the Prince of Wales, 1913	176
16	With Lady Smith-Dorrien and Gren, 1912	177
17	Picture postcard of 1914	192
18	'Mons': still from a film of 1924	193

19	The Cameronians at La-Ferté-sous-Jouarre, 1914	*facing page* 193
20	French cavalry passing through 19th Bde, 1914	208
21	Scots Guards marching down the Menin road, 1914	209
22	Supply column in Flanders	209
23	The popular hero, 1915	224
24	With David, Gibraltar 1918	225
25	Off parade, Gibraltar 1920	225
26	With Marshal Joffre, 1921	256
27	The Man Who Won the War visits Gibraltar	256
28	The old Harrovian with the New Harrovian	257
29	Early days of the British Legion, 1922	257
30	Colonel of the Sherwood Foresters	272
31	Lieutenant Grenville Smith-Dorrien, KRRC	273

ACKNOWLEDGEMENTS

So many people have contributed to the making of this book that it would be tedious to name them all, nor would many of them wish it. First and foremost, I gratefully acknowledge my debt to Major-General Sir Edward L. Spears who, in spite of the many demands on his time, gave generously of it to assist a total stranger and that with a charm and courtesy which the writer will not readily forget. His unparalleled knowledge of men who were to him living people and not merely names in a book is indispensable to any who may seek to write a record of events fresh in the memories of some but as remote as the campaigns of Hannibal or Belisarius to others. To General Smith-Dorrien's last surviving son, Mr David Smith-Dorrien, I also owe much for the information he so readily gave me about his late father as a person. I can only hope that he and his kinsman, Commander T. M. Dorrien-Smith, RN, of Tresco in the Isles of Scilly, who has also been good enough to help with information, will feel that this book may add something towards a belated justice for a greatly wronged officer.

To the Librarian of the Royal United Services Institution, Mr John Dineen and to his Deputy, Miss Stephanie Glover, I tender my grateful thanks for so much help of which they alone can know. The British Museum's Department of Manuscripts, the Ministry of Defence Library, and the Public Records Office have as always been mines of information readily made available. My candid friends, Majors Gregory Blaxland and Derek Poulsen, both of The Buffs, have saved me more than once from falling into error, thanks to their vast knowledge of the Army's past—even at grave risk to their respective eyesights from wading through page upon page of mutilated typescript. Lastly, my deep appreciation to those many former officers and soldiers who served under or alongside General Smith-Dorrien and who, even when having nothing specific to contribute, heartened me by expressing an indignation of the treatment meted out to him which the passage of half a century has in no way blunted.

But, above all, this book owes its existence to the British Army, *quorum pars parva fui*. The continuity of this wonderful institution is illustrated by the fact that, as a young man, Sir Horace served under Sir Evelyn Wood who, in his own youth, had served with Lord Raglan. As Lord Fitzroy Somerset, Lord Raglan had been military secretary to the Duke of Wellington in the Peninsula, and when the infant Arthur Wellesley was taking his first steps, there was being carried to his grave old General Ligonier, who had charged at the head of his company at Malplaquet. And so it goes on until the day comes that the Army which emerged victorious from the wars against the Kings of France, the Empire of Napoleon, the Germany of Kaiser Wilhelm II, and that of his successor is being rapidly destroyed by its own political masters. "And a man's foes shall be those of his own household." It was not always so, however, and to the deathless memory of the men who formed the Second Corps of 1914, living and dead, I respectfully dedicate this book.

PREFACE

On the bookshelves stand the life-stories of the men who, beginning their careers as subalterns in the Army of Queen Victoria, held high commands in the First World War—with one glaring exception. Sir Horace Smith-Dorrien, subaltern at Isandhlwana, company commander on the North-West Frontier, commanding officer of a battalion at Omdurman, brigadier in South Africa, and commander of the Second Corps in 1914 is not there. A biography was written shortly after his death in 1930 by Brigadier-General Ballard but it is no disrespect to General Ballard when I say that he was hedged in by the fact that many of the principal characters were still living and by his own—entirely creditable—reluctance to speak forthrightly at that period. Time has moved on. The men concerned are to most people not individuals whom they once knew but only names in books, and some have left memoirs not then available which throw light into dark corners.

Many years ago I learnt of the shocking injustice which had been meted out to the fine officer whose correct decision to turn and fight at Le Cateau saved 1914 from becoming 1940. I have waited long for some more competent writer, with access to all the information now known and able to tell unpalatable truths without fear of wounding feelings, to reduce into writing all that he did and to tell what manner of man he was. As it now seems unlikely that this will happen I attempt with all proper humility to tell the story myself. In the preparation of this book I have had the advantage of speaking with a number of officers who as young men served under Sir Horace or alongside his command and all have agreed that he was a gallant, highly competent, and popular commander undeservedly brought down by a lesser man. In the library of the Royal United Service Institution there is a copy of Mr (as he then was) Churchill's, *World Crisis*, in which he speaks of Sir John French's wounded feelings when he was relieved of his command. In a pencilled note in the margin, plainly written long ago, some unknown hand has inserted, "What about S-D's?" This seems the verdict of informed opinion. It is the little things that linger in the memory. Almost everyone I have buttonholed for information over many years now has said something like "Smith-Dorrien? Oh, 'Orace you're for 'ome!" Such is fame.

It is fascinating, as always, to speculate on what might have happened but for the unaccountable malice of his C-in-C. Smith-Dorrien was, of course, second in seniority in the BEF and with Sir John French's removal after the Battle of Loos and with Ian Hamilton, the only other obvious successor, away in Gallipoli it would have been hard to resist his claim to the supreme command. Whether his health would have endured it is questionable but he was only fifty-six and had had no serious illness for many years. (Undoubtedly the cause of Sir Horace's notorious rages was a form of neuralgia but he had come through the retreat, Le Cateau, the Marne, the Aisne, and the first two battles of Ypres without losing a day through sickness.) Though no Staff College thinker, he was a thoroughly educated soldier of immense experience and proven courage and ability. In the event, for all his great services, he ended the War in the same rank and with the same honours that he held at its outbreak. No cash grants, freedoms of cities, or other spoils of war came his way and, always a man of moderate means, he who saved the Army and gave his people and their Allies the chance to gain time and win the final victory, found himself unable to afford to live and provide for his family in his own country. A generation which unwittingly owes him much should learn of his life and for that purpose this book is offered.

CHAPTER ONE

On 26th May 1858, there was born at Haresfoot, Berkhampstead, Hertfordshire, to Colonel Robert Algernon Smith-Dorrien (late of the 16th Lancers, 3rd Light Dragoons, and Hertfordshire Militia) and Mary Anne his wife, the eleventh child of a family of six boys and nine girls. The eldest son, after service in the 10th Hussars, became in due time head of the family with his seat at Tresco Abbey in the Isles of Scilly, two of the elder boys entered the Royal Navy, and a third went into the Church. The family was related to that great eccentric Augustus Smith, a country gentleman of Hertfordshire who became Governor of the Isles of Scilly in 1834. Smith found the islands endeavouring to support a population far in excess of their capacity and caused much indignation by transferring many islanders to the mainland. For the remainder, however, he did much and spent a large part of his substantial private fortune in improving his domain. He was a great naturalist and numbered among his friends Charles Darwin. In 1872 he died a bachelor, leaving his estate to a nephew, Mr. T. A. Smith-Dorrien, upon the strange condition that the beneficiary should add the name Smith to his own. The new owner obediently assumed the name of Smith-Dorrien-Smith while his brothers and sisters remained Smith-Dorriens. After a while he pruned his unwieldy patronymic by omitting the first Smith and so the Tresco branch of the family became and remains Dorrien-Smith.

The latest arrival, christened Horace Lockwood, attended a

preparatory school named Egypt House in the Isle of Wight and moved on to Harrow in 1871, at the same time as blue-clad Prussian columns were marching through Paris. At neither establishment did either leave any mark on the other, for he was a wild and mischievous boy (his own description). Sir John Fortescue, his contemporary at Harrow, confirms that Horace was found in every scrape going but was obviously fond of him: Sir John remembers him as "a very black little boy, black clothes, black hair and a very long chin".

Horace's father despaired of his ever becoming a useful member of society and in the autumn of 1875 asked him if he would like to go into the Army (a question which may have been prompted by the fact that a few days previously his youngest son had done his best to drown two of his sisters and himself below the Dance of Death bridge at Lucerne, where the family happened to be staying at the time). Horace was overjoyed, dashed home to an Army crammer, passed the Army examination (he could pass examinations when he had to) and joined the RMC at Sandhurst as a Second Lieutenant on 26th February 1876. At that period one joined as a commissioned officer and if successful in obtaining a special mention secured a year's ante-date on passing out.

Horace had his name on the list for the Rifle Brigade (the old 95th of Peninsular fame) but there was no vacancy in that famous corps and he found himself posted, as a kind of consolation prize, as Lieutenant in the new 95th, formed in 1823 and later to become the 2nd Battalion, Sherwood Foresters. At least the Foresters wore the same Maltese Cross and marched to the same quickstep, *I'm 95*, which has since been borrowed by more than one colonial regiment. The 95th were at Cork and Horace found it agreeable but unexciting duty, though the mess was enlivened for a time by the presence of a former officer whom shortage of cash had compelled to leave the Army to take up the career, unusual for an infantryman, of matador. Apparently the "Matador Ingles" (O'Hara by name), was still a by-word for skill and bravery in the south of Spain half a century later and perhaps he remains so still. O'Hara re-appeared some years later as a physical training instructor in a Dragoon regiment at the Curragh, still wearing his matador's pigtail, rose to the rank of sergeant, and then disappeared from history.

From provincial Cork the 95th moved later in the year to metropolitan Dublin where the Duke of Marlborough was Viceroy and the young American Lady Randolph Churchill the reigning beauty. As Horace himself recorded, "The Castle dances were a thing to dream of." The racing and hunting were no less to his taste for he was a competent horseman, and on the Regiment moving to Athlone he gave proof of his prowess as a sailor, nearly drowning a brother officer and himself by capsizing a boat on Lough Ree. One can see through the years a fearless young scapegrace who was not averse from risking his neck at anything which provided excitement.

In the same year, 1878, he had a taste of excitement of a different kind for war with Russia was a real possibility. Disraeli's Government called out the reserves, those of the 95th being brought to Athlone and trained with the regiment, now 1200 strong. Horace as Acting Adjutant at the age of twenty was fully employed for documentation in the Army of the 1870's was as proliferate as that of modern times even if the training was comparatively rudimentary and left to NCOs. The Congress of Berlin put an end to the enlivening prospect of another Crimea and he had to wait and see his first campaign in very different circumstances.

On the eve of the Zulu War the GOC Natal was Lord Chelmsford who, as Colonel the Hon. F. A. Thesiger, had been Commanding Officer of the 95th. Chelmsford, naturally enough, wanted to obtain officers from his old corps and cabled the War Office specifically requesting three officers for special service; among them was Horace. The present Commanding Officer refused to let his Adjutant (or the others) go, so words passed (Horace's expression) between them, and Horace wired direct to the War Office. His first recorded act of indiscipline paid off and three days later he found himself in a 2,000 ton trooper heading for Cape Town, which he was to see again so often. He did not enjoy the voyage for in spite of his sailing experience he suffered horribly from sea sickness and the passage was a rough one. None of the three officers had the remotest idea what their special service might be and on arrival at Durban, Horace was sent for duty with the transport, working stores to Rorke's Drift on the Buffalo River—the base for the expedition against Cetewayo, King of the Zulu. His task was to control the convoys, loaded with food, forage, ammunition and stores of every kind, and to keep moving the whole supply system along 100 miles of bad roads, half of them through thorn country where the certainty of rinderpest amongst the oxen if they were allowed to graze made it necessary to carry all forage. Quite a responsibility for an officer still some months short of the legal age of manhood. Horace learnt to admire the skill of the Afrikaner drivers of the spans of sixteen oxen to a wagon and to endure the thunderstorms and hail to which Natal is subject during November and December. He also learnt, with a shock, that corruption between contractors and British officers was not unknown; here occurred one of his earlier outbursts of temper (later to become notorious) during which he kicked a rascal out of his tent for attempting to bribe him. Horace was not a prig, but in the tradition of his upbringing and education it had never occurred to him that an officer holding the Queen's Commission could stoop to anything dishonourable.

On the 22nd January 1879, came the disaster of Isandhlwana, from which Horace was fortunate to emerge with his life. It happened through rank carelessness in certain quarters but, as few if any of the officers responsible survived the battle, the reasons for it will never be known for certain. Let it suffice that the garrison of the post on the side of Isandhlwana ("Little Hand") Hill consisted of six companies of the 1/24th Regiment (now the South Wales Borderers), two small guns, and some native levies. What was left of 1/24th remained under command of Captain Gonville Bromhead at Rorke's Drift, while all the other troops of the column, under the personal command of Lord Chelmsford, had gone out to attack the Zulu main army. The garrison stayed with its tents pitched and no serious preparations were made for its defence, though by noon it was plain that a Zulu *impi* was advancing swiftly and in great force.

The Zulu appeared in their usual formation—a mass of spearmen ("the chest") from whom on a signal two strong wings known as "the horns" were thrown out with the object of encircling their enemy. From above it must have looked like a tarantula closing upon a cluster of red ants, for the infantry were fighting in scarlet and carrying colours in battle for the last time. A small proportion of the Zulu carried rifles but their main weapon was the *assegai* and in the hands of these men of magnificent physique and martial pride it could be formidable indeed. Their discipline, skill at arms, and ability to manœuvre at the double were unparalleled in Africa. The 24th were armed with the single shot ·45 Martini-Henry rifle with its long bayonet (an excellent weapon but still using black powder and capable only of a relatively slow rate of fire); moreover, vastly outnumbered and lying in the open as they were, the odds were about equal. The Zulu advanced rapidly and steadily, not shouting but making a low murmuring noise like a swarm of bees drawing nearer and nearer. The 24th were veterans, many of them wearing beards, splendidly disciplined and masters of their weapons. Volley after volley, every shot aimed, took heavy toll of the advance and when about 400 yards from the line the Zulu begin to waver. But the fire slackened and they came on again though, as they admitted later, they would have broken and fled if it had continued even for a little while longer. The reason for this was that the men in the firing line had used up all their ammunition and though there were many thousands of rounds in the wagons, no arrangements had been made to bring it forward, though this is the traditional function of the RSM. Horace, who was there in the camp without any particular duties (he had managed to obtain eleven more rounds for his revolver from Bromhead at the Drift before riding in though he must have had some already), quickly rounded up stragglers to break open the boxes of cartridges and take them forward but now it was too late. The boxes were firmly screwed down and the Quartermaster of the 2/24th forbade Horace to take some of them on the grounds that they belonged to his battalion. Already the right flank was enveloped by one Zulu horn and the terrified drivers with their wagons jockeyed with each other to get away down the road to the Drift, until the left in its turn was outflanked. The 1/24th, now quite out of ammunition, outnumbered by at least thirty to one and with their backs to the rock of Isandhlwana, fixed bayonets. From then it was thrust, parry, and jab (though the advantage had passed to the Zulu as an empty rifle and bayonet can do nothing against a thrown *assegai*) until the last man fell, each with his heap of Zulu dead around him and with his face to the Queen's enemies, less than thirty escaping across the Buffalo River. The Zulu did not regard it as a victory and for years after related how for days the wagons were removing their dead and how their country ran rivers of tears for their losses. The 1/24th lost twenty-one officers and 590 soldiers killed.

When the final Zulu charge took place and the transport had cleared the Nek, Horace mounted his broken-kneed pony and made his way to the crest, where he found some 4,000 Zulu immediately in his path. Into this mass he rode, revolver in hand, but they ignored him, probably because he wore a blue patrol jacket and was taken for a civilian, a species beneath a warrior's dignity to kill. In any case they were far too busy spearing natives, mostly Basutos, who had sided with the British. On the way to the place now called Fugitive's Drift, four miles from Isandhlwana, he passed two officers of the 1/24th, Lieutenants Coghill and Melville, both mounted and the latter carrying one of the cased Colours which was later rescued from his body in the Buffalo River. Horace reached the precipitous descent to the Drift and stopped to put a tourniquet on the wounded arm of a mounted infantryman whom he dragged half way down the bank. A shout from behind of "Get on, man, the Zulus are on top of you" made him turn to see Major Smith, the officer who had commanded the two guns, standing on the skyline bleeding profusely. They were at once surrounded and the gunner, the wounded man, and Horace's pony were killed instantly by *assegais*. The rounds Bromhead had given him for his pistol saved him for he managed to shoot his way through and jump into the Buffalo River, some eighty yards wide. He was carried away by the flood and managed to catch the tail of a loose horse which towed him across. With typical chivalry he gave the horse to a man lying on the other side and sent him on his way. Then Horace was driven off to his left by a large band of Zulu who had crossed higher up the river,

1 Lieutenant H. L. Smith-Dorrien, 95th Foot, School of Musketry, Hythe 1878.

2 Right-hand panel: *An artist's impression of survivors from Isandhlwana crossing the Buffalo River, January 1879;* Left-hand panel: *Egypt 1885.*

twenty of whom pursued him on foot for about three miles being held off by the few remaining rounds from his pistol.

At sundown Horace reached Helpmakaar and safety, having covered twenty miles on foot from the river. But there was no rest for him yet. He found there a small garrison, including four officers who had escaped from the battle, and who promptly pressed him into service. Together they put the place into some sort of defensible condition, Horace, though exhausted beyond words, commanding one face of the *laager*. No attack came that night for the Zulu had turned aside to assail the little garrison of Rorke's Drift. By a happy mistake, two companies of the 24th who had started for the Drift that afternoon and had been turned back by a Staff Officer, arrived to reinforce the small garrison. At long last Horace slept. The following day he rode back to Rorke's Drift and was shocked at the devastation he saw everywhere.

For two separate acts on the 22nd January he was recommended for the Victoria Cross but he did not receive it as the proper channels of communication were not employed. Mr Hamer, the civilian commissary whose life he had saved, wrote copious letters to the Horse Guards and to Horace's family but to no avail. When this became apparent Hamer did his best to obtain for him the Royal Humane Society's medal but was told that it was too late. Many years later Horace wrote that he thought the decision to have been the right one.

At Helpmakaar Horace contracted typhoid fever and was taken by mule wagon some seventy miles to Ladysmith, where he lay for some months between life and death on the stone floor of a Dutch Church turned into a makeshift hospital. Though ordered back to England in May he had no appetite for returning home until the war was over and escaped from the hospital at midnight, his soldier-servant meeting him with horses in the pitch-dark churchyard; somehow he managed to remain in the saddle for forty miles until he reached Dundee, where a friendly transport officer hid him in his tent for a fortnight. By the time the doctors had caught up with him Horace was back in Zululand. His first day there was marred by the tragic death of the young Prince Imperial, the only son of Napoleon III and the

Empress Eugenie. The eighteen-year-old Prince, who was technically still a cadet at Woolwich, had been allowed to accompany the expedition and had gone out with a small party of one officer and a few men to reconnoitre; they stopped at a *kraal* to eat and do some sketching, having apparently taken no precautions against surprise, and were attacked by a few Zulu. The party mounted and galloped away leaving two men dead, but the Prince was unable to mount his restive horse and was left behind on foot to be killed. Long afterwards a Zulu who had been one of the party said that the Prince kept them at bay with his sword until he was struck down with an *assegai*. Sixteen stab wounds were found in his body which had been stripped but, as a mark of respect for his courage, they had left on him the gold medal which he habitually wore and his gold spurs. It fell to Horace on his return home to carry an account of her son's death to the Empress.

It is charitable to believe that the staff officer concerned, Carey by name, genuinely thought that the Prince was with the party but he was court martialled and sentenced to be cashiered.[1] Only the personal intervention of the distraught Empress, who insisted upon visiting the scene shortly afterwards, saved him from so ignominious an end. Carey, though recommended to mercy by the court, had written an incriminating letter to his wife which somehow became public. He forfeited any claim to sympathy on his return home by bombarding everyone, including the widowed Empress and the C-in-C, with hysterical letters asserting ridiculously that the Prince by virtue of his imperial rank was really in command of the party. The damning letter to his wife, however, was now common knowledge and he was regarded only as a neurotic nuisance whose mind had become unbalanced. Carey died of fever in India a few years later.

For the rest of the war Horace continued his transport duties under appalling conditions but without seeing a lot more fighting. The commander of his column, however, was Colonel Evelyn Wood, VC, later to be Field Marshal, who plainly formed a high opinion of the young officer and who, as will appear, was to

---

[1] S-D in his book says that Carey was sentenced to be shot, but here he is mistaken.

stand his friend on more than one occasion in the future. One of Horace's sailor brothers was present with the Naval Brigade and had fought in the battle of Ginginlovo on 2nd April. This brigade never got far for it was very late in starting, the rumour at the time being that the commander would not budge without his full month's supply of pepper. One imagines that this need not be taken too seriously for sailors attempting the work of soldiers must expect a certain amount of leg-hauling.

Horace was present at the final battle of the war at Ulundi when the fire power of guns and rifles plentifully supplied with ammunition broke the Zulu *impis* within twenty minutes at the cost of twelve men killed, all by rifle fire. After two or three months moving stores back from front to rear, Horace returned home in November. He had written a long account of his experiences to his father and must have been bursting to tell him, as one soldier to another, of all that he had seen, the stupidity and blunders no less than the brave deeds. But he never did so, because as the ship called at Madeira he learned to his great grief of his father's death.

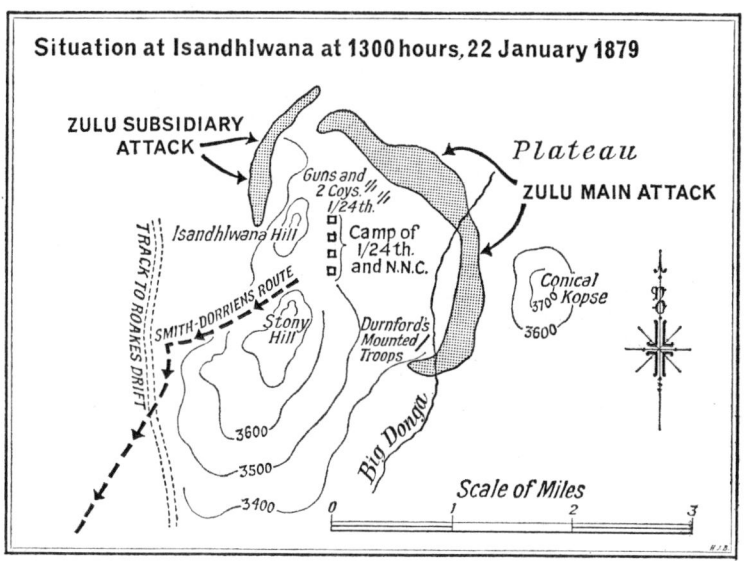

CHAPTER TWO

THE following two years found Horace back with the 95th, first at the Curragh and then at Aldershot. Nothing of moment happened to interrupt the placid life of garrison towns except that out hunting one day he smashed his knee which caused him much trouble for years to come. At the end of the year 1881 the 95th moved to Gibraltar ("I was lucky racing there and enjoyed the gallops with the Calpe hounds") and in July 1882, they found themselves under the command of Sir Garnet Wolseley *en route* for Egypt. The weak and corrupt government of the Khedive Tewfik had led to a threatened Army rebellion under Colonel Ahmed Arabi, Minister of War and the Nasser of the 1880's. There was probably much to be said on Arabi's behalf, but the fact remained that there were some 90,000 Europeans in the country whose safety would be endangered if the government were overthrown. (It was not all that long since Mehemet Ali had assumed power in Egypt and marched to the gates of Constantinople itself.) The British and French Governments agreed that for all his shortcomings, Tewfik must be supported. An Anglo-French squadron sailed to Alexandria on 20th May and serious rioting broke out between the Christian and Moslem communities, great damage being done particularly to the property of the former. The Sultan of Turkey, Egypt's nominal suzerain, would take no part in the matter beyond presenting Arabi with a decoration, of medium importance, presumably to ensure his loyalty to the Sublime Porte. Arabi, letting it be known that any attempt to land troops to restore order would be resisted, began building earthworks. When requested to desist he refused and on 11th July the British squadron of Admiral Sir Beauchamp Seymour bombarded the town, the French ships having sailed away. A British force from Cyprus landed there six days later without any contribution being made by the French whose government had refused to vote funds for the purpose. There was some skirmishing over the same ground where Sir Ralph Abercrombie had defeated the remains of Napoleon's Army in 1801 but when the C-in-C, Sir Garnet Wolseley, arrived he withdrew most of the troops from Alexandria and sailed them to Ismailia, leaving behind a small force under Evelyn Wood. On the arrival of the 95th on 21st August Horace was summoned by his patron, appointed Assistant Chief of Police in Alexandria, and promoted to captain. The police duties were taken over by the Army and courts martial were convened daily. Out of curiosity Horace went to see how Egyptian civil justice worked but hastily withdrew when he saw a witness having his memory improved by the use of thumb screws at the direction of the judge.

Horace did not enjoy police work and after a fortnight received a welcome summons from Wood to a change of duty. Sir Evelyn's difficulty was that he was opposed by some 15,000 Egyptians, mostly mounted, who were harrassing his little garrison up to the city itself and he had nothing but foot soldiers with which to oppose them. To Horace he confided the task of raising a force of mounted infantry, no matter how small, and he was given permission to draw men from his own regiment and from the Manchesters. Horses and horse furniture Wood had none to give. Horace in the course of his police duties had learnt that there were horses and saddles in the stables of the Khedive's bodyguard and there he promptly went with six men, two cabs, and an interpreter. The baffled Egyptian officer in charge eventually gave way and Horace departed with his two cabs full of saddles, his men leading twelve ponies, two mules, and a donkey. Within half an hour he was able to report gleefully that the mounted infantry awaited orders. They marched, if that be the word, past Sir Evelyn with most of the mounted men clinging valiantly to their saddles, and moved on some five miles to plague the Egyptians. Within a couple of days, by dint of raids on the shops of Alexandria, sufficient animals and tack had been collected to increase Horace's command to thirty, with whom he succeeded in pushing back the Egyptian outposts so far that Sir Evelyn was no longer troubled. The mounted infantry continued their scouting work concurrently with instruction in horsemanship for about a fortnight while Wolseley fought the battle of Tel el Kebir, capturing Arabi and seizing Cairo. Horace's MI rode with a squadron of the 13th Bengal Lancers to escort the Khedive to the railway station. History is silent as to whether the donkey enjoyed a glorious hour of martial panoply or whether he had been returned to civil life to perform the duties which fall, or are said to fall, to the donkeys of Alexandria; it is also perhaps as well that no record has been preserved of what the gorgeous Lancers said or thought at finding themselves in this strange juxtaposition.

His second campaign behind him at the age of twenty-four, Horace and the 95th took ship for Bombay, leaving behind two of his naval brothers who had had a hand in the bombardment. The elder of these, Lieutenant H. T. Smith-Dorrien of HMS *Invincible*, varied his normal duties by disguising himself as an Arab fisherman and spying out the land for his Admiral. In the course of this he imprudently ventured on board an American ship and tribute was paid to his disguise by a seaman turning a hose on him on the grounds that he needed a wash. This must have pleased Horace when the news reached him.

On arrival in India the 95th entrained for Poona and marched from there to Lucknow. Early in the march Horace wrenched his troublesome knee pursuing a wounded peacock and to his disgust had to be sent ahead by rail. At Lucknow he addressed himself seriously to polo but the condition of his knee became steadily worse and after two months on his back he was sent home to London with a knee as big as a football. There was talk of amputation but an operation was successful and after many months on crutches he made a complete recovery.

In January 1884, on board a trooper in the Suez Canal on his way back to India, he was spotted by Sir Evelyn Wood, the new

Sirdar, who sent for him and asked him to join the Egyptian Army, now British officered with a view to the eventual reoccupation of the Sudan. Horace was torn between this attractive proposition and a desire to widen his military education at the Staff College, for he realized that his two campaigns bore no relevance to modern military thought. The war of 1870 was long over and its lessons, together with such as European armies condescended to learn from the American Civil War, had been digested by the major military powers, but "civilized" warfare was outside the experience of British officers except for the few remaining Crimean veterans who were in any event due to retire soon. Wood himself had served in the Crimea as a midshipman before leaving the sea service for the Army. In an agony of indecision Horace stayed with the Sirdar for a week, during which he met several times General Charles Gordon, then on his way to Khartoum and his death. In the end Horace agreed to join the Egyptian Army provided that he could go home to read for the Staff College the first year there was no war.

He joined the Staff of Sir Francis Grenfell on 4th February 1884, the same day the Dervishes were happily engaged near Suakin on the Red Sea coast in cutting to pieces 3,500 Egyptian Gendarmerie commanded by Valentine Baker. Baker deserves more than a passing word. Originally he was in the fashionable 10th Hussars and the bright star of London society but came to grief after being convicted of the attempted rape of a young woman in a railway carriage. Baker then joined the Turkish army in their war against Russia and won much fame at the battle of the Shipka Pass. When that war was over he sought other exciting employment and as he still retained the good will of many influential friends (who regarded the railway carriage affair as no more than a slight lapse of taste) he eventually became chief of the Egyptian Gendarmerie. When his troops marched out from Suakin to meet an inferior force of Hadendowa (the original of Kipling's Fuzzy-Wuzzies) he had reason to expect a fairly easy victory. But panic overcame his force and the Gendarmerie took to their heels, 3,000 rifles and a few guns falling into the hands of the Dervishes; Baker and his staff escaped only by charging on horseback through the enemy. This windfall of modern weapons together with those taken a few months earlier at El Obeid, where a very odd army commanded by an ex-Indian Army officer named Hicks had met with the same fate, had given the Mahdi a formidable accretion of strength. This he was not slow to put to use and his *bazingers* (black riflemen) became a valuable addition to an army originally armed only with sword and spear.

It was against this gloomy background that Horace joined his brigade commander, to meet amongst other staff officers a Sapper eight years older than himself named Herbert Horatio Kitchener, just promoted captain. They got on together very well. Within a month the situation was cheered slightly with successes at El Teb and Tamai by a force under Sir Gerald Graham which removed the threat to the Red Sea littoral.

Horace was given the odd duty of raising and training a battalion of Turks. The recruits were of the poorest material and even he could make nothing of them. They were ordered up to Wady Halfa but again Horace's knee gave out and he had to hand over his command, which promptly mutinied and had to be disbanded. This kept him out of any part in the Gordon Relief Expedition and he was appointed Surveyor-General of the Army—a strange title since his duties consisted mostly of supply and transport which were, of course, matters with which he was thoroughly familiar. Being Horace, he tried hard to get into the fighting but he missed the battle of Abu Klea on 17th January where he might have met a cavalry officer named John Denton Pinkstone French receiving his baptism of fire at the age of thirty-three. Horace's only opportunity for combat came in March, when he was appointed Adjutant of the Mounted Infantry. Here he had great fun and a little fighting, but the MI were disbanded in July and he resumed his duties as Surveyor General. By odd coincidences his inspections always took place at times and places where trouble was expected and on one occasion the amused Sirdar let him do duty as Staff Officer to the Egyptian mounted troops in the attack on the Dervish village of Ginniss. For his work in the following pursuit he was thanked in General Orders and awarded the newly-founded DSO.

In February 1886 Horace returned to read for the Staff College at the famous crammer's "Jimmy's". He passed the examination tenth on the list, returned to Egypt for six months to train a new Sudanese battalion and joined the Staff College in February 1887. He was now twenty-nine with ten years service behind him. He enjoyed his two years at the Staff College, not learning as much as he would have liked, working not too hard, originating the Staff College Coach, becoming Master of the Draghounds, and not missing more race meetings than he could help. It is not altogether surprising that he learnt little for the instruction was confined to the campaigns of Moltke and the minutiae of Queen's Regulations, the 1,500 paragraphs of which an officer was expected to learn by rote. Horace Smith-Dorrien was never a bookish man and must have regarded this as largely a waste of his talent; the legend long persisted that at the end of his first three months he was found wandering in the corridors enquiring plaintively the way to the library and it is known that more than once he was up before the commandant for not taking his studies seriously. The College was still living in the shadow of its former Commandant, General Sir E. B. Hamley, who had been an adequate, if not particularly distinguished, staff officer in the Crimea under the Duke of Cambridge (the bow-and-arrow General, as Wolseley rudely called him) and who after the war resolved himself into a military theorist. It was his bad luck to produce his *magnum opus, Operations of War*, just before Konnigratz was fought and he had to revise it very rapidly before it could become the gospel of the next couple of generations of Staff College students. Undoubtedly the Staff College of the eighties smelt of dry rot and it is no wonder that it was regarded by the bulk of the Army as a joke in rather bad taste for its only product was the inculcation in young officers of an exaggerated sense of their own importance. Its progressive outlook can be judged from the fact that when field glasses were introduced into the Army in 1884 their use was deprecated. Wellington had managed very well with a telescope so what need was there of a change to this unfamiliar object? Anyway, there was something rather effeminate about it. The days of such reforming commandants as Rawlinson and Robertson were a long way away. Smith-Dorrien had already given proof of his ability to cram for examinations and he must have done more work than he admitted for he got his certificate.

After his two years at the College he was, like most officers, very hard up for an infantry captain's pay did not begin to cover the cost of hunters, race-meetings, and weekends in London. In accordance with tradition he wanted to get back as quickly as possible to India where pay was higher and sport cheap. It was as well for him that the 95th were still there and his next command was two companies on detachment from Jubbulpore in the jungle of Saugor. Here he added to his accomplishments pig-sticking, crocodile fishing, and the shooting of every kind of jungle beast. He went to Simla to see the Military Secretary, a Colonel Nicholson (whom he would meet again), and was told with a sneer that in India the psc was not an actual bar to Staff employment. Horace did not like Nicholson, but the cherished certificate was undoubtedly held in little esteem in the India of the late 19th century. Lord Roberts, after all, had managed perfectly well without it. Nevertheless Smith-Dorrien did hold a variety of appointments suitable to his rank and seniority over the next few years: Brigade Major at the big Attock manœuvres, Station Staff officer at Fyzabad, Camp Commandant for the Cavalry Manœuvres, and others. In April 1892 he was posted again to Lucknow, this time as DAAG, and there he spent some of the happiest years of his life. Lucknow was the gentleman-rider's Mecca and soon the DAAG was a prominent figure. For a long time he shared a bungalow with "Kitty" Apthorpe of the Royal Irish who was to remain a lifelong friend. The two bachelors entertained lavishly and when the bungalow was full, a small tented camp was pitched in the garden for their many racing companions. Each had his own large stud, their combined total sometimes exceeding thirty horses. Smith-Dorrien was too heavy for the more important races so Hubert Gough became his regular jockey and in the winter of 1895/6 the Smith-Dorrien—Gough team won nineteen races including the Army Cup, netting no less than 13,000 rupees, said to be nearly a record in days of small stakes. The friends were not always so successful for the next season Apthorpe had a pony named Wild Duck which was certain to win the Army Cup. The Royal Irish, who never had any money, borrowed all their credit would stand to back it. When the brute came in at the tail of the race the bungalow was hastily and woefully turned into an auction room, and the stud sold. Never was a regiment as flat broke as the Royal Irish after that meeting.

About this time Horace began to keep a diary, finishing in 1922 and comprising thirty bound volumes. Its pages are filled with events of every sort: sport, travel, war, and social life. He also became a great writer of letters, nearly a thousand every year, long ones to his mother and short ones to his many friends and relations. The next thirty years of his life were to be meticulously documented. He did a spell at Umballa as AAG to General Penn-Symons, who was to be killed a few years later at Talana Hill, was DAA and QMG of a reserve brigade designed as part of the force to relieve the siege of Chitral but never used and, at his own request, returned to regimental duty with the 95th at Bareilly early in 1897.

His duties not being unduly onerous, racing, pig-sticking, and shooting occupied most of his time and his personal stud of horses and ponies, never small, once reached the impressive total for an officer in a foot regiment of thirty-two. He reckoned that their winnings kept him and his guests in comfort. He killed nine tigers in Nepal, was shown where had been hidden the cages for the tigers brought for the Prince of Wales to slay with the minimum of difficulty twenty-five years earlier, broke his leave from England to get quickly to the Tirah campaign of which he had heard rumours, and arrived on the frontier late in October after a journey of nineteen days from the In and Out. Horace was cordially received by his many friends and spent the next six months engaged in the worst kind of mountain warfare in vile conditions against an active, vigilant enemy, who were expert marksmen and well equipped with modern rifles. For the first time since Isandhlwana he found himself more than once engaged in a retreat and concluded that the only way to conduct this difficult operation of war was "as fast as you can lay legs to the ground". At most times, he commanded a detachment of half his regiment but also led *ad hoc* forces in many small engagements. Though the wealther was execrable his diary remains thoroughly light-hearted and his knee did not seem to trouble him. At nearly forty and now a field officer, the mischievous boy was still very much alive in him and he enjoyed an immense popularity with everyone. When he left to go on leave at the end of the campaign much of the regiment went to the station to see him off and the band turned out to play *Auld Lang Syne*. This did not happen to every officer and he was greatly touched.

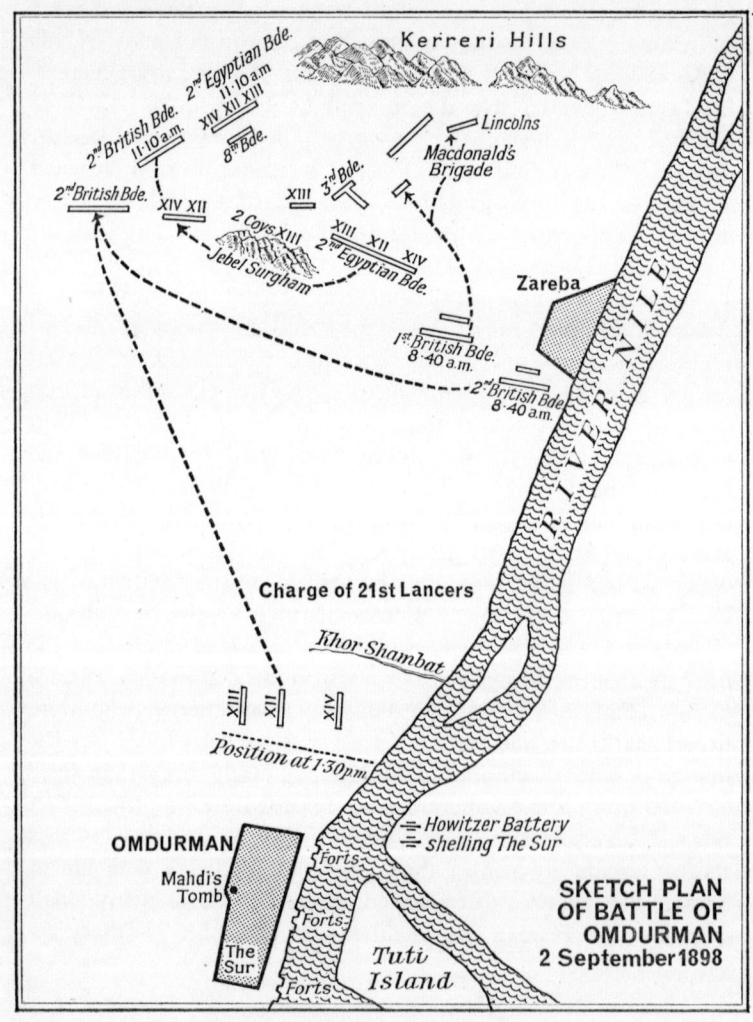

CHAPTER THREE

SMITH-DORRIEN was determined not to miss Kitchener's coming campaign to free the Sudan. He went to Cairo in May 1898 and after much wire-sending and wire-pulling arrived at Wady Halfa in mid-July having just received the brevet of Lieutenant Colonel for his services at Tirah. While he was shaving alongside the train one morning the Sirdar (Captain Kitchener's promotions had been swifter than those of Captain Smith-Dorrien) rode up and told him to take command of the XIIIth Sudanese, the battalion which he had raised and trained in 1886 before going to the Staff College. As always, he was amongst friends including Major Charles Fergusson (later to command the 5th Division BEF in Smith-Dorrien's II Corps), Major Sir Henry Rawlinson, Bart., Hector MacDonald, and Rudolf Slatin, the dapper little Austrian officer and friend of Gordon who had been for ten years a prisoner in Omdurman. In the XIIIth two of Horace's three British officers were to achieve high rank: Capper, who was to be killed in France as a fine Divisional Commander, and Whigham, as Adjutant General. Smith-Dorrien had been too late for the battle of the Atbara, fought while he was still on the north-west frontier, but was well in time for the final blow at the Khalifa's power. By August, Kitchener's force consisted of two Brigades of British infantry, four Brigades of Egyptians (including the Sudanese), a small force of cavalry, and a number of field guns and Maxims. On 23rd August after a review by the Sirdar the Army began its forward movement towards Khartoum. Every night the brigades camped in "attack formation", a rectangle of a battalion each to the north, west and south faces with a thorn *zareba* outside, the Nile itself always forming the eastern face with the gunboats keeping vigil against surprise attack from the eastern bank, their searchlights wheeling lances of brilliance across its ancient waters. After a week of movement in this fashion the formation was changed to echelons of brigades, the right refused, the left as near as possible to the river and each brigade marching in fours, a noble sight familiar for two centuries (even though scarlet was no more worn nor Colours carried) but never to be seen again. On 1st September the Mahdi's Tomb in Omdurman, seven miles away, could be seen from the Kerreri Ridge and word came in that the Khalifa's troops were massed outside the city. The Sambos, as everybody called the Sudanese, became more and more cheerful as they neared their enemy. When all was said and done they had the greatest interest in the outcome of the battle for it was their country which had been turned into an abomination of desolation by the Mahdi and his followers and their people who had been butchered or enslaved.. The three Sudanese battalions, the XIIth, XIIIth, and XIVth (the first named under command of a Lt-Colonel Charles Townsend later to be heard of at Kut) were brigaded together with the 8th Egyptian battalion in the Second Brigade under Colonel Maxwell. They had been on the march since early morning, first in drenching rain and then in torrid heat, as part of the broad front of three brigades, each of them with three battalions in half-battalion column leading and with the remaining one in column of companies in support. The two British brigades were the nearest to the river. The cavalry—the 21st Lancers and eight squadrons of Egyptian horse—maintained a screen some four or five miles ahead, the whole operation as precise as an exercise on some vast sand table.

The immediate object was to take the Kerreri Ridge overlooking Omdurman and it was expected that this would mean a hard fight. In fact the ridge proved unoccupied. The howitzer battery took post on an island in the Nile which had been cleared by friendly Jaalin tribesmen under a British officer, Major

Stuart-Wortley, and within a short time the battery opened fire upon Omdurman itself, the barrage being increased by the quick-firing three-pounders of the gunboats. The cavalry, moving fast, rode to within a mile of the town and were rewarded by the sight of the Dervish Army in full array. As the Dervishes debouched from the town they formed in an orderly line five miles long and made a magnificent spectacle. Mass upon mass of white *jibbahs*, green flags, and twinkling spearpoints caught by the sun, horsemen under their Emirs splendidly caparisoned as had been Saladin's men at the Horns of Hattin seven centuries before, charging out behind the Anglo-Egyptian squadrons as they withdrew to pass on their intelligence.

At about 1700 the Sirdar ordered his force to bivouac for the night and to build either *zarebas* or trenches (as their situation made possible) around the village of Egeiga—about a mile southeast of the ridge. Arms were piled and a meal taken but it was a jumpy night for the Dervishes' best hope of success would have been to attack at night thus nullifying to a large extent the superiority in weapons held by their enemies. The Dervish swordsmen and spearmen, brave strong men adept in the use of their arms and fortified by a blind faith in Allah, were accustomed to night work and would have been formidable particularly against the Egyptians who were not the steadiest troops in the world. But they did not attack and lost their opportunity. Spies, pretending to be deserters, were sent into the Dervishes' camp to inform the Khalifa that the Sirdar himself intended to attack that same night. The courage of these spies was beyond all praise for they knew that if suspected they would meet an unspeakable death by torture. One detects in this mission the hand of Rudolf Slatin who after his ten years' captivity knew more of the mind of the Khalifa and his Emirs than did any other living man. It is no exaggeration to say that these few brave, nameless men made the following day's victory possible.

Smith-Dorrien's thoughts must have moved back to Isandhlwana and although confident of victory he must have considered the possibilty of defeat had a night attack been made. Certainly he did not follow the fashion of underestimating a formidable enemy though this time there would be no running out of ammunition. The Egyptians and Sudanese were still armed with the Martini-Henry rifle but the British troops now carried the Lee-Metford rifle which, with its ten round magazine and smokeless powder, was a far more deadly weapon and the lesson of the screwed-down ammunition boxes had long been digested.

At 0200 hours on 2nd September a great storm burst. Rain lashed down mercilessly and flashes of blue lightning lit up the fitfully sleeping men and the crowded animals. The outpost line peered into the night but the expected attack did not come. From time to time the searchlights of the river steamers silently lit up the emptiness of the desert and the river. At 0330 the Army stood to but nothing happened, and an hour later they stood down again and fed as best they could. The cavalry, horse artillery, and camelry moved out but the infantry remained behind. From the shoulder of the hill men with field glasses could see in the distance the yellow-brown pointed dome of the Mahdi's Tomb and row upon row of mud houses. Between the ridge and the town rose a single black hill with a ridge running from it towards the river masking what lay beyond. This was the Jebel Surgham, whose closer acquaintance Smith-Dorrien was to make within the next few hours. The bugles sounded at 0430, and were joined at once by the music of the drums and fifes of the British regiments and the shriller trumpets of the cavalry.

At 0530 the impatient infantry at last marched out but hardly had they left their trenches when word came back from the cavalry that the Dervish Army was on the move. This sealed its fate for in the open they were far more vulnerable to shrapnel and small arms fire than they would have been behind the walls of Omdurman. The Army had quite expected to have to bombard the town for a day or two before going in with the bayonet but the probable truth is that his recent defeats at the Atbara and Abu Hamed had persuaded the Khalifa that a defensive battle of any sort would not suit the characteristics of an army whose deadliness lay in the hand-to-hand fight, and he preferred to rely on sheer weight of numbers. As soon as this intelligence reached the Sirdar he ordered his force back to their excellent positions to receive the attack. Less than an hour later it came.

3 Isandhlwana: the battlefield from the area to the rear of Page's Company.

4 Queen Victoria's last General, 1901.

At about 0615 the multi-coloured horde surged round the Jebel Surgham and moved rapidly across the front, yelling and singing. The Egyptian cavalry drew back slowly to northward in order not to mask the infantry fire; the 21st Lancers (in whose ranks rode the son of the Lady Randolph Churchill whose beauty had so impressed young Smith-Dorrien at Dublin Castle back in '78) retired in turn along the river bank into the *zareba* under a cloud of prescient vultures who followed them hopefully throughout the day. The vultures were not to be disappointed.

Within half an hour the Dervish Army under the command of the Emir Osman Azrak and moving at great speed reached the foot of the ridge, forming into a huge crescent much like the Zulu "chest" and "horns", the ends of it constantly extending and curling, steadily re-inforced by an inexhaustible supply of black flags and humanity from behind the Jebel Surgham. The green flag of Osman Azrak was borne forward by his mediaeval horsemen; other banners, green and white worked with cabalistic devices, tossed in their multitudes on either side. It was the last charge of the chivalry of the Middle Ages. As they passed beyond the foot of the ridge, Queen Victoria's cannon tore great gaps in their ranks, the sweating gunners of the 32nd Field Battery firing as fast as they could load, and the Guards opening with musketry at the unprecedented range of 2,700 yards. Forward and ever forward in a huge amphitheatre under the blazing sun the masses of fearless men in their gay coloured *jibbahs* followed their reckless horsemen, confident of victory and contemptuous of death. As the range shortened to 900 yards and the screaming targets loomed larger the 1st British Brigade (the Queen's Own Cameron Highlanders, the Seaforths, Royal Warwicks, and Lincolns) the Maxim battery, and the Second Egyptian Brigade (including Smith-Dorrien's Sambos) chimed in with devastating small arms fire. The British troops fired like a machine, disciplined volleys followed by independent fire and back to volleys again as the situation demanded. Their marksmanship and fire discipline were, as always, admirable. At 900 yards men began to fall and as the range closed to 300 nothing could survive the storm of bullets. The Sudanese fired steadily but with an inferior weapon and far less training their shooting was less effective. Nevertheless it brought the charge to a halt and few Dervishes got nearer to the *zareb*a than 200 yards, though they were by no means broken and kept up a steady if inaccurate fire from a fold in the ground some 400 yards away. So ended the first phase of the battle. Some 15,000 Dervishes had been beaten to a halt by the arms of the 19th century. The climax was yet to come.

The Khalifa himself, with Emir Yakub of the Black Flag, had determined that if the frontal attack failed he would fall upon the *zareba* from behind the Jebel Surgham, whilst the Emir Ali-Wad-Helu was ordered to move to the rear among the Kerreri Hills and wait upon events[1]. The Khalifa's men, including his own bodyguard, were the flower of the Dervish Army and Ali-Wad-Helu was a tried and crafty leader. Osman's task was to curve round to the north and assail the *zareba* from that direction. The plan was based on the probability that if the frontal attack collapsed the infidels would over-confidently leave their shelter and move into open country where mechanical superiority would avail them little against the violence and overwhelming numbers of the hordes of Islam. It was a plan that could well have succeeded and Kitchener might have gone the way of Hicks and Gordon.

The Sirdar, however, realized that the most vulnerable part of the *zareba* was on the north or down-stream side, held by Lewis's Egyptian Brigade. In order to avoid the full weight of the attack of the Dervish left wing, Kitchener ordered out the cavalry again to break up its cohesion. The Kerreri Ridge had already been occupied for the same reason by the Camel Corps and a Horse Artillery battery. The ridge consisted of two main features each about 300 feet high, and a mile long, with a gap between them of 1,000 yards. The range is, of course, north of the *zareba* while the frontal attack had come in from the south-west. The Camel Corps were in position on the part of the ridge nearer to the river with the horses and camels in care of their holders in the boulder-strewn gap. The antiquated seven-pounder Krupp guns of the Horse Battery were on the left and Broadwood placed

---

[1] The Khalifa's command included the remains of Osman Azrak's force and amounted to about 30,000 men.

his dismounted troopers along the centre. He expected only to have to deal with small bodies but Osman Azrak, sensibly unwilling to attack the *zareba* with a force still threatening his left and rear, brought up his right beyond the range of rifle fire from the *zareba* and launched his 15,000 men on Broadwood. Kitchener, seeing what was happening, sent a galloper to Broadwood ordering him back to the safety of the *zareba* but this wise officer chose to retire north through the hills, drawing Osman after him. The Dervishes attacked the hills towards the north-east enveloping Broadwood's right and sweeping the gap with fire from their many riflemen, well armed with the windfalls from Hicks and Baker. The Camel Corps were caught in this fire, losing fifty men and many horses and camels. As the Dervishes swarmed over the rocks, faster by far on foot than the camel men, Broadwood decided to send the camelry back to the *zareba* covered by the fire of a gunboat which of its commander's own initiative had now joined in the running fight. The Dervishes rushed to cut off the camelry from the river along the south side of the ridge as the nine squadrons of cavalry mounted and prepared for a self-sacrificing charge (though the Egyptian troopers displayed some economy of enthusiasm for the operation). Happily the gunboat, described by the 21st Lancer attached officer as "a beautiful white devil," and commanded by a young naval officer named Beatty, blazed away with her three-pounders and Maxims into an unmissable target and the Camel Corps managed to reach the *zareba* safely. Then came the turn of the cavalry. Osman's horsemen pursued them three miles to the north drawing off, as Broadwood had hoped, a strong force from attacking the *zareba* at the cost of a couple of guns stuck firmly in a marsh.

A second gunboat arrived and the two of them succeeded in driving Osman's men away from the river allowing Broadwood to trot home, picking up the two guns on the way. He had done well, for Osman's part in the battle was over after the great casualties he had suffered and the Egyptian Brigade remained shielded. It was, of course, a gross violation of orders, a matter on which Smith-Dorrien may have pondered when it fell to him to make a similar decision sixteen years later.

By this time the frontal attack was flagging. The Dervish dead numbered about 2,000 to the Anglo-Egyptian about 150. An enthusiastic if inaccurate fire had been kept up on the *zareba* since the attack began and it was from this that all the casualties came. The artillery searched the broken ground where the riflemen lay and the Maxims cut them down as they were flushed out. No man present could feel but pity for these fine valiant men sacrificed in an unworthy cause.

But defences, no matter how successful, do not win battles (though they may clear the way to victory as Wellington had demonstrated so often) and it was essential to capture the town before nightfall. The 21st Lancers found the Jebel Surgham unoccupied and the plain beyond covered with swarms of wounded and ex-Dervishes making for Omdurman. The 21st succeeded also in getting into a scrape with some 2,700 men hidden in a sunken Khor but they managed to extricate themselves, though not without loss.

Now the Sirdar moved in for the kill. At about 0900 the whole force moved from the *zareba* in echelon. There were some changes in the order of march made by General Hunter, commanding the Division, for he knew there to be many Dervishes still around the Kerreri Hills and he did not wish his Egyptians spoiled. He wanted his best troops and his most reliable commander on the exposed right flank and therefore moved the First Egyptian Brigade to the point of danger. The Egyptian Brigade was comprised in fact of three Sudanese and one Egyptian battalion under command of fire-eating Hector MacDonald. Fighting Mac, as he was known throughout the Army, was a highlander who had risen from the ranks of the Gordons by sheer determination and had been engaged in many Indian campaigns. He rose to Major-General but only five years after Omdurman was to die by his own hand in circumstances that are even now not wholly clear. But this was his day and his finest hour.

The six brigades moved off in echelon from the left, the two British nearest to the river, next to them Maxwell's with Horace's XIIIth on the right, followed by Lewis's, MacDonald being on the right flank with three batteries of artillery and eight Maxims.

The Khalifa with his 15,000 was somewhere behind Jebel Surgham, erroneously believed by many to have fled into the town; Ali wad Helu with about the same number of fresh troops was still lurking in the Kerreri Hills and with him was Osman Sheiked-din, the total number of their combined forces being about 40,000. The echelon formation adopted can best be likened to a step ladder on its side, the top rungs being the two British brigades of Wauchope and Lyttleton, and the bottom one MacDonald's, about a mile behind Lewis in a diagonal line. In the confusion of the change of places Lewis found his brigade some 600 yards further south than it should have been. The regular echelon formation would have brought all the brigades into line very simply and quickly by forming to their right, each making a half turn and marching through a part of a circle until the line was unbroken. On this occasion it was not at all like that. The Lancers were again in front of the infantry, the Egyptian cavalry behind keeping an eye on the Kerreri Ridge.

As the troops moved forward over the carpet of dead and wounded it was necessary to move with care for many wounded were still good for a snap shot or spear stab and quite a number of "dead" came miraculously to life for long enough to perform the same disobliging office. Fire was still coming from the Jebel Surgham so Smith-Dorrien despatched Capper's and Whigham's companies to clear it, which they did quickly, both officers remaining mounted as they climbed the 200 foot hill. On reaching the top they dispersed by fire and yells a large reserve force of Dervishes and were just in time to see the attack break on MacDonald's brigade. At this point Kitchener began to move brigades about as if they were companies. The XIIIth's remaining two companies were doubled into line to the north of Surgham to take the Dervishes in the flank by fire, the other three battalions moved west leaving the hill with the XIIIth remaining on the right. Lewis's brigade was moved into the interval between Smith-Dorrien's battalion, and MacDonald and the 2nd British brigade with some guns were hurried round to the left. Thus all the infantry had turned about and faced north-west. What had happened was that MacDonald's isolated brigade had halted for their wary commander having seen that the forces of the

Khalifa and Yakub were drawn up to the west of Surgham plainly about to attack him, was not going to be caught on the move. He brought his three batteries into action at 1,200 yards five minutes before the Khalifa and Yakub charged his solitary brigade with 15,000 men, Yakub of the Black Flag at their head. The three brigades, now moving west and leaving the river behind them, attacked Yakub's right flank compelling him to form right towards the river and to remove much of the weight of the attack on MacDonald. The gap between Lewis and MacDonald was closed by Wauchope's British troops doubling across the plain into the empty space and the entire force now became heavily engaged in the open. The firing was very heavy, heavier even than during the attack on the *zareba*, and the XIIIth were in the thick of it. The three leading brigades continued to advance steadily westward, looped over the hill, with hordes of Dervishes rushing towards the smoke clouds that hid MacDonald (the Martini-Henry rifle still fired black powder as in Marlborough's day). A battalion of Lewis's brigade, the only one not commanded by a British officer, began to waver but was stiffened by two companies under Major Hickman marching up behind them with fixed bayonets. Yakub began to give ground and the Khalifa realized that his only hope now lay with Ali-wad-Helu, still in the Kerreri Hills.

But MacDonald was not without his own troubles. He had deployed into line with the IXth Sudanese on his right, the guns and Maxims next to them, with the Xth, 2nd Egyptian, and XIth prolonging the line to the left. The IXth had become very excited and made as if to charge forward on their own. Fire discipline broke down and MacDonald, aware that the charge could succeed only if numerous casualties had been caused by fire before taking to the bayonet, rode out in front of his line knocking up rifles and yelling for a cease fire. When some order had been restored he gave the command to order arms and lashed his men with his sharp Scottish tongue. The Dervishes, taking full advantage of the lull pushed to within four hundred yards of the line and began a heavy but aimless fire. Fighting Mac, having restored discipline, ordered firing to recommence by company volleys. Within a few minutes the

Dervishes rose up yelling and rushed forward led by 200 hard-galloping Emirs. They were swept away by a tempest of lead, a few getting within a hundred yards of the line, withdrew, and began again with their musketry. Lewis's brigade was now coming up, three battalions forward, and added their contribution to the fire. Maxwell had got a Maxim to the top of the hill which took a heavy toll by itself. Thousands of Dervishes streamed back towards the town but Yakub and his men disdained to fly and died on their feet, the Black Flag flying to the last over its dead defenders.

MacDonald's battle was not yet over. Away to the right the army of Ali-wad-Helu was pouring out of the Kerreri Hills, its numbers as great as the Khalifa's own corps. Had the two attacks come simultaneously MacDonald's position would have been hopeless for his right rear was unguarded. With great skill and with perfect timing, judging when the Khalifa's attack was languishing enough to permit manœuvre, he turned first the XIth and a battery, then the IXth (whose commander moved of his own accord), and finally the Xth and another battery to face north, the 2nd Egyptians closing the gap at the angle. Heavy firing was continuous but MacDonald still found time to give the rough side of his tongue to the officer commanding the IXth for moving without orders. ("Be so good, sir, as to drill more steadily in brigade!")

The whole rage of the Dervish attack fell on the three Sudanese battalions. These happy warriors revelling in the fight forgot all they had been taught about musketry in their excitement and the officers did what they could by taking rifles from individuals, adjusting their sights for them and doling out cartridges in twos and threes as they squibbed off all their ammunition. Meanwhile the Dervishes, battered by shrapnel and torn by the Maxims, screamed their way forward. Ammunition was down to three rounds a man as the enormous masses, green flags everywhere, poured on. As the Sudanese fixed bayonets, there arrived through the smoke the Lincoln's of Wauchope's brigade, panting, sweating, but intent on business. Doubling round the rear of the Xth Sudanese who grinned and yelled their welcome (the Lincolns are the old 10th Foot and the two regiments sharing the common numeral were friends) they formed line and opened magazine fire at an angle in front of the Sudanese. Ali-wad-Helu's men were no more than 300 yards away when the rapid fire of this fine battalion stopped them in their tracks. Their horsemen made one last charge at the Sudanese who could hardly fail to hit them at that range and all the attackers were killed, to the number of about 400. MacDonald ordered his line to advance; the bands struck up, and the battle was over. The Sirdar observed that he thought the Dervishes had been "given a good dusting" and ordered the resumption of the march on Omdurman. It was 1150. At 1400 the 2nd Brigade entered Omdurman, Smith-Dorrien with them. There was some scrappy fighting in the town but few defenders had any stomach for it now. Next day the cleaning up began and nearly 11,000 Dervish bodies were counted on the ground. The vultures had not been wrong. Though it was his second experience of mass slaughter, Horace felt sick. He was amongst the first to ride into the squalid town, guided by an old telegraph clerk of Gordons whom his troops had found wandering the streets. According to rumour the Khalifa was still in his house so Smith-Dorrien with half a dozen of his Sambos broke open the door of the outer courtyard to find facing them the remains of the bodyguard covering the Khalifa's retreat. Two of the bodyguard charged the small party killing a corporal and wounding two others with their huge spears before they were shot down. The rest then dissolved into the maze of houses and streets; the Khalifa had gone. Smith-Dorrien's only piece of booty from the captured town was a fine Crowned Crane of Africa whose stuffed remains still adorn the family seat in the Scilly Isles.

CHAPTER FOUR

AFTER a week most of the British troops were sent home, Maxwell was appointed Governor of Omdurman, and Smith-Dorrien succeeded him in command of the Brigade. It had not fallen to Smith-Dorrien to play an outstanding part in the battle but his adventures in the Sudan were not yet over. He was given command of the force detailed to take Fashoda, 500 miles above Khartoum. The force comprised a company of the Cameron Highlanders, the XIth and XIIIth Sudanese, and a battery; together with Kitchener and his staff they were carried in four steamers, three of them with barges lashed alongside for the troops. Each night the steamers made fast to the river bank to cut wood for their furnaces. The weather was continually vile. Heat was extreme, rain fell heavily, and strong winds hampered their progress. They were tormented by flies and mosquitos, the kilted Highlanders being the worst sufferers.

Smith-Dorrien had no idea of the reason for this disagreeable cruise until he learnt privately that Kitchener had received reports that a French force was there and wanted to see things for himself. It was typical of the Sirdar not to take the commander of his force into his confidence for he was a man who kept his own secrets. What would have happened if a stray bullet or disrespectful germ had removed Kitchener from the scene is a matter for interesting speculation. After a passage of eight days during which there was some desultory action against bands of Dervishes who were unaware of the Khalifa's disaster and having in the process recaptured Gordon's old steamer the

Saffiyeh, the flotilla reached a village some fifty miles from Fashoda. From there Kitchener sent a runner to warn the French, if any, of his coming. On the 19th September, Kitchener at last sent for his force commander and told him that the sum of his knowledge was that the French commander's name was Marchand, that there were a few other Frenchmen with him, and that his troops consisted of a single company of Senegalese. He could give no definite orders until he discovered Marchand's intentions but if they opened fire Smith-Dorrien was to land his battery and pound them, though the Sirdar was amiable enough to say that he hoped this would not be necessary. If instead there occurred what he described as a "confab", all officers were to take a very official and stand-offish attitude until the ice was broken. Nobody had other than friendly feeling for the French and Smith-Dorrien, like the others, would vastly have preferred inviting them to dine to pounding them. The one thing about which Kitchener was inflexible was that he was there as Governer-General of the Sudan and Marchand must acknowledge the Egyptian flag. Should he prove amenable, Smith-Dorrien was to land all his troops, salute the tricolour, and the Sudanese bands were to play *La Marseillaise*, after which ceremony the Sirdar would offer to transport the entire party to Cairo. If, however, Marchand were to prove intransigent, Smith-Dorrien would receive the signal "Hoist Flag", upon which he was to land, this time drawing up in order of battle and erecting a flagstaff. When all was ready the Sirdar would come and the Egyptian flag would be hoisted to a salute of guns. Smith-Dorrien was then to re-embark, leaving four guns and a battalion to watch the French and continue the voyage with the Sirdar to the mouth of the Sobat river fifty miles further on. Jackson, commanding the troops left behind, was to seal off the French from all communications until orders could be obtained from Cairo.

At about 0900 a small boat flying the French flag approached from up-stream. The oarsmen were Senegalese in bright red jerseys and in the sternsheets sat an officer in spotless white uniform. Engines were stopped, the officer boarded Kitchener's ship, and the flotilla got under way again. Smith-Dorrien could see through his glasses the small fort of Fashoda flying the

French colours. Two more immaculate French officers came from the river bank aboard the flagship and he could see clearly the scene on the open deck, though of course he was out of earshot. There was much bowing and saluting, a map was spread on the table and there followed gesticulations of an obviously inimical kind. Happily a steward arrived at that moment bearing a tray of bottles and glasses; after a short interval the wine appeared to play its genial part and glasses were clinked by the two central figures. Smith-Dorrien, without waiting, landed his troops, hoisted his Egyptian flag and on Kitchener's arrival saluted it with twenty-one guns; the Sudanese obediently gave three cheers for the Khedive in their own tongue and all trooped on board again, except Jackson's contingent. The flotilla moved on south.

The story was current that Kitchener had been unwilling to disclose his intentions directly to Marchand and as he was leaving turned to his ADC, Lord Edward Cecil, saying "By the way, Cecil, haven't you a letter for Monsieur Marchand?" Cecil, well rehearsed, muttered that he believed he had one somewhere and after fumbling in his pockets produced an envelope which he gave to Marchand just after Kitchener had taken his leave. It contained an ultimatum to the effect that there must be no embarkation on the river, no communication with the natives, and no carrying of arms outside the fort, ending with a warning that a force of sufficient strength was present to ensure obedience. Marchand accepted the situation philosophically as he knew full well that but for the victory of Omdurman his little command would have been wiped out. In an odd way, honour was satisfied all round.

All the British officers had much admiration for Marchand and his men who had marched right across Africa and then from the Congo to the Nile carrying their boats in sections. Their splendid appearance, the officers in white uniforms which might just have come from the *blanchisserie* and the men in what appeared to be new red jerseys appealed to every soldierly instinct. Now that the grave and weighty matters were settled—at any rate for the time being—the officers could and did fraternize, the French being found civil and charming as one would expect. In passing it is worth mentioning that one of these officers was called Mangin, a name to become famous though linked with the unpleasing soubriquet of "The Butcher" in a later war. It is difficult to imagine a genial Mangin but of course he was then a much younger man. The British hospitality was more than adequately requited for in some mysterious way which only a Frenchman could understand the French party was handsomely supplied with excellent red wine.

Smith-Dorrien having completed his voyage to the Sobat (where he found nothing but the largest mosquitos in the world) returned to Fashoda a couple of days later. At once there came on board a naval officer, Walter Cowan, whose subsequent career could fill several books, bearing a letter from Marchand which he wished taken down river. Beatty had refused to take it and Smith-Dorrien after some thought excused himself on the ground that he was not going straight to Khartoum and might be delayed for several days. Marchand was vexed and complained to Jackson about the feeble excuses but it was probably for the best. Horace did not tell his chief about it until three years later when he found his action warmly approved. Marchand's men were eventually taken to Cairo leaving Omdurman with full military honours but the affair produced paroxysms of patriotic rage in France which were to endure for a long time, even though their government announced that it was regarded only as a small exploring party. Smith-Dorrien returned to Omdurman and the command of the XIIIth with whom he accompanied Sir Leslie Rundle (later to acquire the name Sir Leisurely Trundle) on his expedition up the Blue Nile hunting outlying bands of Dervishes, and he was greatly shocked by the ruin and devastation the Mahdi and his successor had brought upon their country. On 27th November he took a sad farewell of the Sudanese whom he had come to love and returned to Omdurman for the last time. There he found to his great pleasure that his service in the campaign had brought him the brevet of Colonel and he was to command the 1st Battalion Sherwood Foresters (the old 45th, linked now with his own 95th) in Malta. He wound up his affairs in Egypt, noting ruefully (for he was never a man over-burdened with riches) that he had to sell for sixteen pounds three camels which had cost him forty-one pounds.

He arrived in Malta on New Year's Day 1899 with nothing but Egyptian service uniform. A bilious outgoing Governor refused him leave to go home and kit himself up and he had to await the arrival of his old friend Sir Francis Grenfell, the ex-Sirdar, before he could do so. He went home for a month, got in some excellent shooting, was given, to his great pleasure, a public dinner by the people of Berkhampstead and returned to Malta where he won the Jockey Club Challenge Cup by a short head. He did not like Malta for it gave him fever and neuralgia, probably the result of many years of campaigning in terrible climates. He never really shook these off and was greatly troubled by them during his next campaign though, as he proudly says, he never allowed them to prevent him carrying out his duties.

His regimental soldiering was now nearly over so let us take a look at him in mid-career. Smith-Dorrien was now forty with more than twenty years service behind him, still a bachelor and with no great interest in women. He was, apart from his fever and headaches, in hard physical condition, adept at every form of mounted sport, an excellent shot, and a man of many friendships. He was not very garrulous, sharing with Douglas Haig the constitutional inability to communicate with the private soldier in spite of his undoubted affection for him. His personal courage had been tested time and again and modesty shines through every page of his own account of his life. The loss of his father at an early age had been a heavy blow but his mother, to whom he was devoted and whose capacity for correspondence was considerable, was still living. He was held in the highest regard by the commanders under whom he had served but almost the whole of his military career had been spent in the remote parts of the Empire. This meant that he was not wedded to either the Wolseley ring or that of Lord Roberts (whose distaste for each other did almost as much harm to the Army as the Beresford and Fisher feud was to cause the Navy). Apart from Grenfell and Sir Evelyn Wood, both now almost spent forces, Smith-Dorrien had no patron. The days when he and Kitchener had been captains together were far behind for the ex-Sapper was now a Peer and had flown much higher than a mere brevet Colonel. Smith-Dorrien's view of promotions, appointments, and patronage were those of Wellington himself; "I am what they call in the East, Nimmuk Wallah. I have eaten of the King's salt and I am his servant", but like all of his generation, he did not disdain honours and medals. After Zululand, the Frontier, and two campaigns in Egypt he may well have felt himself entitled to a rest; but round the corner was the next campaign and very different it was to be from the slaughter of half-armed primitive people. Kitchener had offered him the Governorship of Omdurman with the reversion of the Sirdarship, but the rumblings from the Transvaal persuaded Smith-Dorrien that his duty lay further south. The 2nd Battalion Sherwood Foresters—the 95th themselves—arrived from Aden and, after a series of farewell dinners with the Governor and his many friends in the Royal Navy, Horace Smith-Dorrien assumed command and sailed for Durban. The reservists had arrived from England and he was well pleased with them. A detached company was added in Cyprus and the 95th, now 1,200 strong, entered Durban harbour in the troopship *Dunera* on the 13th December. December was the worst month of the war. Sir George White, after the disaster at Nicholson's Nek, was penned in Ladysmith. An Army corps under Sir Redvers Buller had landed, but the 95th did not. They moved on to East London in time to learn that Mafeking and Kimberley were both under siege; that Lord Methuen had been beaten first at the Modder River and then more thoroughly at Magersfontein; that the same had happened to Gatacre at Stormberg and to Buller at Colenso. All these shocks had been administered in one week. It sounded like Omdurman in reverse, this time the decimated masses being dressed in khaki while the invisible Boer riflemen armed with the best Mauser rifles and Schneider-Creusot cannon that the concert of Europe could produce, were playing the role of the defenders of the *zareba*. Something very different from the methods which had won Ulundi and the Atbara were going to be needed here. The former tactics and gallantry of Hector MacDonald, who was of course amongst those present, would be useless and suicidal. But what were the means to be adopted to overthrow the most formidable mounted warriors since the Mongols and who knew of them? Certainly not Sir Redvers Buller.

CHAPTER FIVE

For some three weeks Smith-Dorrien was in command of a mixed force of 5,000 men digging trenches around the Loopersberg where the most eventful thing to happen was his purchase of "a really good horse, Beggarman" from General Gatacre's ADC. As Smith-Dorrien points out, he was going to spend long hours in the saddle and such an animal was worth its weight in gold. On 2nd February to his great delight a wire from Lord Roberts offered him command of the 19th Brigade, recently formed from the Lines of Communication units. These were four good battalions, the 2nd Duke of Cornwall's Light Infantry, the 1st Gordon Highlanders, the 2nd Kings Shropshire Light Infantry, and the Royal Canadian Regiment. The 19th Brigade, together with the Highland Brigade under Hector MacDonald, and a rather scratch collection of divisional troops formed the 9th Division under General Sir Henry Colvile. Two other divisions were forming, both newly arrived in South Africa—the 6th under the experienced General Kelly-Kenny, and the 7th under General Tucker. On the 11th February came Smith-Dorrien's promotion to Major-General. In 1900 the substantive rank of Brigadier-General did not exist and it was common for Brigades to be commanded by Major-Generals and Divisions by Lieutenant-Generals. Hector MacDonald had succeeded to the Highland Brigade on the death of Wauchope—whom we have previously met in the Sudan. Andy Wauchope, one of the richest men in the country and Scotland's darling (his other claim to fame was that he had opposed Gladstone at the Midlothian election), had thrown his life away gallantly and uselessly in Methuen's disastrous attack. At the news of his fall a cry went up from his Highlanders echoing that given on the death of Cameron of Lochiel at Quatre Bras. The Scotsmen had been badly shaken by the punishment they had received from the invisible Boer marksmen, but were still spoiling for a fight.

To join his new formation Smith-Dorrien had to ride eighty-seven miles through country where no solitary horseman was safe and was fortunate in finding a body of mounted infantry heading for the same destination. This just gave him time for a farewell parade of his beloved Foresters and his joy at the prospect of action was tempered by this final leave taking.

His journey on horseback took five days through veldt inches deep in locusts who were devouring every growing thing. With every stride Beggarman took the horrible insects flew into his rider's face with stinging force and the devastation they caused made a considerable mark in his mind. The ride to which he had so looked forward became a nightmare. From Thebus station, his immediate destination, he had a further 250 miles to travel by train to the Orange River where the Army was assembling. There he found a scene of utter confusion, masses of troops, horses, wagons, guns, and oxen busily engaged in sorting themselves out into formations and units. Roberts was preparing for his long march on Bloemfontein.

MacDonald, with eight battalions and a cavalry brigade, had had a skirmish on the 6th at Koedoesberg with the object of causing a distraction from the main advance and also of driving the Boers from their position on the Modder River which was in the direct path of an advance on Kimberley, under siege since Black Week. As Smith-Dorrien ruefully notes "They had not been successful in the latter object"; he had some talent for meiosis.

He spent three days finding and collecting his scattered brigade and meeting his staff, augmented by his nephew Eddy as temporary ADC. At this time he had not the faintest idea what was going on—a state of affairs that he was to encounter again—until put more or less in the picture by Colvile whom he now met for the first time. The three divisions led by a cavalry division were moving on the state capital itself, the 9th marching one day behind the others.

Ahead of the Army lay the strong Magersfontein position from which the Boers, snugly ensconced in weapon pits, had driven back Lord Methuen in bloody retreat. Roberts, however, was no Buller and had no intention of throwing away valuable troops in hopeless frontal attacks. The German official history, a very fair account of the war through the eyes of experienced continental soldiers, pays him the tribute of saying that at last the English had found a general who understood envelopment and to envelop was exactly Bobs' intention. New divisions, to be the 10th and 11th, were forming at home and with the arrival of the last, Britain's manpower barrel had been scraped clean. To complete these two divisions it had been necessary to send out militia battalions and Volunteer Service companies to be joined to the regular units. Canada, Australia, and New Zealand were there laying the foundations of the great military reputations they were to build in the next half-century and many locally enlisted corps of varying military value were spread throughout the Army. Roberts knew well that the home country had been left virtually defenceless and like Wellington before him that he was commanding England's only Army. If he allowed it to be wasted there would be no other to replace it. There must be no more Magersfonteins, no more Stormbergs, no more Colensos. Apart from realistic military judgment and his natural humanity, the death of his only son, the beloved Freddie, in winning his own VC at Colenso weighed heavily on Roberts; many people believed that his main reason for not sacking— or, in the terms of the day, *stellenbosching*—the egregious Buller was that he did not wish it believed that it was an act of vengeance for sending Freddie to his death. He had been overheard on a visit to the field to murmur to himself "it was murder".

While the Army continues its long and wearisome march let us have a brief look at what sort of an Army it was. Numerically it was the strongest force to take the field for many years. The infantry was of high quality, as usual, which is the more remarkable when one considers the raw material from which it was made. The Rowntree Report on the slum conditions in the great cities spoke eloquently of stunted rickety children with rotten teeth and in the days before any sort of welfare state existed many of these children had been compelled to take the shilling under the necessity of dire poverty. As in the Peninsular days the Army and the nation had one over-riding sin—drunkenness. Kipling, who knew more about the Army than his detractors give him credit for, was not wide of the mark when he wrote of the half-baked recruit going out to the East where he acts like a babe and drinks like a beast, but those who survived long enough would grow into his paragon Serjeant [sic] What's-'is-Name. It was little short of miraculous to see the results of the work of a thousand Serjeant What's-'is-Names, turning such unpromising material into sturdy, disciplined riflemen. There were great gaps in the individual training and the troops were not taught self-reliance or encouraged to think for themselves; emphasis was always on mass discipline and indeed at the beginning of the war volley firing was still standard practice, even though the excellent Lee-Metford magazine rifle had made this obsolete over night. The platoon volleys of Marlborough had ruined the French and Bavarians at Blenheim a couple of centuries before but with a weapon capable of fifteen aimed rounds a minute in the hands of a moderately trained man volley fire dissipated all the advantages of the new weapon. However, the Army was swift to learn and the system of rapid independent fire which was to halt a German Army in its tracks a few years later had its genesis on the veldt. A large number of recruits were farmhands and while they were basically sturdier than their urban comrades it was noticeable at the end of a gruelling march that the man carrying two rifles on his shoulder was as often as not the sallow ex-slum boy while the ruddier ex-farmhand gratefully accepted the timely help. The infantryman's equipment was heavy but serviceable and with the reduction of the calibre of the rifle from ·45 to ·303 he was able to carry 160 rounds without undue difficulty. There was no infantry entrenching tool, the Walters spade (a combined spade and mattock) being an RE store. The inevitable moustache was mandatory, paragraph 660 of Queen's Regulations 1896 stating uncompromisingly that "the chin and underlip will be shaved: the upper lip will not be shaved. Whiskers, if worn, will be of moderate length."

The battalion retained its eight company organization but in many cases one company had been permanently detached to become part of a corps of Mounted Infantry. The *Infantry Drill Book* of 1896 prescribed one formation only for the attack—three lines, the first being assault troops, the second for supporting and thickening up the first, and the third being the reserve. A halt at about 500 yards from the enemy "in a good defensive position all along the front whence as from a first parallel in a siege both false and real attacks can be made on the position in front. . . . The critical moment has now come. Orders are given for the final assault. The second line advances and as it strikes the first line carries the assaulting portions of it forward. As this movement is repeated, by the constant accession of fresh troops pressing into the firing line the whole continuously advance and when near enough rush the position. . . . During the delivery of the assault men will cheer, drums be beaten, bugles sounded and the pipes played." The simple art of fire and movement was unknown. The German history notes approvingly that as experience was gained the British practices moved very near to their own regulations of 1870—attacks in mass on a narrow front. The Army had at last an excellent machine gun in the Maxim but its use was not properly understood for it was generally considered simply a reserve of fire power, to be kept for emergencies only. The whole object of an attack was to get at the enemy with the bayonet without loss of time. The fire fight which had clinched the result of so many battles in 1870 was barely considered important. The German doctrine, sounder by far than our own, was that infantry should not be launched into battle until the enemy was a plum ripe for the picking. This, however seemed a lack of fighting spirit to many and was regarded as the hall-mark of continental conscript armies alone.

All transport, of course, was animal-drawn as in the days of Alexander and the problem of providing daily forage for vast numbers of horses, mules, and oxen inhibited many an operation. Curiously enough an old and simple weapon like the mortar, which would have been extremely useful, had vanished from the armoury in common with the grenade. The regimental signallers too could produce nothing better than the flag or the heliograph and a dull, rainy day could and did cause a complete breakdown in communication, though line telephony existed and there were even a couple of crude wireless sets, sent out under the charge of a naval officer for experimental purposes. The experiment was not very successful.

The cavalry, as always, were a law unto themselves. Everything centred on the knee-to-knee charge and all manœuvre was aimed at bringing about this exhilarating experience. This was a horseman's war and the great cavalry horse could easily outpace the Boer's shaggy pony. Lances were carried and used. The Boers, who were occasionally caught in the open and ridden down, reserved their particular hatred for these riders and hunted them down mercilessly whenever they could. A carbine, usually the Martini-Metford was carried, but in the case of the Yeomanry it was the old Westley-Richards monkey-tail—a feeble and despised weapon. As this was the last time that cavalry was to be a principal arm in the field it would be unchivalrous to grudge them their glorious sunset.

In the matter of artillery the Treasury had seen to it, not for the last time, that the Army was less well-equipped than its enemies. The French quick-firing seventy-five had been in service for several years and the house of Krupp had ensured that the German Empire did not lack a similar weapon. The British fifteen-pounder was still of the transitional pattern in which the shell (usually Lyddite which burst with a yellow flash) and the propellant charge had to be loaded separately. The Horse Artillery was even worse off, in some cases having nothing better than a muzzle loading seven-pounder, more suited to the museum than the battlefield. The heavier pieces were 4·7 guns and a few 5 inch howitzers (known throughout the Army as cow-guns) all travelling at a foot pace and loaded like an old Sussex timber wain. To offset the shortage of these necessary weapons Captain Percy Scott, RN, the Navy's gunnery expert, dismounted some of the secondary batteries of HMS *Powerful* and equipped them with home-made land carriages. The only quick-firing guns in the Army were a number of twelve and a half-pounders bought privately from Armstrong-Whitworths by the CIV, to the envy of many a regular gunner. There was a fine war balloon for artillery spotting but this proved more decorative than useful as the observers in their basket were unable to communicate with the batteries, although both Napoleon and Ulysses Grant knew how it was done.

The Sappers performed wonders with precious little. The medical services were devoted and hard working but soon found themselves overwhelmed with cases of enteric fever and other diseases peculiar to Africa for which they had no effective drugs. The greatest weakness of all, however, was the system itself, if such it can be called. For all its size this was an unorganized force hastily thrown together and was more an agglomeration of units than an Army. There was no General Staff system remotely like that which Moltke had taught an amazed Europe to be essential a full generation ago. Each general had his own military family (Smith-Dorrien, for example, had redeemed a promise lightly made in Malta to a young Marine officer named Hood that if he ever got a brigade he would ask for him as ADC) but very little else and no proper division of duties or system obtained for all the forty years of Wolseley's Staff College training. The junior staff officers were little more than gallopers and could not be compared with Moltke's demi-gods—professional liaison officers trained to think and appreciate, knowing precisely their chief's mind and able to enforce his will on subordinate commanders even though they themselves held only junior ranks. They were detested by many generals who regarded them as Moltke's spies, but they achieved his purposes.

Lord Roberts was helped in his planning by the brilliant Colonel Henderson, biographer of Stonewall Jackson, and Lee at second hand, but having been brought up in the empirical ways of the old Bengal Army Roberts was accustomed to see the battle for himself, seize the situation at a glance and send out verbal orders to his few commanders basing his decisions on his own observations. This casualness had served well enough in small Indian wars but was altogether too amateurish in the dawn of this new age of scientific soldiering. The Army had strong limbs but almost no nervous system.

Lord Roberts's plan for the long flank march was an excellent one, worthy of Lee himself. French, with the cavalry division at Rendsburg, and Gatacre at Sterkstroom were only just able to check the Boer commandos which had invaded the north of Cape Colony itself and there was real danger of rebellion. Happily the Boers' system of precedence while it lacked the occult intricacies of Army, regimental, brevet, local, and acting ranks, was sufficiently obscure to produce internecine quarrels and little action. The weakness of Roberts's force lay in the shortage of cavalry but the removal of infantry companies and their conversion into MI produced two MI brigades each of about 1,600 men of a passable degree of equestrianism, and more use was made of Brabant's Colonial Horse, about 3,000 strong. There were also two locally enrolled MI regiments known, hopefully, as Roberts's Horse and Kitchener's Horse. Bobs was going to need them all, for he was carrying the war into the enemy's country to take Bloemfontein and raise the sieges of Ladysmith and Kimberley by drawing off the commandos to protect their own homelands. He rejected the ideas of using the railway from East London for once the Boers realized what he was about they would destroy the railway bridges over the Orange River (they did this in any event), and also the tempting idea of moving from Natal across the Tugela through Ladysmith for the gradients on the railway made it impossible to run trains of more than six carriages, not nearly enough to supply forage alone. In any case the railway ended nearly 200 miles from Bloemfontein.

The route Roberts chose was the most difficult as the lines of communication would be over 600 miles long and there was a large Boer force at Colesberg in the north Cape Colony which if energetically led could threaten his rear. The safety of his communications was of first importance for if these were cut his Army would starve. His wagons would have to carry everything for the ninety miles from Kimberley to Bloemfontein where there was no railway and 4,000 to 5,000 teams would be needed to supply 40,000 men and 15,000 animals. But by this route he would cross the great Orange River bridge which was strongly held by the British and the ninety miles from Kimberley was far less than the 200 by the Ladysmith route. Also the country was far more open and suitable for using his numerical superiority than would have been the high trackless mountains of Natal or the regions about the Orange River.

So the great column moved off on a wide front over the dry rolling veldt. There were no roads but the veldt itself served well enough. The temperature by day varied between 110 and 120 degrees between the hours of 1100 and 1600 and as there had been no rain recently the vegetation was parched and useless for forage. Every afternoon the sky was darkened by heavy black clouds but no rain fell and dust-storms filled the air with grit and sand as dark as a London fog. The nights at least were cool. At last the rain came, rain that is not seen outside Africa, turning the dusty veldt into a morass and bursting the banks of the streams. For ten days it rained, mostly at night, and bivouacs were now cold and wet, but for all that the health of the men remained excellent; they were much tougher now than they had been only a couple of months ago. All this movement was carried out without the Boers' knowledge despite their excellent grapevine.

Roberts feinted with MacDonald's brigade against the left of the Boers' Magersfontein position but the business was bungled. (This was the Koedesberg affair which Smith-Dorrien had heard about on his way forward). The German account of it says heavily, "The resolute but unsuccessful attack of General MacDonald was not in accordance with the purely demonstrative object of the enterprise." Fighting Mac would not have taken kindly to shadow-boxing. The main effort was to be a long turning movement round the east of the position to compel Cronje, who commanded the Boer forces there and before Kimberley, to abandon his position and open the road to the besieged town.

Roberts kept his plan to himself and his staff until the last minute and gave his orders on the evening of 8th February. French's cavalry was to relieve Kimberley and the 6th and 7th Divisions were to follow with the 9th behind them as soon as it arrived. On 12th February, French swept over the Riet River through the unoccupied De Kiel's Drift driving de Wet with 500 men and a couple of guns back towards Winter Hoek; unfortunately, French made no further attempt to find out what the latter was planning, assuming him to have fled before the terrible horsemen. De Wet had done no such thing and was crouched to spring upon the British rear as soon as the opportunity arose. Patrolling is always a trying business and French's cavalry officers could not be bothered with it. One of them is quoted as saying that it is better to get into a tight place now and then by neglect of these duties than to have to endure the constant irksomeness which they entail. On this occasion de Wet was going to make them pay for chasing him and for their lack of respect.

A German observer on the British side said severely that he was inclined to connect this slackness with the national and ineradicable optimism of the British.

On the morning of the 13th, Smith-Dorrien marched his 19th Brigade eastwards across the Riet River at Waterval Drift in intense heat and drought, the marching conditions being so gruelling that it was not until after nightfall on the 14th that its tail was across the river. Early next morning when the march was resumed he observed in his rear a convoy of ox-wagons crossing the drift apparently guarded only by some irregular horse, and knowing more about the vulnerability of transport in Southern Africa than most men he dropped off a company of Gordons to guard it. At about 1000 news reached him that the convoy was under attack by the ubiquitous de Wet. A battalion and some MI were hurried back but it was too late; the convoy had already changed hands. As it contained 28,000 rations for men and 88,000 for horses its loss was a serious blow to Roberts. He took the brave decision to cut his losses and in spite of all efforts to improvise another convoy the Army was on half rations until Bloemfontein fell.

On the 17th, 19 Brigade reached the Modder River at Klip Drift but to understand its actions and those of the individuals concerned it is necessary to look back over the last few days. On the 14th, the day the convoy was lost, the 6th Division and the MI had reached the river and on the same day the 15th Brigade of General Wavell (famous father of a more famous son) had taken Jacobsdal. Cronje had abandoned the Magersfontein position and moved his laager a couple of miles back from the river. Now the cavalry had their chance. Kitchener loosed French with orders to relieve Kimberley. Charging at the gallop with two Lancer regiments leading, and covered by the guns of the 6th Division, six thousand horsemen burst through the 900 riflemen holding the Boer line. The dust kicked up by the horses hid everything from view and when it cleared French and his men were seen rallying a mile beyond the Boer position. Their casualties were sixteen men and twenty horses wounded. As Horace ungrudgingly records "it was a bold conception splendidly carried out and rightly raised the reputation of the General commanding the Cavalry Division." The official historian in a moment of euphoria wrote "The part played by cavalry in the main attack where conditions of ground are favourable is one that will grow in importance in wars of the future." French's Chief of Staff was a Major Douglas Haig who at this time would have heartily applauded the sentiment. Colonel Horne, later to command the First Army in France, who had joined the cavalry before Colesberg and who was both eye witness and participant, subsequently maintained that it was Haig's knowledge and sagacity combined with French's energy and daring which won for the cavalry their great success. The orders which Haig issued on behalf of his commander were almost always written in his own hand and were models of lucidity. *O si sic omnes.* The cynical could say that this was no Balaclava or Mars-la-Tour as the charge was unopposed save by fire. The fact remains that it achieved its object and French entered Kimberley that same evening. This must have been in every sense a relief to the garrison commander, Colonel Kekewich, whose greatest cross was the captive and hysterical Cecil Rhodes. These two had fallen out long ago for Rhodes considered himself, amongst other things, a military genius. His genial forms of address, ("Kekewich, you damned cur" is only one of them) and his constant interference had led that long-suffering officer to consider putting Rhodes in gaol when the dust of French's men was seen on the horizon. A few weeks after the siege was over Rhodes pretended not to know who Kekewich was, saying "You don't remember the man who blacks your boots."

CHAPTER SIX

UNFORTUNATELY, French now felt that he could for the moment rest on his new laurels. Du Toit and Ferreira, the Boer generals investing Kimberley, had fled before him but were undamaged and still to be reckoned with. Much more important was the fact that Cronje's laager was at that moment indefensible and could have been taken by cavalry alone. As usual, however, the commander on the spot knew no more than he could see through his field glasses and the chance was lost.

Next morning the bewildered Cronje took the decision to retire on Bloemfontein. The old warrior was now a pathetic figure, vacillating between one plan and another as his advisers heatedly had their say. One report speaks of him sitting in his tent all day with his wife patting his head and making soothing noises. The Boer force had grown fat since Magersfontein with its accumulated loot and numbers of women and children had joined it during the lull in the fighting. There were now with Cronje some 5,000 men, of whom one-third were on foot, nearly 500 wagons with their teams, numerous women and children, and a herd of cattle. However, de Wet, du Toit, and Ferreira were still hovering somewhere on the flanks of the British and if they could somehow join up he might still escape to the east.

That night the entire mass, less about eighty wagons for which no teams could be found, moved in bright moonlight across the open veldt in front of the British Army and were not seen. Such a move ought to have been stark madness but Cronje knew the slack habits of his enemy, took his chance and succeeded. At 0600 (about half an hour after dawn) vedettes of the MI saw the great dust cloud and reported back that Cronje was on the move but equally incredibly no action was taken for several hours. The MI were then sent off to work round Cronje's left but one gun and a pom-pom were brought into action against them and they fled in disorder. At 0900, the Buffs were ordered to cross the river and take the *kopjes* to the north of it, an operation which they carried out as if on parade.

By the worst of ill-fortune Lord Roberts was at this moment attacked by a severe chill and took to his bed at Jacobsdal where Colvile and 19 Brigade were bivouacked. Before doing so, however, he sent a message to French ordering him to move with all speed to head off the laager. In the belief that this was being done the C-in-C succumbed to his illness; his recovery would have been the slower had he known that the telegraph wire was cut. Roberts's Chief of Staff was now in his element and prepared to hurl battalions and batteries around the battlefield with more energy than tactical skill. This time, however, he was no longer the Sirdar and the Army's exotic system of rank and command asserted itself. Kitchener was a substantive Major-General, as were Kelly-Kenny and Colvile. It had, however, been decided that commanders of divisions should all be given the local rank of Lieutenant-General. Thus it happened that Kelly-Kenny, far superior to Kitchener in skill and experience but ranking below him in the Army List as Major-General, was the next in seniority to Roberts himself. French was a mere Colonel in Army rank but as a local Lieutenant-General he too could have claimed precedence had he been there. Kelly-Kenny, quite properly, insisted that as the C-in-C was a casualty the command devolved on him; Kitchener in return retorted that as Chief of Staff he was the voice of the C-in-C who was no more than temporarily absent. In the end Bobs sent a personal letter to Kelly-Kenny courteously supporting Kitchener's view; Kelly-Kenny replied huffily that he would even submit to humiliation for the good of the service. Kitchener, never even in his calmer moments noted for his urbanity, was by now thoroughly excited. Kelly-Kenny was forced to accept the position but became sulky and played no part in the coming battle. In any case he would have had little chance to exercise even the command of his own division for the ex-Sirdar, never dissatisfied with his own questionable tactics at Omdurman, was about to do it again.

Kitchener began by pushing Stephenson's and Hannay's tired MI along the south bank to Paardeberg Drift. As Hannay predicted, they got as far as Klip Kraal, were counter-attacked and promptly pushed back to their starting point. They had not yet got over their performance earlier that morning. By evening Roberts's message reached French who, by aimless gallopings about north of Kimberley, had reduced his men and horses to a state of utter exhaustion; he had also failed to make contact with du Toit or Ferreira. Still, he managed to muster a few hundred tired men and at 1900 they rode out towards the southeast. Cronje was still moving eastward and had reached Wolves' Kraal intending to cross the river at Vendutie when the shelling from French's few little horse guns halted him in his tracks. Fortunately for Cronje a strong position (another of those river banks beloved of the Boers) was at hand and into it he moved, laagering his wagons as his father had done against Dingaan and digging into the steep banks of the river with such tools as could be found. While he was doing this French was in his turn attacked by Ferreira who had appeared out of the blue. Ferreira was not the most resolute of commanders for French's handful was at his mercy had he pressed his attack home. Boer generals were nearly always nervous of being attacked by cavalry in the open and probably French's reputation, after the stories of the charge had been repeated by terrified burghers who would not have minimised their ordeal, saved him. Be that as it may, Ferreira drew off, having gained Cronje some valuable time.

Now that French's guns could be heard Kitchener's nervous energy re-doubled. Smith-Dorrien's brigade, on orders direct from Lord Roberts, marched through the moonlit night and the following day the twenty-six miles to Paardeberg Drift with Hector MacDonald's troops just ahead; they had marched sixty-miles in five days, mostly after dark. After a brief halt (in the course of which Ridley of the MI inadvertently trousered his Brigadier's tobacco pouch after filling his pipe from it) they moved south-east again. By morning on the 18th the 6th Division lay opposite the laager, which occupied both banks of the river. Smith-Dorrien, in common with almost all those present, had no idea what was afoot until there arrived Hubert Hamilton, one of Kitchener's staff officers, with orders for Smith-Dorrien to take his brigade and a battery across the river and "establish yourself on the other side." On enquiring where he was supposed to cross, the general received the helpful reply, "The river is in flood and as far as I have heard Paardeberg Drift, the only one available, is unfordable; but Lord Kitchener, knowing your resourcefulness is sure you will get across somehow." Smith-Dorrien returned what he describes in his diary as "a jeering answer" which sad to relate has now been lost for posterity. He did, however record that he told Hamilton that his reply was that of a "courtier"—one of the most pejorative expressions in his vocabulary.

With the brigade following he galloped to the river and, plunged into it as he had done into the flooded Buffalo twenty years ago. The result was much the same for again he was nearly swept away but somehow he regained the bank and moving down to the Drift itself found that Beggarman could just get across without swimming. The Sappers got a rope across the fifty yard wide river (as Sappers always manage to do in some manner that only another Sapper can comprehend) and the brigade and the battery crossed, the rushing water up to their armpits and the current trying to sweep them away towards the laager. The three machine guns were carried in one of Admiral James's excellent collapsible boats. The DCLI was left behind with two companies of the Shropshires as a baggage-guard, and the rest of the brigade took up a position running roughly north and south—Otter's Canadians nearest to the river, next the Shropshires, then the battery, and lastly the Gordons. Smith-Dorrien had established himself on the other side; he had been given no further orders.

Meanwhile, to the south of the river Kitchener was losing his troops in impressive numbers. Kelly-Kenny, wishing to invest the laager and force its surrender by fire and starvation, was still playing Achilles in his tent. Kitchener had boasted to his staff at 0730 that he would be in the laager by 1000 hours; he was going to do it or others would die in the attempt. First he hurled in Hector MacDonald's Highland Brigade—they were promptly mown down by the men who had performed the same office for them at Magersfontein. Encouraged by this Kitchener issued identical orders direct to 13th Brigade. They in turn rose up and were shot where they stood, making no progress at all. There remained only the MI.

Earlier in the day Kitchener had sent both Hannay's and Stephenson's Brigades to the East of the laager; at about 1000 he sent a galloper to bring them back. Learning of French's arrival he sent a further galloper to cancel the order and rode out himself to order the MI to press down both banks. Hannay protested that the order was madness, which it was. Although Kitchener claims in a subsequent letter to have been completely calm, eye witnesses are unanimous in holding that he had worked himself into a rage bordering on apoplexy and Hannay, feeling that his personal courage had been questioned, rode at the Boer position. At first they did not fire, thinking he must be out of his senses but then one man fired, others joined in, and Hannay and some forty men fell riddled with bullets. His grave is still preserved and honoured. Did John Buchan, perhaps unconsciously, remember his name?

Baulked at the south and east ends of the laager, Kitchener turned his attention to Smith-Dorrien's part of the field. He learnt that de Wet was attacking from the south and had taken Kitchener's *kopje*. This ought to have been the Atbara again but instead it was Omdurman, with Ali-wad-Helu in a slouch hat, coming from the wrong direction, but with the same object of upsetting Kitchener's attack. It never developed into a serious threat for de Wet was still learning his trade fast and knew his limitations. Smith-Dorrien, waiting impatiently for orders—the Official History criticizes him for lack of dash but does not say what form it should have taken—swore a mighty oath that he would not shave again until the laager had been taken. Smith-Dorrien had been told nothing and knew no more about the disposition of enemy or his own troops than did his own horse holder. It was only on the following day that he learnt that the guns which he had heard to the north-east were French's. At 1600, on his own initiative, he made a small forward movement with the Shropshires to draw fire from the Canadians and MacDonald but an hour later to his shock and rage he saw his entire line, including the troops he had left to guard the transport, rise up and charge forward cheering. Kitchener had taken a hand. He had personally given orders to Smith-Dorrien's troops, even bringing the DCLI over the river, and had ordered them to attack. The only man who was not told what 19 Brigade was to do was its commander. Colonel Aldworth was shot dead encouraging his Cornishmen forward, and the charge quickly petered out in the face of the Mausers, having achieved nothing. The Army's casualties that day were twenty officers and 300 other ranks killed and fifty-two officers and 890 other ranks wounded, some eight per cent of the 15,000 men engaged and the highest of any day in the War. All were sacrificed to the monumental incompetence of one man and the wretchedness of the system of staff and command. The units of 19 Brigade involved lost twenty-two per cent of their strength.

Smith-Dorrien's terrifying bursts of rage were well known throughout the Army. As if he had not had enough to try him already, he received at dusk an order to report personally to Colvile on the other side of the river. He did not like Colvile but hoped that at least he would get some information and orders. It was nothing of the kind; Colvile merely wanted a report on the day's proceedings to obtain which he had put a general officer to the trouble of crossing and re-crossing the swollen Modder and deprived him of much-needed sleep. It is not difficult to guess the kind of report Smith-Dorrien gave him. His photograph in the *Times History of the War* shows a heavy pugnacious face over a lean, horseman's body. This was not a man to suffer fools and he had seen fool's work that day. Smith-Dorrien returned at midnight and lay down on Gun Hill with his saddle doing duty for a pillow. He was a very angry general.

The following day was comparatively uneventful save that at 1100 he had his first meal for two days except, as he carefully records, a mouthful at dawn on the 17th and a biscuit at mid-day on the 19th. The loss of the convoy was making itself felt. But at least Lord Roberts had recovered from his chill and was back in the saddle. Smith-Dorrien's line, under Roberts's order, spent most of the next day moving gingerly towards the laager while their commander attended a summons to the presence of the C-in-C. There he found Bobs, Kitchener, Colvile and French at a council of war. Bobs came at once to the point and asked whether Smith-Dorrien thought he could carry the laager by direct assault. Smith-Dorrien replied straightforwardly that losses would be great and chances of success small. Kitchener, naturally, spoke heatedly to the effect that it could and should be done. Colvile, who was to give proof soon afterwards that he was a man utterly devoid of humanity, supported him. French, oddly enough for such a thruster, did not favour it. The C-in-C mindful of the previous day's casualties, was against it and would not be argued out of his conclusion. Smith-Dorrien advised a few days' bombardment and harrassing while he sapped forward to a position from which he could attack. As he mounted to ride back Kitchener told him that if he would attack at once he would be a made man. Smith-Dorrien with one of his rare smiles answered "You heard my views and I shall only attack now if ordered to." Nobody seems to have commented on the state of his beard.

And so it fell out. Correspondence passed between Roberts and Cronje over a proposed armistice for the burial of the Boer dead but Roberts felt he had to refuse this as he believed it was only intended to gain time for de Wet, or Ferreira, or both to come to the rescue. Cronje accused Roberts of unkindness and invited him to bombard away. On the 21st Roberts wrote that he had learnt of the presence of women and children in the laager and offered them safe conduct. Cronje refused, as he refused an offer to send in doctors and medical supplies unless they remained in the laager. The Boers, not to be outdone in chivalry, did not fire on thirsty men filling their water bottles from the stinking river polluted by the corpses of horses and cattle but they probably achieved the same object without expending precious ammunition as casualties from enteric fever, caused by drinking such filth, far exceeded those from musketry. The bombardment and the trenching continued and on the 27th Smith-

5   The Smith-Dorrien—Apthorpe—Gough team, Lucknow, 1895.

6   A civic reception at Berkhampstead, June 1901.

7 Boer War General.

Dorrien attacked under cover of darkness, the place of honour falling to the Canadians. The laager surrendered. One white flag followed by another and then another appeared along the river bank drawing from him the observation that "It's just like the Resurrection." The casualties were only twelve killed. Smith-Dorrien galloped a couple of miles, shouted for a razor, and removed his nine day beard. It was the anniversary of Majuba.

By a happy chance someone with a camera was present to record for all time the meeting of the dapper little Field Marshal in plain uniform with his Kandahar sword by his side and the burly, vastly-bearded, and untidy Cronje. "I am glad to see you: you have made a gallant defence, Sir", followed by breakfast. A captured German officer records that the Boers were treated with the utmost humanity, British officers and private soldiers alike behaving like thorough gentlemen. It was, as General Fuller said, the last of the gentlemen's wars. The first of the cad's wars was still some way off. Cronje was sent to Saint Helena, Mr. Punch enriching the occasion with a cartoon showing him greeting the previous tenant of Longwood over the caption "Same enemy, Sire: same result".

The condition of the captured laager was dreadful, even such a connoisseur of smells as Smith-Dorrien remarking that his vocabulary was inadequate to describe them. There were captured 4,200 burghers, four generals and 5,000 rifles. The immediate result was that away over in Natal the forces besieging Ladysmith were withdrawn, giving Buller a walk-over on 1st March.

For the next few days the Army rested; it had well deserved it. The march on Bloemfontein began again on 6th March and it was now that the loss of the convoy really told, for not only were the men hungry but the half-starved horses could barely raise a trot and frequent halts were essential. The Boers (since Ferreira's death under de Wet's own command) were by no means defeated but were now very sensitive to having their flanks turned. As Horace put it, it was like a grouse drive where the game was disturbed and alarmed before the guns had taken up their position in the butts. Smith-Dorrien's dislike of Colvile was in no way mitigated by the latter's continuous refusal to reveal what orders had been given to him and by having to watch opportunities slip away by Colvile's constant refusal of permission to move. Such permission, however, was granted at the capture of the Leeuwkop taken by 19 Brigade after some very expert manœuvring; it was now a formation of the highest quality. Apart from some skirmishing there was no serious work to be done before Bloemfontein and the town was taken over without a fight on 16th March. Smith-Dorrien speaks lovingly of turkeys at fifteen shillings, Aylesbury ducks at three shillings each and the addition of a chaplain who was an excellent Mess President and skilful forager. (Later he became a Bishop and no doubt was an admirable pastor.)

The weather was very wet and the tired men succumbed in large numbers to enteric fever which was never eradicated from the Army, the usual cause being the use of water from polluted rivers and pools. In the whole war there were over 8,000 deaths from enteric fever alone compared to only a little over 1,000 in the entire First World War. Inoculation would have been more useful than any other modern weapon. It was practised on small numbers of men by disciples of Professor Wright with complete success but was never employed on a large scale, nor was it made compulsory. Dr Conan Doyle of Langman's Hospital is on record as saying that Bloemfontein could be smelt long before it was entered, for men were dying at a prodigious rate. (It would not be accurate to say that they died like flies for in that febrile city flies seemed immortal and multiplied readily.) Between April and May there were buried more than 5,000 men.

CHAPTER SEVEN

On the last day of March Roberts began the next stage of the advance on Pretoria itself, this time with the 9th Division leading. After some six hours marching, Colvile ordered Smith-Dorrien and MacDonald to join him on the top of Boesman's Kop, fourteen miles from the town. From the summit they could see the tall chimneys of the waterworks seven miles away and a lot of mounted troops about two miles further on in the same direction. Colvile announced that they were Broadwood's men and that "he had sent for that officer". Already there was a rumour about some disaster to the guns, believed to have happened about six miles to the north-east of Waterval Drift. His brigadiers both urged Colvile to ride on, find Broadwood and ascertain what had taken place. Colvile's bland reply was that Broadwood was in a state of collapse and he would get nothing out of him. After twenty impatient minutes Martyr's MI led the division on towards the Drift. The enemy were in some strength there and were driven off after a sharp fight, much delay had been caused by Colvile who remained a long way behind and kept all the guns with him. It was 1700 when the guns at last appeared, just in time to lob a few shells at the retiring Boers. While this was going on Broadwood rode up, looking very fit and enquiring for the divisional commander. From him, Smith-Dorrien learnt that the calamity had occurred on the Korn Spruit, five or six miles south-east of the Drift. At Sannah's Post there was a small garrison of 200 men whom de Wet intended to take in order to cut off the town's water supply. Under his own hand he had 350 men with four or five guns while another 1,150 burghers lay on the other side of the river. His plan was simple and effective, to set an ambush along both sides of the Korn Spruit into which his guns would drive the garrison which would then be shot down by his riflemen. While this was going on de Wet learnt from his spies that Broadwood was falling back from Ladybrand before General Olivier and was heading for Thaba Nchu, thirteen miles east of the Waterworks, and he saw rightly that a nobler prey than a couple of hundred infantry was going to blunder into his trap.

At first light de Wet saw Broadwood's entire force 3,000 yards away. Down the Spruit came a number of carts containing women and children who were allowed to pass, with the warning that if they attempted to signal they would be fired on. Broadwood's men followed them at some distance, into the Spruit where they were greeted with the challenge "Hands up." De Wet says that a forest of hands at once rose into the air and 200 men were quickly disarmed. He was only 100 yards away and five guns and 100 wagons were added to his bag. The remainder of Broadwood's men then fell back to the station, recaptured two guns by a counter-attack and opened up with shrapnel. De Wet had fewer men but more guns and he managed to drive the British from the station. The fire fight lasted for three hours during which his men from east of the river managed with great difficulty to get across. Then Broadwood ran the gauntlet of the ambush, those who succeeded in doing so running straight into the arms of de Wet's reinforcement who put them to flight in disorder. The booty consisted of 480 unwounded prisoners, seven guns, and 117 wagons. The Boer casualties were three killed and five wounded to about 350 killed and wounded on the British side. Once again the British were heavily punished for their slackness in patrolling, this being the worst example of it in the whole war.

Smith-Dorrien's men continued on to Waterval Drift which was very steep and difficult to cross, but by midnight they were over, although bivouacked in an exposed position. Though ordered to be ready to move at first light, the force spent the hours from dawn till 1000 watching a large force of Boers moving about on the high ground six or seven miles ahead. Colvile then arrived and gave orders to go back across the river and occupy the waterworks which he believed to be clear of the enemy. At 1400 they had re-crossed and were a couple of miles west of the waterworks when a further order arrived to the effect that the waterworks were occupied after all and they should move back to Boesman's Kop. Smith-Dorrien did so, putting a strong guard across the donga where the ambush had taken place. When he arrived to take up the position he found there Brigadier-General Porter, four RHA guns, and about eighty cavalry, survivors of the rout. Porter told him that there were eighty-seven cavalry lying wounded in some corrugated iron houses about 1,400 yards to the front, roughly halfway between himself and a force of Boers with whom an exchange of artillery fire was going on at a range of about 4,000 yards. Smith-Dorrien sent both his ADCs back for all available ambulances and carts, but before they had got very far Colvile arrived and said that as the wounded belonged to the mounted troops they were no concern of his and they must get them away themselves. Shortly after this a written order arrived to withdraw all troops at once to Boesman's Kop, though it was clear that Porter's little party alone had no chance of saving their wounded. Smith-Dorrien says "I shall never forget the indignation of General Porter and his men when they heard of this inhuman order." Smith-Dorrien obeyed the letter of his orders, but sent his troops back very slowly and extracted all the wounded under heavy fire without loss. The cavalry were suitably grateful. In fact the wounded would probably have suffered no harm had they been captured for this was a war in which there was little mutual hatred and each side did the best it could within the limits of its resources to care for those who fell into its hands. To men who had learnt their trade against Zulus, Afridis, and Dervishes (whose methods were different) abandonment of wounded would have been the ultimate in shame and a man guilty of such a crime would never dare show his face in any mess again. Smith-Dorrien could never understand why Colvile had not marched straight ahead to the scene of the disaster instead of going on a wild goose chase to Waterval. Nor could Lord Roberts, who demanded a written explanation which proved unsatisfactory.

When the work of saving the wounded was completed, Smith-Dorrien attempted to report his return only to learn that Colvile was snugly asleep in a farmhouse leaving orders that on no account was he to be disturbed. This was probably as well, for Horace had much to say to him. The next day as they were riding together Colvile observed "I hear you got away those wounded fellows last night and think it was a good thing to have done." His audience remained silent. He had just been ordered back to Bloemfontein when the situation plainly demanded an attack on the waterworks which it was well within his capacity to execute.

The day after he arrived, de Wet captured intact a battalion of the Irish Rifles at Reddersburg. The fact that the Boers treated their prisoners humanely was generally known and occasions were not wanting when a few individuals were willing to exchange the comparative comfort and security of a prison camp for the hardships and hazards of a soldier's life. When the example had been set it was rapidly contagious; besides once the white flag had been shown even the more stout-hearted felt obliged to lay down their arms for fear of firing under the protection of a flag of truce. Many a position would have been held to the last if the defenders knew that surrender meant certain slow death by torture and mutilation.

The occupation of Sannah's Post by de Wet had cut off the town's water supply and was filling the hospitals and the graveyards with enteric cases. Even after the lapse of so many years it is impossible to understand why Sannah's Post was not retaken. De Wet certainly expected it to be and the failure to assault it with the large number of troops available can be neither explained nor excused. For good measure, de Wet had picked up another 400 prisoners—again near Reddersburg—through Gatacre's carelessness, and was also laying siege to the township of Wepener which would have to be relieved before an advance to the north could be made.

French was sent off on 27th April with his mounted troops to effect this, joined by a new formation called the 11th Division (in reality the Guards Brigade and Stephenson's Brigade of the 6th Division), under the command of the Cornishman Pole-Carew. French also had what was left of Gatacre's old 3rd Division (Gatacre had been *stellenbosched* for two failures) diluted with militia. Gatacre had been unlucky: after Atbara, Kitchener had sent him the finest coat of mail and most beautifully finished spear he could find and added his warmest thanks for the splendid gallantry and good judgment with which Gatacre had led his brigade. He was a fine soldier, much loved by his men but had been too often outwitted by de Wet and had to be sent home to encourage the others. All these things were tiresome setbacks but a sense of proportion had to be preserved. In the words of the Official Historian "Smith-Dorrien alone seems to have yet realized that the Boers had been morally shattered by the very struggles which had impressed the need for caution on the victors. His success, small as it was, enforces the truth of a favourite principle of General Grant, the man who brought to an end the great American war, that the time for pressing boldly on is that when you feel that your own men have had about enough because it is certain that the enemy will be in the same state and then the side that goes in wins."

A turning point in the war now came for Smith-Dorrien. He had served for the last time under the unspeakable Colvile. A word about the remainder of this officer's career may not be out of place and it comes from his own pen. Colvile, as has been said, was called to account by Roberts for his behaviour at Sannah's Post and was told officially that he had acted injudiciously. He was to have one more chance. On 23rd May at Lindley he received a message that a Yeomanry Regiment under Colonel Spragge was surrounded and needed help. Having said loftily "And who is Colonel Spragge?", Colvile deserted him to his fate. Again de Wet scooped up a complete unit. Unfortunately for Colvile but fortunately for the Army this regiment consisted mostly of blue-blooded men of means who did themselves well and gave all their pay to charity. Disapproval was rife; Roberts sent for Colvile, expressed thorough disapproval of all his work, sent him home and broke up his division.

Colvile's last defiance was a book which he published immediately on his return home, claiming all the credit for the rescue of Broadwood's wounded and setting out menacingly in an appendix, Section Forty-Two of the Army Act, the one which gives an aggrieved officer the right of appeal to the Sovereign. Nobody took any notice: if Colvile had ever been a force at all he was now a spent one and the publication of the book damned him out of hand with the Army. His only friend, Count Gleichen, with whom he had served in the Brigade of Guards for seventeen years and who was himself to command Sir Horace's 15th Brigade in France later on, has left a recollection of him. Colvile was in the line of great Victorian eccentrics in company with such men as Baker, Brabazon, and Burnaby, in whom remained the last vestiges of the Regency Buck. As a young man he was accustomed to show his contempt for danger by performing such feats as walking along narrow ledges of very high buildings, travelling in disguise through the almost unexplored parts of Morocco, and photographing Spanish fighting bulls from point blank range. (It is not impossible that when performing this interesting feat he sought the assistance of O'Hara, the "Matador Ingles", for one imagines that a Spanish professional would have given scant encouragement to such a performance.) He is also said to have spent his honeymoon in a balloon but happily Gleichen does not enlarge on this. Before taking up his command in South Africa, Colvile had had a brigade at Gibraltar and immediately before this had been Governor of Uganda. During his time there he had fought a bloody battle against a native chief and suffered from fever to such an extent that he was found one day wandering in a forest in a state of nature and delirium. This together with a notorious disregard for anything in the shape of the welfare of those under his command did not seem to disqualify him for his appointment. Gleichen admits that after the Uganda episode his friend's temper had become uncontrollable and he was no longer the man he had been before. Over the Spragge affair, Gleichen takes the view that Colvile was badly treated and hints darkly at a forged telegram having been sent in his name. Gleichen may have been right but it was the last of a series of demonstrations of unfitness for command and Lord Roberts cannot be criticized for returning him to store. More difficult to explain was the fact that Spragge received a decoration. Colvile, protesting to the last, lived for another seven years. He took a considerable interest in the newly invented motorcycle and obtained his quietus by driving one day at a furious speed on the wrong side of the road in order to set up a record. Unhappily for him he collided with a motor car emerging from a side road and was killed on the spot. The driver of the motor car was no other than Sir Henry Rawlinson.

Smith-Dorrien to his intense pleasure now found the brigade under the command of his old friend Johnnie Hamilton. It seems to have been a phenomenon in the late Victorian wars, shared by the Second World War but not by the First, that it was always the same old faces that one found at the business end of the Army. Hamilton was a man after his own heart: from now on, Smith-Dorrien said, he enjoyed every moment of the campaign. "He was a delightful leader to follow, always definite and clear in his instructions, always ready to listen and willing to adopt suggestions and, what is more important, always ready to go for the enemy and extremely quick at seizing a tactical advantage and, with it all, always in a good temper." Conan Doyle saw his brigade march off, not prettified as in the illustrated papers but tangle-bearded, pipe in mouth, and with veldt sores on their hands.

They took the Waterworks without difficulty next day and on the morrow Smith-Dorrien learnt that the Boers were retiring north with French in pursuit and with Rundle (GOC the new 8th Division) and Pole-Carew following. This plainly meant finding the Boers in strength at Thaba Nchu and Smith-Dorrien was not surprised to receive a message from Hamilton, who had gone on ahead with the MI calling for him to come as soon as his supplies arrived.

The brigade, duly supplied, left at 0900 on 25th April, learning from the MI that the Boers were in force at Israel's Poort (a poort is a gap in the hills) seven miles beyond the Waterworks. The brigade, supported by a field battery, attacked at 1330 and by a skilful application of fire and movement—probably for the first time in this War—drove the enemy out within three hours. Their commander gives a special word of praise for Colonel Otter and his Royal Canadians, one of whose companies was French speaking. Next day the brigade camped just short of Thaba Nchu itself. Lord Roberts's grand design was now becoming clear. He intended to strike at the enemy's citadel in the best tradition of Clausewitz, for with Pretoria in his hands, Johannesburg must fall and after that he intended to have Komati Poort and Delagoa Bay. If this succeeded he would have cut off the Boers' supply of home-produced ammunition, mostly made at the Pretoria Mint, and once he reached the sea the supplies from abroad and the constant flow of foreign volunteers would be stopped. Further, if he did not strike swiftly the unruly element in Johannesburg might get out of hand and wreck the mines. He had no intention of rounding up every ragged band of Boers which might be lurking in this enormous area but intended to conduct the nearest thing to a *blitzkrieg* possible to an Army capable of no higher speed than Julius Caesar's. Roberts had, however, one weapon in his armoury which had only loomed large in military thought since the time of Grant and Moltke. Railways were the key to success and without them the war might have dragged on for a generation. Bobs did not have the highly-trained and specialized railway staff which had done so much to make possible Moltke's victories, but he did have Percy Girouard who had built and operated the desert railway for Kitchener not long ago.

From now on it was going to be a tussle between the Boer commandos, bent on tearing up tracks and dynamiting bridges, and such troops as could be spared to prevent their doing such flagitious things. For this purpose twenty-three battalions of militia, not exactly crack troops but the only ones then available, were sent from the home country. They were not fit to take the field but were good enough to guard the lines of communication. If the supply lines were severed Roberts's Army would be cut flowers in a vase, to borrow the description used by the correspondent of the *Morning-Post*-cum-cornet of light-horse of Admiral von Spee some years later.

It is reasonable to suppose that Roberts foresaw the quick end of the war once these things had been effected for the Boers had begun to drift away in large numbers since Paardeberg. Christiaan de Wet had hard things to say about many of his compatriots at this stage though it is true that Sannah's Post and Reddersburg had caused a number to take heart of grace and saddle up again. No one could have been expected to see that the end of the pitched battles would lead to the beginning of a larger and grimmer campaign. De Wet's siege operations around Wepener and Dewetsdorp had done him as much harm as good for while he was busily engaged in this way the railway was left largely untouched and troops and supplies poured into Bloemfontein. These were very necessary for the sick list was now depleting every unit and caused Roberts to delay in Bloemfontein for nearly seven weeks before he could set out for Kruger's own stronghold. This did at least give Roberts time to axe out some of the dead wood. Five Divisional Generals, six cavalry Brigadiers, eleven cavalry regimental commanders and six infantry battalion commanders were weeded out. (Smith-Dorrien was never in any danger for his reputation stood high amongst the senior officers.) Both armies paused for breath.

Roberts's plan was for a concentric attack by several columns like spokes in a wheel converging on the hub—Pretoria. From left to right there were Hunter's 10th Division with Methuen's 1st in support and numbering about 20,000 men with sixty-eight field guns. Roberts himself was in the centre with Tucker's 7th and Pole-Carew's 11th Division, Ian Hamilton forming a flank-guard to the right, and finally Buller with 35,000 men and 100 guns if he could be persuaded to move from Ladysmith. The centre column numbered in all about 65,000 with 210 guns while the total of all four neared 200,000 including 55,000 in garrison on the lines of communication and 23,000 in hospital. Hamilton's column because of its peculiar role had the most mounted troops and was the first to move. His infantry were now experienced practitioners and their skills from the individual soldier and subaltern to the generals at the top had been widely increased by six months' fighting and marching.

Against this force the Boers under Christiaan and Piet de Wet, Grobler, Olivier and Philip Botha mustered about 30,000 actually in the field. De Wet, with a good strategical sense, wanted to invade Cape Colony itself but President Steyn vetoed the suggestion on the grounds that the Free State commandos would be accused by the Transvaalers of leaving them in the lurch now that their own country was in enemy hands. He was particularly anxious to prevent the granary of the OFS between Ladybrand and Bethlehem falling into British hands for there had been a fine harvest that year (reaped by women and Kaffirs as the men were on commando). In fact there was so much corn that when the force he left for its protection had been driven off the British burnt it by the thousands of sacksful: de Wet was of opinion that if the corn had been saved the war could have continued. Things were not going well for the republicans now; the lethargic and gluttonous Buller had relieved Ladysmith on 1st March, or, more accurately, the Natal Field Force had relieved the town in spite of Buller. Sir George White, the commander of the hungry garrison, being at pains to do their reliever honour, provided him with a refection including some iced cakes conjured up by somebody from somewhere: the affable hero snorted and observed "I thought this was supposed to be a starving city."

On 5th March, Stormberg Junction had at last yielded to Gatacre and on the same day Lord Roberts issued his proclamation that burghers who would hand in their rifles, return to their farms, and swear never to fight again would not be molested. Many took advantage of this and de Wet, by far the sternest critic of his own people, swore that after Paardeberg panic had set in and at Poplar Grove on the 7th there was such a flight as he had never seen before. He did many burghers an injustice: they handed in rifles in large numbers it is true. They handed in flint-locks and percussion muzzle loaders which had done duty against Mozelikatze and Dingaan, venerable double-barrelled Roers of astounding length and weight which had slain many beasts during the Great Trek came in sufficient quantities to fill a good sized museum. But the *aachterlaais*, the fine modern Mausers, were buried under farmhouse floors or hidden in walls and roofs against the day when they might come in useful again. The Calvinist consciences of the Boers did not find an oath taken under this kind of duress binding but appeals to the Deity to strike down the foresworn British whenever a burgher was taken off on suspicion of concealing arms or preparing to go on commando again went up loudly across the veldt. The British always have the misfortune to get the worse of double standards. De Wet, however, was far from even considering surrender. He was convinced that Cronje need never have been captured but for the fact that, like King Joseph at Vittoria, he was hopelessly encumbered with wagons full of everything imaginable. If he could have brought himself to part with property—in Boer eyes the unforgivable sin—and ride with just his horse—commandos, a substantial force could have joined up with Ferreira and de Wet and kept an army in being. (Ferreira was now dead, killed by an accident to one of his own Krupp guns outside Kimberley, and Weilbach had deserted at Poplar Grove.)

De Wet, de la Rey, and de Villiers (curious how general the prefix was amongst the best Boer leaders; Huguenot blood, descendants of Henry IV possibly) hardened their hearts. There must be no more wagon camps, no more women and children, if possible no more *voetgangers*. Horse commandos, mobile Krupp guns, and Maxim-Nordenfeldts must do the business from now on. A protest went up from the burghers, not without reason for their wagons contained everything they had been able to bring from their farms in the sure knowledge that the filthy British would certainly have taken the wagons and possibly the rest. De Wet and his men, remember, were Free Staters and the war was now being waged over their own holdings. De Wet managed to impose a discipline on his free and independent men far more rigid than that of any other Boer general, for he was a dedicated man: he was well-off and had no previous military experience but he rose quickly by acclamation and election. He did not hate the British, though he execrated Brabant's Colonial Division as Cains willing to murder their brethren for five shillings a day. But even against prisoners from these Corps he was no more than rough. The British, whom he captured in large numbers, really rather liked him and certainly admired his courage and skill in the way that their grandsons admired Rommel. He knew that the opportunity of winning the War had passed and his one article of faith was that the independence of the two republics must be preserved and he hoped, not without reason, that when the fighting ended the Commandos would be such a thorn in the English flesh that with the help of Mr Lloyd George and the Liberal Party independence at least might be saved. In common with many other leading Boers he would not have minded handing over the gold mines which he regarded as a canker on the state and the cause of all their ills.

Brave, skilful, humane, and high-minded though he was, it would have been better for the South African Republic if Christiaan Rudolf de Wet had never been born. For the moment, however, that did not seem to be the case except to the exasperated Army. After Sannah's Post 500 oath-takers dug up their rifles, saddled up and joined him at Alexandrie, about five miles from Thaba Nchu (Black Mountain) and by bringing in his none-too-successful besiegers he was able to concentrate over 4,000 mounted men there by 25th April. It was this force that Hamilton was ordered to seek out and destroy. His own command consisted of 11,000 men, 4,600 horses, 8,000 mules, two five-inch howitzers, thirty-six field guns, and half a dozen captured pompoms (one inch Nordenfeldts) now to be turned on their original purchasers. Smith-Dorrien's 19th Brigade marched east on the same day as de Wet concentrated at Alexandrie. The latter had no intention of fighting it out at this point for Thaba Nchu was only forty-five miles from Bloemfontein and so well within the reach of supplies. It would do him no good to try and cut Hamilton's supply line here; it would be far better policy to let his advance continue, harrassing him and weakening him all the way, and to fight him at the Zand River when his men and animals would be tired and isolated. So for three days he fought a delaying action around Thaba Nchu and Thoba mountain, forcing Hamilton to deploy and mount a regular attack. The Boer rearguards were most effective in holding up vastly superior numbers for a long time. Hamilton may have learned from these lessons which he turned to advantage in 1916 when he conducted the evacuation of Cape Helles without loss.

The next day was a repetition of the performance at Houtnek and by 1st May Hamilton was through the pass. Smith-Dorrien had fought his brigade throughout with his usual professional competence but there was nothing about the operations that need detain us. A new brigade, the 21st, arrived after Houtnek and Smith-Dorrien was given command of what was called the division, Colonel Spens of the Shropshires succeeding to 19 Brigade. The task remained the same—to act as a flank guard to the east of Roberts's main column tramping steadily up the railway towards Kroonstadt, about half way to Johannesburg. Hamilton was to sweep wide through the pleasant little town of Winburg, and French was to collect his scattered horsemen to cover the advance of the main column. The activities of the other columns need not concern us here, but the small engagement at Senekal deserves mention for the reason that there the gallant and chivalrous de Villiers was wounded so grievously that it was beyond the capacity of the Boers meagre medical resources to treat him. Without hesitation de Wet had him taken to the nearest British outpost where equally without hesitation he was received and given all the care and skill at their disposal. Sad to relate his wound was mortal and beyond cure. All that the British could do was to inter his body with full honours. There is no reason to doubt that if the position had been reversed any Boer general would have done the same. So as the twentieth century dawned the last chivalrous tradition of war between Christian people died and was buried: it was the last time armies would fight to the death without rancour. To the credit of everyone concerned no attempt was made on either side to whip up the deliberate hatred with which later generations were to become painfully familiar nor did the troops of either side conduct themselves in a manner to excite it spontaneously. That had to wait until humanity had moved on a few years.

The next natural obstacle to Roberts's advance, and the one where a successful defence or at least a substantial delaying action was possible, was the Zand River. Apart from its natural aptitude for defence, this was a very special place of almost mystic significance to the Boers; it was here that the Convention of 1852 which gave them their cherished freedom had been signed. Here de Wet and Botha wished to turn and fight it out. The dispirited commandos, however, would not stand even under the lashing of that sardonic tongue and Hamilton's men forced the crossing with ease. Roberts entered Kroonstadt without a fight though the physical difficulties of getting so many wagons across the drift imposed considerable delay made no easier by the fact that de Wet had dynamited the bridge over the Valsch River. Smith-Dorrien entered Heilbron, the temporary state capital on 23rd May, President Steyn moving out under de Wet's protection with all the state paraphernalia in a few wagons. Not since Genghis Khan can a capital have been so peripatetic as that of the Orange Free State.

Mafeking was relieved on 18th May by Colonel Bryan Mahon and added a new word to the language. These victories were timely, for after Sannah's Post and Reddersburg the German bands in the London streets exhibited a lamentable tendency to disregard the martial, though over-familiar, "Soldiers of The Queen" in favour of a lugubrious ditty called "The Boers Have Got My Daddy". Mafeking might soon rectify this undesirable situation.

8 Lady Smith-Dorrien, shortly after her marriage.

9 *Aldershot: with Sir Evelyn Wood, about 1908.*

CHAPTER EIGHT

On 26th May, Smith-Dorrien's forty-second birthday, he crossed the Vaal River into Kruger's own Republic. At Doornkop, the scene of Jameson's surrender, there was a workmanlike little action in which the Gordons and the CIV particularly distinguished themselves. Horace confided to his diary that the extended movements of the latter compared favourably with some of the regulars. At dawn the next day they occupied the Main Rand Ridge (a tautologous expression as Rand is Afrikaans for Ridge) and by lunch time were bivouacking amongst the gold mines, looking down on a town which young Winston Churchill claimed to remind him of Oldham. The curious inspected the unattractive place which combined the least pleasing features of any northern industrial town and any Wild West frontier one. Bars and brothels abounded but Smith-Dorrien's men had no opportunity of sampling these simple joys for they had two days marching immediately ahead of them, over twenty-seven miles to Six Mile Spruit, three miles from Pretoria itself. On 4th June Pretoria was entered without serious opposition. Smith-Dorrien led the impressive parade past the C-in-C. As the last days of Hamilton's force were near we might have a detailed look at them. CIV Mounted Infantry, 19th Infantry Brigade, 74th Field Battery RA, the Gordon Highlanders, three more Field Batteries, the two invaluable five-inch cow guns, the 21st Infantry Brigade, and lastly the ammunition column. This was now a veteran army for all its short life. It received an accretion of strength in the shape of 5,000 prisoners of war who were formed into provisional battalions.

Hamilton's column had marched 380 miles in thirty-seven days, halted on eight days only and fought six engagements. Mortimer Mempes, the artist and an accomplished rifleman in match shooting, wanted to know why the telescopic sight, readily available, was not used in such perfect conditions for it. Nobody answered him. Mempes, whose delightful sketches repay study, affirmed that the boots of the infantry were shoddy affairs made of cardboard and even allowing the artist some licence they must have been of poor stuff. The march is one of the Army's classics. Marlborough's march to the Danube in 1704 was longer but better organized in something like peace-time conditions, and Wellington's six year journey from Mondego Bay to Bordeaux is hardly comparable. Roberts had taken great risks and his gamble had succeeded so that he stood at the zenith of his fame. It cannot be denied that luck had played a great part in it but after all Napoleon's first question about any general was "Is he lucky?"

De Wet, according to his habit, went far to spoil the celebrations. It had been decided that the OFS commandos should not cross into the Transvaal; in all they amounted to about 8,000 hard men readily comparable to Jubal Early's desperate soldiers in the twilight of the Confederacy. On 4th June, just as de Lisle was cautiously entering Pretoria, de Wet added to his game bag fifty-six wagons and 200 Highlanders near Rhenoster Spruit. Three days later, with 600 horsemen and two Krupp guns, he captured the railway station at Roodewal where, with an inexcusably small guard there were stores to the value of £750,000 and including all the warm clothing Lord Roberts's men would need for the coming winter and all their mail. Of the British force, 187 were killed or wounded and 500 taken prisoner. Though de Wet burnt all that was not needed, the party, captors and captives alike, left the station with all the loot they could carry, the horses being so loaded that all went on foot. A field cornet, improbably named Smith, deserted with his twenty men and again de Wet complained of flagrant refusal to obey his orders. This indiscipline deprived him of the finest bag of all, for on 13th June his commandos, not under his immediate eye, stopped a train on the main line but failed to press home their attack. Part of its load was the Chief of Staff, Kitchener of Khartoum himself, who managed to escape on horseback. De Wet insisted to the end of his life that if his orders had been obeyed Roberts would have been cut off and starved to death in Pretoria. This certainly overstates the case, for with the advance of Buller the Natal lines became cleared and sea power could have shifted his base from Cape Town to the Natal ports as Wellington had shifted his from Lisbon to the Spanish Biscayan coast. But de Wet was essentially a landsman and in the long run an unlucky general. To complete the tally, Froneman burnt the bridge at Leeuwsspruit collecting eighty-seven prisoners in the process and then wrecked the line at America Siding, though Olivier was driven off from Honingspruit.

These exercises in removing the gilt from Roberts's gingerbread came too late. Even the surrender of the 13th MI at Lindley to Piet de Wet a few days before Pretoria fell did little to stiffen flagging spirits. The Free State army withdrew into the horseshoe shaped valley behind the Roodeberg mountains known as Brandwater Basin. The Caledon River runs through the valley and it is one of the most beautiful areas in South Africa; one could wish for no better spot to withdraw for rest and meditation. For some reason one of the usual Boer quarrels over command broke out and an election of doubtful validity deposed de Wet (who was not universally loved) in favour of the aged Martinus Prinsloo. The force was divided up in order to slip through the British-held passes and de Wet did so at Slabbert's Nek expecting Prinsloo to follow suit. That ancient man, however, merely waited to be sure that his redoubtable brother officer had really gone and then promptly surrendered to Hunter his entire command of 5,000 men. There was a diverting interlude when a former commandant (who was also a minister of religion) named Roux tried to explain to Hunter that no one was sure whether Prinsloo was really Commander-in-Chief or not and there should be an armistice to find out. Hunter gave him a short answer. More burghers surrendered to MacDonald at Harrismith within the next few days and although Danie Theron caught a train on the 19th July taking ninety-eight prisoners, the balance was handsomely in favour of the English if only on the basis of counting heads. Roberts's manpower difficulties were great but the surrendered burghers were irreplaceable in addition to which the windfall of 5,000 ex-prisoners from Pretoria was a very useful accretion. Many of the stoutest-hearted Boer leaders were seriously wondering whether any good purpose would be served by prolonging the War and indeed feelers had been put out after the capture of Bloemfontein. Hopes of a reasonable settlement foundered on the issue of independence which the British Government would not accept at any price. Many of the longer-headed men would have been willing to settle even on these terms but did not press their point for fear of being accused of faint-heartedness or even of treason. It is a thousand pities that they did not have the courage of their convictions for they would at least have been spared the ravaging of their country and the terrible bitterness with which the heart-breaking business would end. Piet de Wet, whose devotion to the cause was beyond question was one of these and voiced his misgiving to his brother Christiaan. The result was a furious quarrel in the course of which Christiaan, beside himself with rage, threatened that he would shoot Piet "like a dog" if he were to lay down his arms.

The regular pitched battles were now nearly over. Had the Boers been an urban people the war would have been nearly over too but the vastness of the country enabled the commandos to disappear, rest, and reorganize amongst a friendly people. The diehards hoped for another 1812: but it was 1865 instead. All hope of foreign intervention, in which de Wet for one had never really believed, was gone. The Boers were on their own.

Hamilton's force had ceased to exist and Smith-Dorrien's experiences now became varied. Nominally he had reverted to command of his 19th Brigade, but in fact he had become Roberts's all-purpose general. He commanded columns of a few hundred horsemen, a few guns, and a couple of battalions for baggage guards whose composition was constantly changing and covered great tracts of country on horseback; he was sent west after de Wet and de la Rey, whom he narrowly missed for the usual reason of bad communications. His health had suffered again from the rigours of campaigning but somehow by sheer willpower he kept in the saddle. On the last day of July he underwent the experience, unique in his career, of having a Boer under a flag of truce ride up to him in camp near Frederikstad, while he was shaving in the early morning, to demand his surrender. One feels rather sorry for the Boer for if it would have been impolitic to make such a demand of the general at any time, to do it before breakfast was the height of imprudence; one is left to imagine what he said or the manner in which he said it, but the records show that the Boers were driven off in a two hour fight with some loss. Nobody ever had the hardihood to make such a demand of him again. He kept the chastened emissary with him until the affair was over and then packed him back to his commandant to bear the news of Prinsloo's surrender.

He burnt four farms as a reprisal for the murder of some soldiers. It was rough, but it was justice. On 12th August he learnt from Roberts that Hamilton was moving to block the pass over the Magaliesbergs at Olifant's Nek from the south. His own information about his wily adversary was better than any available at Pretoria and he made an urgent signal asking that Hamilton keep to the north of the range and block the Nek from that side (which in any case would have meant a shorter march for him).

Roberts refused and de Wet passed unhindered through the Nek on the evening of the 14th. Smith-Dorrien reckoned, probably rightly, that if his advice had been taken de Wet could not have escaped and the war would have been shortened by six months.

A brother officer gives us a picture of him at this time: "The chief recollection that remains in my mind is of his unfailing good temper when conditions were bad. Transport broke down in an impossible drift, supplies ran short, rain came down in torrents and Smith-Dorrien was seen roaring with laughter. Then the weather cleared and he drove us with whip and spur; a badly posted picket or an overloaded wagon meant serious trouble for somebody." He was undoubtedly a soldier's general. He got wind of the Boxer Rebellion in China and believing the War in South Africa to be nearly over cabled his old chief Sir Francis Grenfell, whom he understood was going out in command, offering his service. Nothing came of it and he was not to finish with the veldt just yet.

The usual slackness after victory to which British Armies seem peculiarly vulnerable now set in and there were several disgraceful surrenders. Smith-Dorrien, however, had so impressed his personality on his command that no one dared to ease off and his reputation in high places rose as others fell. At the end of August he found himself again under Hamilton helping the plethoric Buller in the mountainous country around Belfast where, as he said, his old Indian frontier lessons stood him in good stead. A bullet narrowly missed him while he was taking his morning bath at the lovely town of Spitzkop, 6,000 feet above sea level and the next day his men took the Mauchberg. Smith-Dorrien compared it to a sledgehammer cracking an egg and the resemblance to an Aldershot Field Day was completed by a Staff Officer who rode up, saluted and said "March back to camp, please, Sir." And so they did.

Buller now came to the conclusion that he could manage on his own and the brigade moved by Machadodorp to Helvetia on the way to Komati Poort and Delagoa Bay. In these operations 19 Brigade had covered on foot more than 1,200 miles, about the distance from Calais to Cadiz. They covered another 140 to Komati Poort going steadily downhill to the fever-ridden coastal plain and on the way he met Kitchener "having a look round and imagining he was creating order out of chaos". A railway bridge was broken and Smith-Dorrien had begun its repair when Kitchener appeared again. "I disappeared. This was not done in any spirit of disrespect to him but he was apt to issue instructions to the nearest person to him, quite oblivious of the fact that that particular person's duties might lie in another direction." Horace had the measure of his erratic chief.

Komati is on the Portuguese border, and it contained all the debris left behind by Kruger when he had taken ship for Holland in the Dutch cruiser *Gelderland*, put at his disposal by the Queen of the Netherlands. There was enough rolling stock to make up 130 trains but the departing Boers had destroyed bridges and torn up lines which left Girouard's men much to do before they could be moved to Pretoria.

Early in October Smith-Dorrien was ordered back to Pretoria arriving just in time for Lord Roberts's farewell parade. The war seemed at an end. The old chief had fought his last campaign and was going home with his staff and the CIV leaving Kitchener to complete any unfinished business. The last and worst phase of the War was about to start.

Smith-Dorrien's column was next engaged in scrappy fighting around Belfast where some of his Canadians, escaping after having been captured, brought in uneasy reports that the Boers far from being disheartened were in excellent spirits each man having two horses, two rifles (the second usually a Lee-Metford) and a Kaffir servant.[1] They were by no means out of the fight yet. They were making a speciality of raiding the railway using friendly farms as bases. Smith-Dorrien hardened his heart, burnt every farm known to be used for this purpose and for good measure a couple of flour mills as well. This was the beginning of the great bitterness. Smith-Dorrien returned to his base in Belfast towards the end of November where all his mounted troops were taken from him including the 5th Lancers (he had replaced their traditional weapon with the long rifle, rather surprisingly they accepted this without demur and even submitted to musketry instruction).

For a month he had nothing to do: on 15th December news came that de la Rey had driven Clements back west of Pretoria with 600 casualties. Kitchener, who had no finer feelings about such things, sent Clements home at once in spite of his fine record. (Even Kitchener's friend Gatacre had complained of a "rough and uncomradely attitude" when he had suffered the same fate.) A few days later a post at Helvetia was rushed with the loss of 250 men and a 4·7 gun. The prisoners were released shortly afterwards as the Boers could not cope with them and the gun had no ammunition, but it was a disagreeable incident. On the night of 7th January 1901 Botha, Smuts (a new name but coming rapidly into prominence), and Ben Viljoen raided

---

[1] I cannot resist the temptation to quote a riddle which was enveloped in many crackers at Christmas 1900.

"Why does President Kruger wear thick socks?"
"To keep de Wet (the wet) from defeat (the feet)!"

five railway stations simultaneously—Machadodorp, Dalmanutha, Belfast, Wonderfontein and Ran—but were repulsed from all of them in some hard fighting. Smith-Dorrien conducted the defence of Belfast. It is interesting to note that he spoke of one strong point being protected by "impenetrable barbed wire."

On 22nd January, the anniversary of Isandhlwana, he was placed in command of a column of 5,000 men of all arms and 500 wagons to sweep round to the border of Swaziland (south of Komati) destroying as he went all crops and livestock to prevent the enemy from living off the country. This was the first time a British army had been compelled to undertake this disagreeable task since Marlborough had ravaged Bavaria after Blenheim. Every day the hateful work continued, acre upon acre of crops being laid waste with fire, sword, and bayonet; thousands of sheep were slaughtered. Smith-Dorrien's column was rushed in a night attack by 2,000 Boers under Botha and Smuts on the 6th February: the horses of the 5th Lancers stampeded and under cover of their wild careerings the Boers rushed in. The outpost, Suffolks and West Yorkshires, many of them recruits, stood firm and drove the attackers off. With the dawn came a thick fog which hindered pursuit. Fifty-four horses had been killed, about the same number wounded, and 200 had been lost: the commandos lost twenty-eight killed.

Within the next few days Smith-Dorrien collected 5,000 cattle, 14,000 sheep, and sixty or seventy wagons with a few wounded prisoners. Driving all this livestock was a considerable problem but the general personally instructed his transport officers how to make a wagon laager to contain the cattle from a pattern he had learned in the Zulu war. They could not cope with the sheep and had to slaughter 15,000 before they moved on, but the following day they acquired another 23,000 sheep and 4,000 cattle. It must have looked more like the migration of the Children of Israel than a twentieth-century army and one suspects that most of the soldiers lost their taste for mutton. Smith-Dorrien was able to send the Queen of Swaziland fifty highly prized black oxen and 1,000 sheep with a request that she should allow no Boers into her country and hand over any who might be there already. The Swazis were polite but evasive: white men's quarrels were no business of theirs. The heir to the throne, very corpulent, very black, and nattily dressed in a pinafore of monkey tails crowned by a bowler hat, fired a five-inch gun with much glee.

Smith-Dorrien now came under the command of French for the first time and the two seem to have got on well enough. French offered the advice that the advance south should be slow, that every family should be removed, every crop destroyed, and the farms of those still in arms confiscated and sold. The suggestion actually originated from, of all sources, Louis Botha, who was known to have said that one of two things would end the war quickly—the capture of Steyn and de Wet or the confiscation of land. Smith-Dorrien could be as ruthless as Sherman when it was necessary. And so the miserable business went on.

On 6th March he met French again in Pietretief and found him most affable and so well pleased with his subordinate's work that he placed him in command of half the entire force, to operate independently. No shadow of jealousy seemed to mar their relationship. Smith-Dorrien picked up tit-bits of news; de Wet had been chased out of Cape Colony with the loss of all his guns and transport, a convoy had reached Pietretief safely under an officer fortuitously named Colonel Bullock, and the Swazi Queen, fired by her heir's prowess as an artillery man, had called out her *Impis* and driven the Boers from her country. Food was running short and there was plainly some shady work going on somewhere in supply circles for such biscuit as arrived was almost uneatable and every bale or bag was under weight. Smith-Dorrien could get no remounts so one third of his cavalry were reduced to walking and his chances of a successful operation in the north were very slim. (Here he met for the first time a successful cavalry Colonel named Edmund Allenby, already known as The Bull.) Smith-Dorrien was not at all well at the time; his last operations had achieved nothing, and on 22nd April he was summoned to Pretoria to learn with mixed feelings that he was to be sent at once to India as Adjutant-General. It was the top staff appointment in the Army but Sir Horace had no great taste for staff work and in any event, out of sorts though he was, he had no wish to leave South Africa with so much of the business unfinished. Smith-Dorrien was fortunate in that he came out of the South African War with a greatly enhanced reputation in sharp contrast with many others. He had missed the disasters of Black Week and was to miss the last horrible year with its block-houses, drives, concentration camps, and other "methods of barbarism." By May 1902 the country was for the most part near to starvation, the Kaffirs had banded themselves together and were raiding farms occupied only by women and children, and after a long conference at Vereeniging the Boer leaders were forced to accept unconditional surrender. The British government gave generous help and apart from a small minority of irreconcileables the country settled down again to cultivate its farms. In 1914 Smuts was able to say that he would side with England against Germany as a country which "when we were at their mercy treated us as a Christian people should."

CHAPTER NINE

Before moving on to India it might be as well to pause and look at the Grandees of the Army when the War eventually petered out. Roberts returned to be Commander-in-Chief in place of Wolseley and was soon eased out when that office was abolished. Buller, who had been a good man in his day though risen far above his ceiling (he had been well described as a superb major, a mediocre colonel and an abysmally poor general) was soon to follow. None of the other divisional commanders were to rise to the heights: Kitchener, of whom there is much more to tell, was shortly to go to India as C-in-C. The two top men remaining were French, the cavalryman, and Ian Hamilton the Highlander.

French had been a late developer and apart from his service in the recent war he carried little in the way of personal battle honours. He had been born at Ripple in Kent on 28th September 1852, only at a very short remove both in time and place from the last days of the Duke of Wellington who died at nearby Walmer Castle that same year. French's father who was a postcaptain in the Royal Navy and of Irish descent, duly entered him as a cadet in HMS *Britannia* in 1866 at the very moment that Roon and Moltke were giving the European powers their first lesson in the warfare of the future. A tendency to vertigo in the days when sail had not yet given way to steam settled his fate as a future admiral and he was commissioned in 1874 in the 8th Hussars by the backdoor of the Suffolk Artillery

Militia. He remained only a few weeks with the 8th and then transferred to the 19th Hussars with whom he was to spend all his time as a regimental officer. Lack of means prevented his cutting a dash at Aldershot and he spent much of his leisure reading military history. Sir Evelyn Wood, noticing him one day ten years or so later asked his Colonel "Of what value?" "Forever reading military books", was the answer. He was with his regiment in Ireland from 1876–1881 in which year he became a Yeomanry Adjutant to the Northumberland Hussars—an appointment which lasted three years and which he seems to have enjoyed, although it kept him out of the 1882 campaign in Egypt where his regiment was engaged at Tel-el-Kebir. At the end of 1884 French rejoined the 19th in Egypt and was with them at Abu Klea in January 1885. He was thus a major of thirty-two before he smelt powder and his practical military education was of an antique kind. Even after Abu Klea he had not been seriously engaged for it was an infantry battle of the traditional Sudan kind, the infantry square versus the Dervish horde. Here he came under the command of Buller who paid him the compliment of saying that "the force owes much to Major French and his 13 troopers". French always maintained later that he owed his career to Buller, which is not surprising for the two men had much in common.

French remained at home doing the aimless things which passed for training in the cavalry of the eighties; the charges of von Bredow's dragoons at Mars-la-Tour in 1870 and the death-or-glory (both, in fact) ride of the Marquis de Gallifet's Chasseurs d'Afrique at Floing in the same year were considered more perfect examples for cavalry to follow than the less showy but far more effective lessons given by Sheridan and Stuart on the wrong side of the Atlantic. Cavalry charged their enemy knee-to-knee as Cromwell had done at Naseby, Cadogan at Blenheim, the Marquis of Granby at Warburg, Lord Uxbridge at Waterloo, and Lord Cardigan at Balaclava. Everything else was ancillary to this sublime moment of military achievement. True, Rupert had thrown away more than one battle by carrying the business too far; the Duke had had some very harsh things to say about his cavalry in the Peninsula and so had Lord Raglan in the Crimea. But Rupert was an amateur, the Duke was an infantryman, and as for Lord Raglan. . . .

French's only service abroad apart from his brief spell in the Sudan was in Bangalore between 1891–1893 when his command of the 19th expired and he went home on half-pay. This was a very serious matter for a man of such small means and French saw his career ending with a strident lack of distinction at the age of forty-three. At a time when his half-pay period was nearly over and with compulsory retirement staring him in the face, manna fell from heaven in the shape of an appointment as AAG at the Horse Guards. The hand of Buller must have been in this, as it was in his next appointment two years later to the command of the 2nd Cavalry Brigade at Canterbury. Nothing happened there to ruffle the waters of peacetime garrison life, nor was this placid situation altered when he was translated to Aldershot in 1899. The bulky figure of Buller occupied the seat of the GOC and on his Brigade Staff was a Major Haig. It was during his time at Aldershot that French became very hard pressed indeed for money. He was noted as a man whose gallantry was not confined to the battlefield (even when he was rising seventy and Viceroy of Ireland, a plot was laid to lure him from Dublin Castle, the bait being the offer of kindnesses from a lady of surpassing beauty) and such things have to be paid for. Fortunately for him, Haig was a man of substance and provided his embarrassed Brigadier the timely loan of £2,000. The debt remained unpaid in 1914 but some consolation to the subordinate-creditor was provided in the shape of a piece of plate, suitably inscribed. French had, it appears, also speculated unwisely in—of all things—Transvaal Gold Shares. In December 1899 the outraged shareholder was on his way to inspect the company's undertaking for himself, with three regiments of cavalry at his back.

Within a few days he found himself in command of a small force at Elandslaagte where he scored a small victory, the 5th Lancers having the heartening experience of riding down Boers fleeing from the field and spitting them like bundles of hay. With his creditor he left Ladysmith in the last train to the south. In November he was appointed local Lieutenant-General in command of the Cavalry Division, three British regiments, an Australian and a New Zealand squadron, and two companies of MI. His writings, more or less contemporary, show his attitude to his command and include these elegant extracts: "I am absolutely convinced that the cavalry spirit is and may be encouraged to the utmost without in the least degree prejudicing either training in dismounted duties or the acquirement of such tactical knowledge on the part of leaders as will enable them to discern when and where to resort to dismounted methods. How, I ask, can the cavalry perform its role in war until the enemy cavalry is defeated and paralysed? . . . Cavalry soldiers must of course learn to be expert rifle shots but the attainment of this desirable object will be brought no nearer by ignoring the horse, the sword or the lance."

If the Aldershot musketry returns are to be trusted, neither of these last three could complain of neglect. On an annual allowance of forty rounds a man (thirty being fired at ranges between 500 and 800 yards) that "of course" sounds a bit strong.

Writing of foreign cavalry (by inference the Union cavalry of the American War) French continues "they were devoid of real cavalry training, they thought of nothing but getting off their horses and shooting; hence they lamentably failed in enterprises which demanded, before all, a display of the highest form of cavalry spirit." It is interesting to speculate how Sherman, Sheridan, or Pleasanton would have managed the Poplar Grove affair or that of Thaba Nchu. At least their horses would have been less exhausted by manifesting the cavalry spirit day after day.

"Another most important point must be noticed. I allude to the increasing tendency of umpires and superior officers to insist on cavalry manœuvres and elsewhere being ultra-cautious. They try to inculcate such a respect for infantry fire that cavalry is taught to shirk exposure and the moment infantry came within sight, squadrons are made either to retire altogether or dismount and shoot, regardless of what the cavalry value of the ground happens to be . . . we ought to be on our guard against false teaching of this nature, seeing that there are many grave warnings to be found by history of the inevitable consequences of thus placing the weapon above the man." Yakub of the Black

Flag had shared this view but French had been at Canterbury while Yakub may have briefly shifted to a different point of view.

There is no need to follow French right through the War. Denys Reitz, who had the misfortune to come before him as a prisoner describes him as "squat and ill-tempered looking". It cannot, however, be denied that he came out of the War a popular hero and it was not undeserved. The pity of it is that his military career did not end then and he could have retired suitably honoured and rewarded. He had reached his ceiling. However, he had a long course ahead of him, apparently determined that the talents of Buller should not be wasted but would be faithfully carried on by his disciple. Nevertheless, it is only fair to say that the cavalry did not at this date offer anyone who was obviously his superior.

Ian Hamilton—Johnny Hamilton to his friends, and they were many—was a man of an entirely different kind. A year younger than French he had been born into the 92nd Highlanders (the Gordons) which his father was commanding at Corfu, educated at Wellington and in Germany, and was one of the first students of the RMC at Sandhurst. Originally commissioned in the Suffolks, he was transferred to the Gordons in 1873 and sent straight to India where the second-in-command was a Major George White, later of Ladysmith fame. Hamilton became perfect in Hindustani, travelled much in wild places, and as a subaltern served the then Major-General Roberts in the Second Afghan war of 1878–1880. He came early to the notice of Bobs for an act of personal bravery, and was present at the battle of Charasia (where White got his VC, and Hector MacDonald his commission) as ADC to Brigadier-General "Redan" Massey—a Crimean veteran as his nickname implies. After being boarded home, Hamilton treated his medical advisers in precisely the way Smith-Dorrien was doing in Zululand at the same moment and rejoined the Gordons just in time for the battle at the end of Roberts's famous march from Kabul to Kandahar.

He was wounded at Majuba on the 26th February 1881 (Cronje surrendered at Paardeberg on its anniversary), his hand, like Smith-Dorrien's leg, was threatened with amputation, and he too was recommended for a VC which he never received. In 1882 he was ADC to Roberts at Madras where the other ADC was Neville Chamberlain—the inventor of snooker at Ootacamund Club. Hamilton's particular subject was musketry (he had seen the uselessness of the cavalry sword in Afghanistan) and he wrote a book on the subject. Being one of Roberts's men, he fell out with Buller, a leading light in the Wolseley "ring" who from Horse Guards vetoed Hamilton's appointment as Assistant Military Secretary to Roberts on the ground that at thirty-two, and with two hard campaigns behind him, he was too inexperienced. Johnny Hamilton as a young subaltern had met Gordon (who became his hero) and he managed to smuggle himself into the sister battalion of the Gordons for the relief expedition, going up the Nile in a whaler. This, was, of course, with the River Column and not the Desert Column which fought at Abu Klea, though he was in the thick of it at Kirbekan. Back then to India as ADC to Roberts, now C-in-C, whom he followed next year to the Second Burma War where the British took Mandalay for the first time. It was to be much harder sixty years later.

Next year Hamilton was back in India still with his old chief, published a book of by no means despicable poetry, and became AAG (Musketry) in which appointment he improved the standard throughout the sub-continent with the blessing of Roberts to whom the subject was very near the heart. When Roberts went home in 1893 Hamilton became Military Secretary to his successor the now Sir George White, VC, a brother Gordon. He was a staff officer at the relief of Chitral in 1895 and commanded a brigade under Penn-Symons in the Tirah campaign of 1897 where his Gordons and Gurkhas stormed the heights of Dargai to the music of the pipes.

In 1898 Hamilton became commander of the School of Musketry at Hythe, passing up the opportunity of being QMG in India at four times the salary. He was a brilliant success there and did much to raise the standard—not very high—throughout the Army but was denied the time to see the fruits of his work. On the outbreak of the South African War he went out on the staff of Sir George White arriving at Ladysmith on the day the Boer ultimatum expired. Before the month was out he was given command of the 7th Brigade (which included his old 92nd Highlanders) as a local Major-General. His path and that of French crossed for the first time at Elandslaagte for there, symbolically, French commanded the horse and Hamilton the foot. Between them they won a neat little victory, Hamilton's men charging to the sound of the pipes and French's to the shrill cavalry trumpet. There is no need to follow him any further for the moment. Hamilton could not have been a more different type of man from his cavalry colleague; lean and spare, affable with everybody, and with a charm and courtesy as marked as its antithesis in the other man, he was one of the last of that exotic race—the British poet-generals. He had the soul of an artist in words which seemed in some fashion perfectly congruous in a man of many campaigns. Between the wars he was to go as official observer attached to General Nogi in Manchuria during the Russo-Japanese War of 1904 where he saw an Oriental people, only fifty years ago living in their own kind of mediaevalism, carrying on the military education of the world from the point where Moltke had left off. Here he observed, apart from prodigies of valour comparable to the Dervishes, demonstrations of the use of artillery, machine guns, and barbed wire (unconsidered legacies from the American Civil War) which were changing the face of warfare. Hamilton's experiences written more than sixty years ago in *A Staff Officer's Scrap Book* make all the many books written on the Boer War seem by comparison as remote as the campaigns of Belisarius. There was never to be a repetition of South African conditions, but Manchuria was 1916 writ small and Hamilton missed none of it. His description of the Japanese as the "world-conquering Army of 1920" (the year the Anglo-Japanese treaty was due to expire) was regrettably forgotten by 1941. Hamilton was a man of such charm that he made but one enemy in his life; to his eventual undoing, that enemy had to be William Nicholson. Nicholson had been a brother member of Lord Roberts's staff in India in the 1880's and for some reason long forgotten he felt that he had been slighted by Hamilton. From his surname alone it was inevitable that he should be called "Old Nick" but he was what Samuel Johnson called an unclubbable man and a born trouble maker, though it is only just to say that no officer ever sat a chair better or few a horse worse. He was the head of the mission to Manchuria and having no mind to watch the battle of the Motienling tried to make it impossible for his junior to see it either. In the end Hamilton went alone. Nicholson's carefully matured hatred blew up when many years later he became a member of the Dardanelles Committee. In the meantime, Nicholson became the Chief of the General Staff in succession to Lyttleton in 1908 (the "Imperial" being added in 1909). It is highly probable that this personal spite had much to do with the fact that Hamilton, in every way the obvious choice, did not command the BEF in 1914. There were some very dedicated haters in King Edward's Army.

If the necessity of sending an expeditionary force overseas in the next few years should arise the command must inevitably go to one or other of these two men. With the advantage of looking through the microscope of history, it is hard to avoid the conclusion that in the event it went to the wrong one.

CHAPTER TEN

THE Cardwell reforms of 1874, which had in its day outraged military opinion by the introduction of the short service engagement and the two battalion regiment, ensured that those who at the turn of the century wished to see the British Army in the pride of its manhood must go to India to find it. The regular infantryman or gunner learnt his trade—as did the soldiers of no other Army—in one small campaign after another on the North-West Frontier, an incomparable training ground. The battalions at home were charged with training their recruits and, as soon as they were fit for service, with drafting them to the linked battalion in India. Year after year the young Cockney, Irishman, or Highlander emerged from the regimental depot, scrubbed, dressed, and drilled ready to join his home battalion. There, physically fit, master of the comparatively simple weapons of the day and already possessed of a fierce and uncompromising pride of regiment the trained soldier found himself one day marched behind a band on board the *Malabar*, the *Jumna*, or another of the famous troopers to endure the long sea voyage to Bombay. On arrival it did not take him long to learn that "trained soldier" was an entirely relative term and that he was, in truth, pretty green. He added to his vocabulary of Hindustani words (acquired from the company storeman who had smelt powder at Chitral in '95 and was not slow to give the recruit the benefit of his recollections, remembered with advantages in most cases). *Char, pani, roti, juldi* and all the old now half-forgotten words soon came tripping naturally off his tongue. Eventually he would be pretty sure to find himself on the Frontier: no longer Blackdown, Catterick, or Aldershot but Razmak, Peshawar, and Rawal Pindi now felt the weight of his ammunition boots. In time he mastered the gentle arts of picketing heights, constructing sangars, enduring night-long sniping and, above all, marching, marching, and marching, with the straps of the new webbing equipment boring into his shoulders: thirst, heat, cold, aching feet—none of which must ever be allowed to affect his alertness or instant obedience to the quick order. As the private soldier (a curious expression for the man whose greatest lack was privacy) learnt his business, so did the young officer. "The eye of the tribesman is always watching you," was more than a wry joke. It was a matter of life and death, present at all hours. Tough though it was, the life produced a race of hard, disciplined, and thoroughly trained soldiers whose like will not be seen again. To the cavalry a posting to India was a disagreeable experience mitigated only by the excellence of the polo and pig sticking.

Beside the Army in India, lay the far larger Indian Army and this, at the turn of the century, was of uneven quality. The men in high command were for the most part old—some very old; Lord Roberts himself had only recently handed over his command and he remembered the grim days of the Mutiny. To him John Nicholson, Herbert Hodson, the siege of Lucknow, and the massacre of Cawnpore were not historical personages or events—they were men he had known and experiences he had shared. The organization of the Indian Army was ramshackle and designed, if for anything at all, to maintain law and order should there be any repetition of the events of 1857. It had provided a small expeditionary force for Lord Napier's Abyssinian campaign in 1868 and sent troops to the second Burma War in 1885. There were fine regiments which would have been ornaments to any Army, but there were also many units, particularly in the south of the country, that were unfit to take the field against the feeblest enemy. The Guides, the Punjab Frontier Force (Piffers), the Sikhs and the Gurkhas, would have allowed no affectations of superiority from any British regiment, household or line. Taken as a whole, however, it was not an Army as the twentieth century understands the word. It was deployed in cantonments throughout India in locations which had no strategic meaning nor relation to any intelligible order of battle.

To rectify this there arrived two men, vastly different in background and experience but each in his own way honestly set to form this mass into a modern fighting force. George Nathaniel, Marquess Curzon, sometime of Balliol College, became Viceroy and Governor General in 1898. He knew nothing of armies save that they, and all connected with them, deserved no more than his aristocratic disdain and hauteur; armies were a body of inferior beings who must learn their place—which was not an exalted one. Sir William Lockhart, the C-in-C, had died suddenly in March 1900 and had been succeeded by Sir Arthur Power Palmer, a charming and easy-going gentleman whose brief was merely to maintain the *status quo* until Lord Kitchener had disposed of the Boers. In the autumn of 1902 Kitchener arrived in India. Kitchener's singular talents cannot be compared with those of any other general. The son of a half-pay Irish Colonel he was totally uneducated in boyhood and during the Franco-Prussian war, while still a cadet at Woolwich, he visited his father in France and joined Chanzy's Army of the Loire as a volunteer. He saw a little skirmishing around Le Mans in which the French (ominously named Troupes Territoriaux) ran away, caught pleurisy as a result of a freezing ascent in a balloon and earned a genial reproof from the Duke of Cambridge. His commission in the Royal Engineers was not prejudiced, however, and he spent many years in the peripherally military task of map-making in Cyprus, Palestine, and other unsurveyed places. Governor of Suakin on the Red Sea littoral in 1885 at the age of thirty-five, he lived much in desert places and amongst uncouth people. Completely autocratic in his command of the Sudan Expedition in 1898 though he had been, he had never commanded so much as a platoon (except when he had interfered so disastrously at Paardeberg), nor enjoyed the most rudimentary staff training, nor had any experience of the British Army comparable to that of officers whose careers had been of a more conventional nature. Add to this a temper of outstanding ferocity, a profound if misplaced belief in his powers of organization, a relentless ambition, and one could hardly imagine anyone more antipathetic to the overbearing aristocrat who was now his master. It was, of course, mutual.

The eccentric arrangements for the command and administration of the Indian Army comprehended a Commander-in-Chief and a Military Department whose head was a general officer junior to the C-in-C but who controlled all matters of finance. The head of the Military Department, General Elles, speedily quarrelled with his new chief and before long the two men would not speak to each other. Smith-Dorrien tells a story which illustrates this interesting dichotomy. "Indian cavalry regiments had in addition to their horses eight camels each. Their function was for orderly duties, long distance dispatches and other tasks more suited to the camel than to the horse. The C-in-C was of the opinion that economy and efficiency would be served by increasing the establishment of camels to sixteen and the number of horses correspondingly reduced. The question was put to every cavalry regiment in India: all favoured the proposal. The C-in-C (then Sir Power Palmer) was a cavalryman with many campaigns behind him and spoke with the authority of decades of experience in making his recommendation. It had to be referred to the Military Department even though it involved a reduction in cost. The proposal came back with a brief minute signed by a Captain in the Military Department saying that the Government of India did not agree—and that was the end of that."

Curzon hated the Army and treated it with studied contempt and arrogance. Sir Power with the assistance of his Adjutant-General tried hard to keep the peace during his last days, but in vain. The stories of Curzon's behaviour to the soldiers are legion but the atmosphere can best be understood by the story of the Commanding Officer of an infantry battalion who requested that it might be selected to attend the Delhi Durbar. The reply was that economy was the chief consideration and if the battalion happened to be quartered a long way off it would only be selected if its record closely connected it with wars in India. The Colonel conceded that he had no claim on that score but pointed out that they were due for new Colours and would much like to receive them from the hands of the Prince of Wales at the Durbar. Smith-Dorrien replied that the Colonel was mistaken in believing that the Prince would be present but it would make no difference as His Excellency the Viceroy would be asked to present the Colours. He said, "I shall never forget the man's face. He did not speak but looked aghast. At once the stories I had heard flashed through my mind and I blurted out 'Surely things are not as bad as that?' to which his reply was 'If we have to receive our new Colours from the Viceroy, we would rather not go'. Further experiences on that tour subsequently convinced me that other units had much the same feeling of resentment." Smith-Dorrien put the blame for this squarely upon Curzon, "a masterful self-centred man with no-one to say him 'Nay' would not pause to reflect that any attitude of his could be open to criticism or that cutting and disparaging remarks and minutes from the head of a great Government cannot be answered but do all the more harm on that account for the iron enters deeply into the souls of the people reflected on when no reply is possible." It cannot be denied that Lord Curzon was a cad. Curzon best revealed himself in the remark he once made to Winston Churchill, "I tipped him a touch of the Grand Seigneur." Needless to say, the subject of the conversation was not the Viscount of Khartoum, though the result of such a rencontre might have been interesting.

Such was the legacy Kitchener inherited. Irresistibly determined to command in fact as well as in name, he came directly into collision with the immovable determination that the Army should remain under the Viceroy's control like any other government department. Smith-Dorrien, when he had completed his agreed tour as Adjutant General in 1903, assumed command of the 4th Division at Quetta and moved away from the centre of the storm. It was at this time that he renewed his acquaintance with the Inspector General of Cavalry, Major-General Douglas Haig who stayed with him in March 1904. (The views of the two men on the training of cavalry for war coincided exactly.) As time passed the quarrel between the Viceroy and the Army widened to the extent that the 9th Lancers, believing themselves unjustly punished by the Viceroy's direct order, are said to have hissed him as they passed the saluting point. This was greeted with cheers from the spectators.

Smith-Dorrien now found himself for the first time in his life chained to an office desk and his advances in rank since the happy days of the bachelor bungalow in Lucknow drastically curtailed the sport he had enjoyed as a mere Major. But there came a compensation for on 3rd September 1902, "the happiest day of my life," he married Miss Olive Schneider, god-daughter of Sir Donald Stewart, Governor of the Gold Coast, with whom he had served in Egypt in 1885 when she was four years old. The wedding was at St Peters, Eaton Square and the church was packed with relations and friends. Immediately on his return the General and his bride were caught up in the overwhelming magnificence of the Coronation Durbar. Did he remember the carefully caged tigers put out for the royal guest to shikar all those years ago?

News of his marriage caused some consternation in South Africa where the press, misreading Schneider for Schreiner, announced the General's impending nuptials with the famous authoress and speculated with interest on the role of her existing husband. Their five years at Quetta were very pleasant but not full of event, though they entertained many guests, official and private, including the future King George V and Queen Mary, the Prince becoming a firm and valuable friend to both. Their first son "Gren" (after Sir Francis Grenfell), was born on 11th February 1904, followed in due time by Peter and David, in 1907 and 1911. Smith-Dorrien attended the C-in-C's formal visit to the Maharajah of Bikaner, the elaborate programme for which remains in the Scrap Book. Amongst such diversions as the display by the Ganga Rissala (the State Camel Corps), appears this ambiguous entry, "Saturday 30 November. Visit to jail. Shooting for rest of party".

Kitchener was supported by both Smith-Dorrien (who found him "a pleasant Chief to serve—much less secretive than I had imagined") and Haig, though the former felt that his chief went rather too far in some things. When he sent a memorandum asking all officers of the rank of Major-General or above to approve his measures the answer of the GOC 4th Division was polite but evasive. By 1906 the lamentable battle was over: Curzon ceased to be Viceroy, Kitchener remained C-in-C but the wings of the Military Department were clipped. The Indian Staff College at Quetta was inaugurated by the joint efforts of Kitchener and Smith-Dorrien and this was perhaps the most essential step in the conversion of the land forces in India from a number of disparate units into an Army. The reward came eight years later. Smith-Dorrien devoted a part of his leave in 1905 to attending the annual Kaisermanöver of the German Army at Potsdam. He could not fail to be struck by its power but the skill of the troops did not overawe his experienced scrutiny.

CHAPTER ELEVEN

MEANWHILE back at Aldershot, French was now GOC-in-C in succession to his guru, Buller, and the cavalry were being trained to deliver knee-to-knee charges, rarely dismounting. The large number of trees growing everywhere hampered the training of the infantry. The Provost-Marshal's police patrolled the streets nightly: drunkenness and fights were commonplace. The Artillery, Infantry and Engineers being of no great interest to the GOC were left to get on with their training as best they could. Roberts, before he had been eased out, instructed Colonel G. F. R. Henderson to produce a new work to be called *Infantry Training* in substitution for the old *Infantry Drill Book* (which had been found so wanting) and in which would be found the distilled wisdom of the lessons learned in the late War. Henderson did not progress very far with the book for he returned to South Africa, fell sick, and died in Egypt on his way home in 1903. The work was taken over by a committee whose secretary was a Colonel Stopford who appeared to have forgotten its contents by the time he came to command at Suvla Bay in 1915. Roberts wrote a foreword deprecating mechanical obedience to orders and requiring commanders to use their wits. This was a tremendous break with all tradition. The German Von Lobell spoke admiringly in 1904 of the infantry's skill in the use of ground and avoidance of frontal attacks (no more Magersfontein's—yet) and mentioned the sensible abolition of volley firing, a waste of the virtues of the magazine rifle. All this happened in spite of rather than because of the two consecutive General Officers

Commanding-in-Chief. Messing arrangements varied from good to indifferent, depending upon the interest of the officers. Still no such thing as an entrenching tool existed, though the need for such a basic piece of equipment had been demonstrated over and over again in South Africa. The Vickers-Maxim machine gun (in service at the rate of two to a battalion) was twice the weight of the Vickers gun then available and very little thought had been given to its tactical use. The Aldershot command was regarded as the cream of the Army at home and would provide on mobilization the first corps of any expeditionary force—but between 1901 and 1907 it reflected mostly the personality of its commanders and would have been of little use against any first-class military power.

In 1903 the Elgin Committee was appointed to study the state of the post-war Army and its reserves and to advise how it could profit from the sharp lessons of South Africa. In 1899 the Regular Army had comprised three Regiments of Household Cavalry, twenty-eight of Cavalry of the Line, twenty-one batteries of Royal Horse Artillery, ninety-four of Field Artillery, ten batteries of Mountain Artillery, ninety-nine companies of Garrison Artillery, nine battalions of Foot Guards and 148 Infantry of the Line, which with the usual additional corps made a grand total of nearly 234,000. (In 1936 it was 204,000: it is now about 180,000. *Ehev fugaces.*) In 1896 the government bought Salisbury Plain as somewhere to stage manœuvres at home. The soldiers were now all short-service seven-year men but the Regular Army had a reserve organization of its own; the First Class Reserve totalled about 25,000, though by the time soldiers unfit for foreign service for medical or other reasons had been weeded out these warriors did little more than ensure that the totals did not actually fall. When Tucker's 7th Division and Rundle's 8th were sent out after Black Week there were three battalions of Regulars left in the country. Just under 43,000 Reservists of one kind or another had been sent to South Africa by the beginning of 1900 and this included the Militia Reserve.

The Militia was a military oddity: it claimed the second title of Old Constitutional Force and persuaded itself that it followed in the pure line of descent from the Saxon *fyrd*. It had at various times past been the subject of compulsory service or ballot and theoretically was still so. On paper it was over 100,000 strong and included all arms except cavalry. It had a regular cadre of about thirty to a battalion, men were enlisted for six years and the recruit usually did six weeks' training at the regimental depot to which his Militia battalion belonged to qualify for a small bounty. Battalions did twenty-eight days' collective training each year, usually at or near the same depot. The junior officers generally had no military credentials beyond belonging to county (or aspiring-to-be-county) families, and no training took place between annual camps. It was a useful recruiting agency for the Regular Army in that the man who was doubtful about whether he was cut out for a military life could sip at it by joining the Militia (from which discharge could be cheaply purchased) before draining the whole draught to find the shilling at the bottom. The time-expired Militiaman transferred to the Militia Reserve on which the Regular Army drew, with the individual's consent, and for this liability he received an extra bounty of one pound annually. Again in theory (there was much about the Militia that was more theoretical than factual) they were subject to fairly stiff discipline and in 1898 there were over 800 convictions before courts-martial and over 700 sentences of imprisonment, mostly for absence without leave, or desertion. It was, as has been noticed, a convenient back door to commissioned rank and the Militia gave to the Army, in addition to Sir John French, the future General Lord Byng of Vimy and Field Marshal Sir Henry Wilson, to say nothing of Captain W. S. Gilbert of the Argyllshire Militia who might well have been a future CIGS had his talents not taken a different direction in conjunction with a bandmaster's son named Arthur Sullivan.

In a society becoming increasingly urban and industrial the Militia was a diminishing force for employers could not be expected to contemplate with equanimity the disappearance of their people for six weeks at a stretch, usually in May and June. Still, when in the words of General Kelly-Kenny, "We should have come to the end of our tether if we had not had extraneous aid", sixty Militia battalions volunteered for and served in South Africa.

They were living proof of the aphorism that there are no bad troops only bad officers, for these were not only inadequately trained but in numbers woefully below establishment. The Militia were employed mainly on lines of communication—which had to be garrisoned by someone—and if they did nothing else they at least freed about the same number of Regular battalions to make war.

About 13,000 Militia Reservists went to South Africa in drafts for Regular units and another 10,000 for Militia Battalions there. Hamilton says that their quality was quite excellent.

The Yeomanry, entirely a mounted force, comprised thirty-eight regiments varying greatly in size and with a Regular staff much smaller than that of the Militia. In its early days before Sir Robert Peel's new police force, it existed mainly for internal security such as dispersing riots at the behest of the civil magistrates and it had no liability for overseas service. There was a school of instruction for Yeomanry officers at Aldershot and the recruit was required to do a dozen drills and fire a basic musketry course. Each trooper provided his own horse on something like the silladar system of the Indian Irregular Cavalry and there were eight days' annual training. There was no organization above regimental level, no transport, and the Yeomanry naturally tended to take their cue from the Regular cavalry.

Last came the Volunteers, about a quarter of a million strong and essentially an urban force, distinct from the Yeomanry who recruited mainly in agricultural districts. Their organization and discipline, previously nobody's business but their own, were regulated by the Volunteer Act 1863 and they had a place in the defence of London organization set up by the Stanhope Committee. The required training was slight but most units, based on their own privately purchased drill halls, did far more than the bare minimum. Training at week-ends and in the evenings with a school of instruction in London for officers and an annual camp, they reached on the whole a state of moderate efficiency—indeed some of the richer London units provided themselves out of their own funds with the first machine guns and bicycles used by British troops.

On the outbreak of war Colonel Vincent, MP, of the Queen's

Westminsters offered to raise a battalion for service in South Africa and Colonel Balfour of the London Scottish offered a service company of that regiment to go with its parent, the Gordon Highlanders. After Black Week and in the face of some economy of governmental enthusiasm, the City Imperial Volunteers came into being almost overnight, raised by the Lord Mayor and paid for by a Mansion House fund. The Lord Mayor's Committee bought clothing, including the dashing Smasher slouch hats turned up at one side, other Volunteer units helped out with equipment, rifles were drawn from the Tower, four twelve and a half-pounder quick-firers were bought from Vickers and Maxim and in January 1900 three troopships took them to Table Bay. Lord Roberts said, "They were extraordinarily intelligent fellows and quite excellent." Hamilton, under whom the greater part served, said, "They got better and better every day and in the end they were quite famous." In their ranks were to be found one Law Officer of the Crown, nine barristers, sixteen solicitors, five Writers to the Signet, sixteen Surveyors, seven Architects, twenty-nine bank clerks, two bankers, one shipowner, four schoolmasters, thirty civil servants, and 308 Clerks. With them went the Imperial Yeomanry and many Volunteer units sent service companies to join the Regular battalions of their parent regiments.

After the capture of Pretoria when the war seemed almost over the Guards and the CIV were sent prematurely home. Their presence in South Africa had caused some awkwardnesses mainly because their rates of pay were very high—five shillings a day for a trooper against one shilling for a Regular private—and they were rather unjustly suspected of being shielded from loud noises. They were in Africa only about ten months and they fought two battles—Diamond Hill and Doornkop. The infantry battalion marched 523 miles in forty days. If only they had stayed on for another year or eighteen months they would have become in every sense a *corps d'élite*. The loss of Spragge's 13th MI at Lindley was the saddest entry on the other side of the ledger.

An Australian officer wrote a bitter parody of the parable of the prodigal son which enlarged on the difference in treatment of the favourite sons of John Bull (CIV and IY) in contrast to that given to the younger prodigals who had come from far countries to fight the old man's battles for him.

The auxiliaries thus had played a useful part in the war but less than they might have; they were never mobilized for each unit could be mobilized only if it wished to be. Between the wars it had to be the business of the government to see that the springs of patriotism were all channelled into the same stream and the government could only act through its soldiers. The new Secretary for War, St John Brodrick, set up the Norfolk Committee to enquire into these matters and appointed to it Spencer Wilkinson, a Volunteer officer of unusual gifts. Wilkinson, the same age as Hamilton, was the son of a Manchester banker and at Oxford he began a life-long devotion to things military. He joined a Volunteer Corps soon after being called to the bar and was shocked at the difference between the conduct of modern war, about which he was very well read, and the comically antiquated instruction given to him in his unit. He founded a body with the improbable title of the Manchester Tactical Society, translated at his own expense all the French and German military textbooks on which he could lay his hands (keeping himself alive in the meantime as a drama critic and, as Military Correspondent of the *Manchester Guardian*, published a criticism of the Egyptian campaign of 1882 which won high praise from General Sir Frederick Maurice, himself one of the profoundest military thinkers and most prolific writers of the late Victorian Army.

In 1893 Wilkinson produced *The German Order of Field Service* which was adopted by the War Office, enjoyed the friendship of Hamilton (who wrote to him from South Africa urging him to use his influence to get Buller recalled before he did any more mischief) and of Lord Roberts, although he felt the latter paid too much attention to antiquated drill movements and not enough to the use of the pick and shovel. The report of the committee was in the main Wilkinson's work and it cleared the path for Lord Haldane. In 1909 Wilkinson became Chichele Professor of Military History at Oxford and continued from there to campaign for an increase in both Regular and Reserve

Forces for he was one of the clairvoyant few who saw the coming of another and greater war and the necessity for Britain to raise armies of sizes as yet undreamed. Little Lord Roberts stumped the country preaching the gospel of compulsory military service but all he got for his pains from a Liberal Government was a motion in the House by a particularly bilious member demanding that his pension as a Field Marshal on the active list be stopped.

This was the heritage to which Smith-Dorrien succeeded when he moved into Government House at Aldershot in 1907. His appointment to the command was by no means a foregone conclusion for, as the then Prince of Wales wrote to him, every politician in the cabinet put forward two names—first that of his own favourite General, second that of Smith-Dorrien. As there was no unanimity about the first choice Kitchener's advice was sought and he came out strongly in favour of the man who had done so much to improve the state of Quetta District even though he could ill spare him. A letter from Sir Arthur Bigge (later Lord Stamfordham) survives with Sir Horace's papers reminding him of the rare gifts of his immediate predecessor but saying that the King expected new ideas from the east. The Monarch never regretted his choice (so strongly urged on him by the heir-apparent) of Smith-Dorrien as the new General Officer Commanding-in-Chief. In the same year he was rewarded for his past service with the KCB. Smith-Dorrien was now fifty. He had thirty years of service behind him, including six very rough campaigns, in which he had miraculously escaped wounds but suffered much from sickness; he had retained his spare horseman's figure though his hair and heavy moustache were now grey. His jaw still stuck out like the ram of an Athenian galley and it cannot be denied that his manner, except amongst his peers, was ungracious; remember that apart from his two years at the Staff College in the eighties he had not served in England for twenty-seven years. His aspect was rough and his temper ferocious—anyone, including members of his own family, could find himself at the receiving end of it without warning. Even the redoubtable "Wully" Robertson, himself an adept performer, had a taste of it: but it was a quick temper and Smith-Dorrien was easily mollified if it appeared that the victim had the right of it, and few held it against him. His old Harrow schoolfellow Sir John Fortescue tells a story of him at the Delhi Durbar of 1911 which can be only one of many such incidents. "I was driving back to the King's camp after some function or another with Smith-Dorrien and one or two others in a closed motor all of us, of course, in uniform. On the way we overtook a squadron of dragoons trotting gently back to their own place and just as we overhauled the tail of the column the head wheeled to the left blocking our road and bringing our motor to a standstill. Horace became restive at once. Surely, I thought, he is not going to make a scene. The whole place is humming with motors full of magnates of every description and travelling in all directions. If an officer is to be looking out for all of them he will never get his men back to camp. But no! In a moment Horace's head was out of the window and the question 'Who commands that squadron?' rose at the third repetition to a formidable fortissimo. The unfortunate officer came round to the window, explained and apologized and after a few seconds of rapidly cooling wrath Horace dismissed him with a bland 'All right'. It was a fire of straw, burnt out in a few minutes but regrettable because quite unnecessary. . . . As to anything deeper than irritability, it was not in his nature to be ungenerous, rancorous, froward or vindictive: and he had a keen sense of the ridiculous."

And in the condition of his new command he found much that *was* ridiculous, but this time it did not amuse him. He took no great interest in politics but having known Gordon he was no admirer of Gladstone or any of his adherents: the pro-Boer faction of Lloyd George and his friends upon whom the mantle of the GOM (or MOG—Murderer of Gordon, as the transposition had it) had descended can hardly have made any greater appeal to him. He viewed the Press with considerable and justified misgivings, though he did not carry them to the tempting conclusion of his old chief Kitchener who barged his way through a group of war correspondents waiting expectantly outside his tent in the Sudan with the genial greeting "Out of my way, you drunken swabs!" Horace fell foul of them just before succeeding to the Aldershot command when, having made an after-dinner speech advocating compulsory military service to a gathering which he understood to be private, he found its contents blazoned across the next day's papers. He was summoned before the Adjutant-General, Kelly-Kenny, who invited an explanation as to why a General Officer on the active list had publicly advocated a policy diametrically opposed to that of the government. Knowing Smith-Dorrien to be the soul of honour, Lord Roberts readily accepted his explanation that he had been no more than naïve, but the lesson was digested. Again it is an odd coincidence that both Hamilton and Smith-Dorrien, when their high decisions became the subject of press scrutiny, were hounded by malevolent newspaper men—Ashmead Bartlett and Murdoch in the case of Hamilton and Lovat Frazer in that of Smith-Dorrien.

Hamilton too was lean and hard and he and Smith-Dorrien presented a striking contrast to Sir John French who was having much trouble with his weight (so much so that he even took, surreptitiously, to learning to ride the bicycle). French was now CIGS and was thus able to continue the tradition of his beloved Buller (to whom he had written a fulsome letter when his patron had secured Aldershot for him some years previously) not merely in the spirit but in the flesh. The Army had the doubtful satisfaction of seeing a man of corpulence at its head. A tendency to adiposity is not necessarily fatal for a soldier; John Sobieski when he relieved Vienna in 1683 was mountainous and few would have called Joffre underweight, but heaviness seldom lends itself to mental agility as a natural compensation. Judging from the imprint French had left for his successor at Aldershot, Sir John seems to have seen war as the campaigns of Seydlitz profusely illustrated by Caton Woodville. However, Sir John was able to draw heavily on his substantial reserves of vanity and to present a majestic front to the world. The years of good living had had their effect and he was no longer in the judgment of any but himself—the Rupert of King Edward's Army.

After the South African war commissions and committees came and went in the cause of reform, the Elgin Commission on the condition of the Regular Army, the Esher Committee on War Office reform, and the Norfolk Committee on the auxiliary forces. The lamentable state of the artillery whose weapons were inadequate and obsolete came under particular scrutiny (there were no less than sixteen types of piece in service and at the end of the war heavy howitzers had been bought from the Skoda works, shortly to find a better customer). Brodrick, and his successor Arnold-Forster, had begun useful improvements but the election of 1906 swept them out of office by an avalanche of Liberal votes. The new government of Campbell-Bannerman was dedicated to peace, retrenchment, and reform and when his patronage came to the distribution of officers he found none of these new mild men who would touch the War Office "with a pole". "Then give it to me," said Richard Burdon Haldane, the Chancery Silk. His request was granted.

CHAPTER TWELVE

HALDANE, complete with his seals and in a hired brougham, arrived at the War Office in the thickest fog he could remember. He groped through the mud, round the horse's head and into the door of the building then located in Pall Mall. Overcome by his exertions, Haldane handed over the seals to an Under-Secretary and asked the ex-Guardsman in attendance whether he might have a glass of water. "Certainly, Sir, Irish or Scotch?" came the answer and Haldane's opinion of the military rose at once.

The next day at a meeting of the Army Council Haldane met for the first time not one General but several and questions were put to him about his ideas in the anxious voices of men perplexed at the appearance of one trained in so different a stable. Haldane was prepared for this and produced his famous answer that he was a young and blushing virgin recently united to a bronzed warrior and that no result of the union should be expected for at least nine months. The *mot* reached King Edward who was much amused. On the following day Haldane was asked, also by a General, what sort of Army he wanted to see. "An Hegelian Army," replied the philosopher, after which conversation fell off. He asked them to advise him of an officer whom he might appoint his Military Private Secretary and was given the name of Major Gerald Ellison—a choice he never had cause to regret. Haldane took to applying his keen lawyer's mind to the refreshing works of Clausewitz, Bronsart Von Schellendorf, van der Goltz, and by way of balance the Frenchman, Ardent

Du Picq. Thus enlightened he turned to the matter of the reform of the Army and its reserves for the state of both had shocked him. His brief was to reduce expenditure and he learnt from his financial advisers that there was much waste which if prevented could be used to increase efficiency without adding to the estimates. He learnt all about the Militia, the Yeomanry, and the Volunteers; he learnt too that the regular artillery had, on paper, ninety-nine batteries but for lack of men and reserves only forty-two of these could take the field and that this was symptomatic of the state of the entire service.

And so he assembled his team which from the available talent could hardly have been bettered: Haig ("a first-class General Staff mind") was brought from India "to do our thinking for us"; Nicholson, the Chief of the General Staff ("a very clever man, not by nature a soldier": Haldane told him he ought to have been a lawyer—he meant it as a compliment) Spencer Ewart, Sir Charles Douglas, plus the invaluable Ellison. These men, forgotten now, were responsible for the new model Army which was to be mobilized in 1914 and their names should be inscribed in the country's archives in letters of gold. Haldane himself, Doctor of Philosophy and Master of Arts of the University of Göttingen, made it his business to pick the brains of the foremost practitioners in the business. He wrote a number of newspaper articles friendly to Germany and was rewarded by an invitation to Berlin from the Supreme War Lord himself. Haldane was shown everything he wished to see including the splendid War Office where commanders and staff manœuvred not brigades and divisions but whole armies of millions. He could not fail to be tremendously impressed by what he saw but was not overawed; when he was dined by the Minister of War, the Chief of the Great General Staff, and no less than thirty-eight Corps Commanders, he came away with the impression that although of a high standard they were not up to that of the General Officers of 1870. The reform Haldane would have most liked to borrow was the complete separation of the General Staff (whose business was purely strategy) from the Administrative services— the Intendantur—an idea perfected by the elder Moltke in the 1860's and borrowed by the British in the Middle East in 1942.

He was presented to the Kaiser and met the younger Moltke. The Kaiser, addressing him (perhaps because of his aggressively civilian status) in a tone different from that which he usually employed with visiting British Generals, observed affably, "A splendid machine I have in this Army, Mr Haldane, isn't it so? And what should I do without it situated as I am between the Russians and the French? But the French are your Allies, so I beg pardon." The old Queen's grandson was not entirely devoid of humour. Haldane, of course, was obliged to return the hospitality but when the German Generals arrived they were not very interested in military establishments. What they all wanted most to see were Harrods and Maples.

This is not the place for a full exegesis of the Haldane reforms for they deserve a book to themselves. He would have been the first to acknowledge that much valuable clearing of the ground had been done by his predecessors Brodrick and Arnold Forster and would not have denied that many improvements in equipment were largely due to the money voted by the governments of Lord Salisbury and his nephew Arthur Balfour. Money was by far his biggest single difficulty for the new Liberal administration (some of whose members had not long ago gloried in the name of pro-Boers) regarded themselves as having been elected to raise the standard of the working man by the congenial process of soaking the rich—a task which could safely be left to the eager hands of Lloyd George. Armies, to the minds of men like John Morley and John Burns, were parasitical growths battening on the nation's earnings and serving no purpose in a modern world. The Navy was in a rather better position for even Burns had heard of Trafalgar and shared the view of A. G. McDonnell that one of the few subjects amongst the English not suitable for laughter was Lord Nelson. The strident voice of the Royal Navy raised by Admiral Sir John Fisher (augmented a little later by that terrible ex-Cornet of Horse whom we glimpsed at Omdurman) did not fall on entirely deaf ears especially with the clanging of hammers on steel echoing from the shipyards of Hamburg and Bremen. The Navy demanded, fairly enough, eight dreadnoughts if it were to guarantee that the working man could ply his trade in peace and in the fullness of time draw his newly created old age pension. The Navy received its battleships but against screams of protest only slightly muted by the fact that building capital ships provided employment for many and was an improvement on Louis Blanc's Ateliers Nationaux. The Army, however, was quite another matter. Every good Liberal knew that the brotherhood of man was just around the corner and that there would never be another war. If by any remote chance they were wrong, Fisher's dreadnoughts would see that the war stayed on the continent where such things belong. Every Liberal, that is, except two—the political head of the Navy (recently proselytised from the Conservatives), and the political head of the Army.

So it resolved itself into a question of what could be done within the Budget of 1899 by eliminating useless expenditure and on this the philosopher and his military and financial advisers did much thinking. First, they must make the best use possible of available manpower. A conscript Army on continental lines was out of the question not merely on political grounds, as it would only supply huge numbers of short-service men who would have been no use in garrisoning India or other remote places. Old Sir Colin Campbell had described the Prussian Army of just before 1870 as "verra good militia" and everybody knew the troubles Mr Lincoln and Mr Davis had had with such forces; they had to aim for a small, well-trained, properly balanced Regular Army with an adequate flow of reserves. The quality of the officers and men of the Regulars had never been higher for, under the Cardwell system, recruits made their way through the regimental depot to a home battalion for a spell of more advanced work, and then to India for a turn on the Frontier. This resulted in skilled, highly-trained soldiers. Moreover, after leaving the colours the soldier was available for recall by Royal Proclamation and he would not take too long to settle down in the ranks again.

The non-regular reserves were, however, in a far less happy condition; the Militia as we have already seen was a dwindling force and served only for draft-finding for the Regular Army. The Yeomanry and Volunteers had made a useful contribution to the War (even though Colonel Allenby thought the former "quite useless") but they could have been more efficient had they been organized as an Army and not as a series of private members clubs loosely affiliated to a central body. Mr Punch, perhaps something of a distorting mirror at this time, waxed very humorous about them but drew a clear distinction between Militia and Volunteers. The former were usually pictured as comical yokels led by skinny young men with disproportionate eyeglasses, a sample caption being,

Officer: "I hear you have had previous service. What were you?"

Stout Militiaman: "Mrs Wiggin's coachman, zur."

The Volunteers were usually shown with an officer, vastly corpulent, urban, and looking as if he was doing very well in trade, insecurely seated on a hired horse receiving the pleasantries of a crowd of ragged urchins, such as "Wipe the blood off yer sword for yer, General?" The rank and file (when they appeared at all) were represented in a recumbent and dishevelled posture behind a bush in a state of advanced insobriety making witty drunken remarks in barely intelligible Cockney. It can hardly be a matter of surprise that little public confidence could be placed in either and it is all the more creditable to our grandfathers that they kept in being something upon which a new generation could build. Haldane and his military colleagues knew this hodge-podge must be replaced by a new Reserve Army created as complete as possible in all its arms, ready and able to take over the defence of the island when the Regular Army embarked the Expeditionary Force. If after more training they could be fitted to take their place in the line then so much the better, but this was a secondary object. The difficulties to be overcome were enormous particularly in the case of the Militia for in both houses of Parliament colonels of the Old Constitutional Force abounded and they defended their hopeless cause to the last ditch. Valuable advice had been given by the Duke of Norfolk's Committee (largely the work of Wilkinson) and the government paid more heed to it than in very recent times it has done to that given by a subsequent holder of the title. This may seem a little strange when the loudest voice in the cabinet was proclaiming that a fully equipped Duke cost more to maintain than a fully equipped battleship but Lloyd George's prejudices were well known. From another, more authoritative source, Lord Roberts himself, came further criticism of the scheme for while he had no objection to the provision of quantities of semi-trained infantry, since his National Service League was plainly not going to succeed over conscription, the thought of his beloved artillery being turned over to a mob of shop assistants, clerks, and farmhands officered by lawyers, farmers, and business men was abhorrent.

Haldane and his advisers, however, had faith in the scheme and were determined to have their way. As no soldier was capable of doing the job for him Haldane farmed out the drafting of the necessary bill to one of his former devils in Lincoln's Inn and by an arrangement with the sympathetic Balfour, now Leader of the Opposition, the Territorial and Reserve Forces Bill 1907 was quietly, almost furtively, made law. The Militia was to be disbanded, except for the formation of a special reserve of individuals and some conversions of old regiments into the extra services (such as ammunition columns) which the new quick-firers would need to feed them with shells. It is true that the additional factories for making these shells did not exist and it would be difficult next time to repeat the Boer War expedient of buying them from Germany, but this was something beyond even Haldane's powers and at least the organization to move the shells from railhead to battery was in being. The business caused much heart-burning but on the whole was cheerfully accepted for most of the people concerned had sufficient wit and patriotism to see that the change, though lacking in drama, was a considerable step towards the creation of a Twentieth-Century Army.

On All Fool's Day 1908, the new Territorial Force was born and it throve from the start. Its people felt that at last they were a serious and serviceable military organization. Their intendantur was the County Association, a name admittedly of Cromwellian origin, whose charge it was to provide the drill halls, clothing, and other basic quasi-civilian essentials while armament and training were to be the business of the War Office. Regular adjutants and permanent Staff Instructors were freely provided, divisional and brigade organizations set up, Schools of Instruction were opened to territorial officers and the best arms available were supplied.

The spirit was high and recruiting was encouraged by patriotic plays like "An Englishman's Home" which sought to make the point that a German invasion was not a fanciful impossibility. The original plan for twenty Divisions was modified to a more practical fourteen, and within two years 276,000 effectives were under arms. The Territorial Force return for 1908 shows a figure of 188,785 men serving on different types of engagement, of whom about sixty per cent were ex-Volunteers. Lancashire and the West Riding of Yorkshire had by far the best recruiting figures. By the end of September 1910 the force mustered 9,759 officers and 257,337 other ranks. The two midland districts each had more than ninety-two per cent of their establishments.

The drill halls—from the wealthy London units where an entire battalion could be accommodated under one roof, to the small building at the back of the pub in a Wealden village— acted as magnets to the best of the island's young men. Their motives were entirely patriotic for the annual bounty and a fortnight's camp at Regular Army rates of pay were not much of a financial inducement to join. Miners, ploughboys, counter hands, clerks, fishermen, they all came and with them a number of time-expired Regulars anxious to keep up in some fashion the old comradeship of the regiment. The TF could not become a carbon copy of the Regular Army, for inevitably it had a discipline of a more elastic kind, something half-way between the Guards and the Working Men's Institute. It would be absurd to expect the Territorial Company-Sergeant-Major, who had perhaps left the Army on pension years ago as a corporal and who was engaged in civil work of quite a humble kind, to be treated off parade with the deference that was his due by a man who may have occupied a superior position in the same organization during the rest of the week. The TF had a mystique of its own about these things for on parade it sought to be more regular than the Guards while, after the drill was over, all would drink together on terms of equality. Some of the more clannish London units indeed went to the length of having no officers or sergeants messes at all and when the last notes of No Parade died away they became all members of the same club whose discipline was maintained only by the natural good manners of all concerned. The oddest thing about it was that it worked very well in practice; as it has been aerodynamically proved that a bumble-bee cannot fly, so this incomprehensible peace-time behaviour proved to carry within itself a disciplined obedience equal when tested to any in the world.

The TF had both enemies and friends in high places. The Commandant of the Staff College, Henry Wilson, saw it his duty to ridicule the TF and to interlard his lectures with spirited imitations given in his own singular way of Generals Haldane and Lloyd George leading a charge of Territorials. He must have inculcated in many good officers of medium rank a contempt for his auxiliaries. Ian Hamilton, who had seen more fighting as a leader of troops in any two years of his career than Wilson was to experience in a life-time, came, saw, and was converted—even to the point of falling out over the matter with his beloved old chief, Lord Roberts. He did not go all the way with Haldane, deprecating the emphasis on home defence and saying wisely that a shield is not easily convertible into a sword. "There is hardly a Territorial who does not at the bottom of his heart hope to go into one historic battle during his military existence." Some were to have their chance. Haig too, while he would have preferred to have seen some form of compulsory service realized the political impossibility of such a plan and threw the great weight of his prestige and authority into making the system work. Even Punch altered its view slightly with a cartoon showing Mr Punch commiserating with a group of Territorial officers on their fatigue at the end of an exhausting exercise and receiving the reply, "At least we have strength enough left to write our cheques for our expenses." Hamilton, as Inspector General of Overseas Forces, introduced the idea to the self-governing Dominions who adopted similar plans with variants to suit their national characteristics. Smith-Dorrien did not immediately make their acquaintance but when at Southern Command a few years later he wrote,

"The great advantage I gained was getting into touch with

Territorial troops. Hitherto, excepting my five years at Aldershot, when I had practically nothing but Regular troops to deal with, I had, since I came to years of discretion—in other words, since I became a senior officer—served entirely abroad and I really knew nothing of Territorials. In the Southern Command, however, I soon got to know and to appreciate them. Their keen study of soldiering, their earnestness, thoroughness, and considering the short time they were embodied each year, their remarkable standard of efficiency impressed me very soon. The more I saw of them the higher the opinion I formed of them and the greater did my confidence become that in them we really had a most valuable asset should the nation be in trouble. Yeomanry, Artillery, Infantry, Engineers, ASC, and Medical Units were all heart and soul in their work and showed great *esprit de corps*. It was on account of this high opinion formed between the time I took up the command and the outbreak of the Great War in 1914, about two and a quarter years, that I urged Lord Kitchener in August 1914 to use them as the basis for expanding the Army."

Now at last there was a real Army of Reserve dressed throughout in serviceable khaki with its own horse, foot, guns, and supplies. Surgeon-General Keogh persuaded many local doctors to join and began an efficient medical and nursing service. The days of the private Volunteer Corps, each fantastically dressed according to its own whims (though none approached the company of patriotic Frenchmen who arrived in Tours at the end of 1870 gorgeously if not very serviceably attired in the fashion of D'Artagnan's Musketeers) were now very far away.

Such was the situation of the men of King Edward's army and now let us inspect its material. The long Lee-Enfield rifle was a good weapon with the smoothest bolt action in the world but it was unhandy; the cavalry's Martini-Metford carbine (though better than the French Mousqueton which was fit only for rabbiting) was a poor weapon; the introduction in 1903 of the new Short Lee-Enfield, the old rifle with five inches lopped from its barrel, produced a weapon admirably suited to both arms for it was as accurate, or very nearly so, as its predecessor and could be carried in a leather bucket by a horseman without difficulty. In 1908 arrived the Mills equipment made of canvas webbing instead of leather and providing a specific place for every item carried by the infantryman (though the Cavalry clung to their smarter leather bandolier) and the D-III field telephone, quite an efficient instrument. It was also the year of the new artillery—long overdue—and the RFA was issued the excellent eighteen pounder QF with a range of 6,500 yards, the 4·5 howitzer, and the sixty-pounder medium gun with its team of a dozen horses. The new cavalry gun, the thirteen pounder, brought into service in 1904, was the best of its kind available. There were still not enough of these new arms to go round and the TF had to make do with the fifteen-pounder (converted to quick-firing as a result of experiments with the German Erhardt gun) and an improved 4·7 but they were weapons not to be despised and with them the TF went to war. The machine-gun remained the Maxim, heavy but capable of 600 rounds per minute (when it was first on the market Sir Hiram Maxim demonstrated one to the King of Denmark who observed "A splendid gun, Sir Hiram, but it would bankrupt my little kingdom in half a day"). There were two to a battalion accompanied by an unsound doctrine for their use. Omitted, doubtless for the usual financial reasons, were more sophisticated forms of signal equipment (although wireless was no longer a toy and was used in the Royal Navy and in the German Army), any form of light automatic, hand grenade, signalling pistol or mortar, any means of enabling the artillery to use indirect fire, and better RE equipment. The necessity for these things, like that for the steel helmet, had not yet been proved though all were available. Such heavy artillery as existed was antiquated and no great use was made of motor transport. A demonstration was given at Aldershot by a private firm of the Caterpillar tractor but little notice was taken. The Army was breathing with a new life and the little red manuals were coming out thick and fast from Gale and Polden. *Infantry Training 1911, Artillery Training 1908,* and above all *Field Service Regulations 1909* which for the first time prescribed a common doctrine throughout the Army of what was required of every commander at all levels in the usual operations of war. The ASC and Ordnance Corps, once nobody's children, were properly allocated and the Royal Engineers with their usual virility, fathered the infant flying service.

In order to ensure the availability of a pool of men of education who would be the young officers of the TF in a few years time and who would have enjoyed some military training before being commissioned, he approached the Headmasters' Conference and the University authorities. From this came the Officers Training Corps, the public schools providing the Junior Division and the Universities the Senior. Membership of the Junior Division was usually compulsory and the schoolboy at the age of seventeen or thereabouts took his Certificate A examination which comprised both a written and a practical test. The instruction was of high quality and most boys left school fairly competent in drill, musketry, map reading, sanitation, hygiene, and other basic subjects. The Regular Army was generous in its provision of instructors and demonstrations both during the twice-weekly parades of term time and the fortnight's annual camp, ensured a boy was fit for an immediate commission in the lowest rank without fear of being a passenger. Membership of a University Corps carried the young man's education beyond the infantry training he had received at school, into artillery and other arms, giving the advantage of an ante-date should he join the TF. The Corps also provided a good flying start for those determined on a professional military career and it was very largely its work that the Armies, Regular, Territorial or New, did not degenerate into armed mobs for want of competent leaders. Many a young man, pitchforked into a position of sudden responsibility, learned to bless the School Corps (however lacking in ardour he may have been during his active membership) for teaching him how to drill a squad, march on a compass bearing, conduct a range practice, or build a latrine, not to mention the arts of assembling and blanco-ing web equipment and rolling on puttees in the one correct way. The unknown schoolmaster also deserves his place of honour. On 23 May 1914 Sir Horace inspected the University OTC at Oxford and there marched past him behind their Corps of Drums over 1,000 cadets, horse, foot and guns, including Private HRH, the Prince of Wales. The General thought them "a very fine lot of young men." Every year when the 11th

November comes round and the long rolls of names are read out in schools and colleges proof is given that he did not err in his judgment.

By 1912 Haldane's work was done and he was translated to the office he had always sought—the Lord Chancellorship. On the evening of the Victory Parade through London in July 1919 Haig called unannounced at his house leaving a bound volume of his Despatches in which he had written: "To Viscount Haldane of Cloan—the greatest Secretary of State for War England has ever had. In grateful remembrance of his successful efforts in organizing the Military Forces for a War on the Continent notwithstanding much opposition from the Army Council and the half-hearted support of his Parliamentary friends—Haig, F.M." The spontaneous gesture and the sentiments with which few will quarrel do honour to both men.

CHAPTER THIRTEEN

LET us return to Smith-Dorrien taking over his new command at Aldershot. In his scrap book is a letter of welcome from his predecessor Sir John French written in the most cordial terms. It was to be the last message of its kind from that source for Sir Horace was aghast at what he found. First, it cost him over £3,000—and he was not a rich man—to fit up Government House (which was merely an empty shell) and to equip himself in a manner becoming to a C-in-C with a young and beautiful wife. Though he had not done a day's duty in the UK for twenty-seven years, save for a couple of years as a student at the Staff College, it was at once plain to him that in order to make his corps—the only complete regular corps in the Army—fit to take the field in the face of a European enemy, much must be put to rights. Still, he felt a certain diffidence about it after so long an absence from the country. Of his first reform let him speak for himself.

> I was very much struck on arriving there to find every night the roads and streets being patrolled by innumerable small piquets of an NCO and four to six men and on looking at the duty states I saw that over 700 men weekly were employed on this irksome duty. From a long experience of the rank and file who always play up if trusted I abolished the piquets forthwith—at the same time publishing an order saying that I did so as I trusted the men to behave but that if events proved that I had formed too high an appreciation of the British soldier I should cancel the order. The Provost-

10   Aldershot: with General Nogi, 1 July 1911.

11 *Sir Horace with his mother,* Haresfoot *1901.*

Marshal, a first-rate officer, was much upset and protested that without piquets he could not be responsible for discipline which amused me much and a little later he again protested because I was abolishing another order. This latter was to the effect that when troops were moving about the country doing military training all public houses were placed out of bounds. My train of thought which I explained to my PM was that, even if out of bounds, a thirsty man would enter a public house and knowing he could not do so often for fear of the Military Police would drink as much as he could in a short space of time and probably get roaring drunk whereas if there were no restrictions and he could get his glass of beer whenever he liked no evil effect would result. I regarded both the piquets and the public house prohibition order as productive of military offences.

There was inevitably a great wrangle but the end of the story was a letter of appreciation from Haldane and another from the Town Council when Sir Horace vacated his command. The matter also caught the imagination of the national press which thoroughly approved what had been accomplished; long articles and editorials (all carefully pasted into his scrap book) appeared extolling his actions and usually printed under some such heading as "The British Soldier is a Gentleman Says General Smith-Dorrien." Cartoons appeared showing the general, axe in hand, cutting through red tape, and toasts being drunk to him in canteens by a red-coated Thomas Atkins with a halo. Even so unlikely a paper as Robert Sievier's *Winning Post* devoted a full page and a half to his career—though not surprisingly more space was taken up by his prowess on the turf than in the field. He became over-night the symbol of the New Army and no dissentient voice was raised. The feelings of his vain, rancorous predecessor can be imagined, and French could only consider that the affair had been deliberately arranged to insult him. One day he would have his revenge.

Next the new GOC determined to make barracks more attractive and to provide healthy recreation for the off-duty soldier. Every piece of ground large enough for cricket, football or hockey was taken up, levelled, and grassed. With the assistance of Captain R. J. Kentish, a name not forgotten by sportsmen,

Smith-Dorrien increased the playing fields area by 150 per cent. Larger and more comfortable regimental institutes, better lighting, dining halls instead of men having to eat where they slept, more baths and showers all followed and were appreciated. Messing was greatly improved, thanks to General Burnett, once Quartermaster-General, and cross country running introduced. Down came the trees which made any sort of training impossible between Government House and Norris Bridge. The chief engineer claimed that it would take the RE years to cut them down and that no contractor would buy them standing. Both divisions were ordered to carry out an operation designed to take up a position on the edge of the wood and clear such a field of fire as would remove their obnoxious presence; all the trees were down in six hours and more came down later to create the airfield between Farnborough Common and Norris Bridge. For himself and his successors Smith-Dorrien had courts built where he could play his favourite game of squash, which he kept up until late in life. It is still almost possible to trace the commands he held by the trail of new squash courts he left behind him. It is a pity one was not there in Sir John French's day for it might have helped him with his weight problem. Important though these things were, however, they helped only indirectly in the production of trained soldiers. The general condition of the artillery and infantry was good, thanks to divisional generals of the calibre of Grierson and Stephenson with their subordinate commanders, (one Brigadier was Sir Henry Rawlinson) and to the Artillery Adviser, Colonel Horne, later to be Peer and general and the only gunner officer to command an Army.

But the state of the cavalry, at any rate from the viewpoint of the fighting soldier, was sad indeed. True their appearance was superb—Blücher could he have returned would have again said that every troop horse was "goot for Feld-Marschall"—and their drill left nothing to be desired. Even on dismounted occasions such as church parades, at which they marched to compulsory worship behind their bands in full dress, they caused a stir in the most sluggish pulse. For any operation of twentieth-century warfare the kindest thing that could be said of the cavalry was that they were no worse than their French or German counterparts. Smith-Dorrien, no mean horseman himself, was horrified. He had no great regard for an officer who had an indifferent seat on a horse as appears from his comments on "our pen-loving CIGS, Field-Marshal Lord Nicholson," who "was not fond of inspecting troops and except once when ordered to be in attendance on the King never came near Aldershot all the time I was there. The truth was he disliked a horse and that on the one occasion referred to telegrams were flying for days to unearth the most docile animal in the Army. The Royal Military College produced the favoured quadruped but I gathered it was not approved of as the CIGS only came out with HM one morning, looked thoroughly unhappy and pleading urgent business went back to his office the same afternoon." Perhaps Haldane had been right and Nicholson should have been a lawyer after all. This does not mean that the absurd charges with lance or sabre which formed almost the only part of a cavalryman's training won Sir Horace's approval, for they hardly ever dismounted and their musketry was abysmal. Here no doubt came the best help and advice available in the Army for the Chief of the General Staff was no less than Brigadier-General W. R. Robertson. "Wully" Robertson had enlisted in the 16th Lancers (the Scarlet Lancers to the Army and once the Regiment of Sir Horace's father) in 1877 at Aldershot, where his first weapon had been a muzzle-loading horse pistol and where he had endured precisely the same training as was now being meted out to the next generation. Eleven years later, in India, he was commissioned into the 3rd Dragoon Guards and began an almost unprecedented career to the heights of CIGS.

In 1909 Wully and Rawlinson accompanied their chief on a private inspection of the cockpit of Europe, motoring all along the Meuse from Spa to the Belgian frontier. They arrived at Waterloo Station early one morning and found only a few ancient cabs to be had. Smith-Dorrien and Wully selected what seemed the least disreputable hansom and as they drove up the slope both shafts broke, the cab falling over backwards and coming to rest on the driver's seat. The aged driver rolled off down the hill and the generals were left lying on their backs with their legs sticking straight into the air wedged firmly together and roaring with laughter to be liberated eventually by another decrepit man who happened by. Rawlinson drew one of his spirited cartoons of them in this helpless and undignified posture which remains to this day in Sir Horace's scrap book.

Sir Horace, as has been noted, had a fearsome temper. This seems strangely out of character in a man of so humorous and kindly a disposition (when his old chief, Sir Arthur Power Palmer died leaving two orphaned daughters Sir Horace and his wife at once adopted them into their own family). His temper was undoubtedly the result of the hideously painful complaint of neuralgia. Wully had a taste of Horace's temper early on in their association but the two men soon became and remained fast friends. Sir Horace took the problem of cavalry training by the throat and on 21st August 1909 summoned all cavalry officers to meet him at the mess of Wully's old regiment where "I gave them my views pretty clearly." Certainly by the time Sir Horace had finished no one could have been left with much doubt that the fun was over and serious training for a European war was to take its place. The cavalry, having been for so long encouraged by French to indulge in their customary exciting but futile antics, were furious, but dared not disobey this new fearsome chief and nearly went to the head of the annual musketry returns. News of this latest outrage was not slow to reach Sir John who added it to the score which some day would be settled. French's antagonism to Sir Horace was not hidden for when the latter attended the meetings of the the selection board for the promotion of officers (over which Sir John presided as CIGS) it quickly became plain that a recommendation by Horace for the promotion of any officer was the kiss of death. Sir John also went to some pains to see that his former friend was denied the opportunity of gaining practical experience in the handling of large bodies of troops at the annual manœuvres by forbidding him on specious grounds to exercise his right to command. The only other punishment he could inflict was to deprive Government House of the sunshine of his presence for he never paid the customary social visits except when attendance on the King compelled it. Sir Horace, no doubt, bore this absence with his customary fortitude. In 1910 Wully Robertson relieved Henry Wilson as Commandant of the Staff College while the latter moved to the War Office as Director of Military Operations, but not before leaving on the hall table at Camberley a bill for £250 for various items left behind. The "items" consisted of a greenhouse and some rose trees given to Lady Wilson by Lady Rawlinson and furniture which had been left by past commandants. When Robertson wrote to Rawlinson to verify Wilson's claims, the answer came, "That fellow Henry! My wife built that greenhouse and gave it to Lady Wilson. My wife put in those rose trees and gave them to Lady Wilson. . . . You had better dig up the potato patch and see if the seed potatoes are still there". (Wully cut Wilson at the next garden party: this can hardly have made for easier relations on the staff of GHQ-BEF a few years later.)

Smith-Dorrien's tour at Aldershot, however, was not confined to cutting down trees and cursing cavalry: the post necessitated a great deal of entertaining—both official and private. To Sir Horace this was no hardship for he and his wife, who for all her mere twenty-six years of age was an accomplished hostess, loved it. Dinner parties of thirty and forty were commonplace and in addition to their private friends many men of high rank and influence were their constant guests. Sir Horace was now one of the great men in the land, well-known to and liked by his King and whose guest he frequently was when in London. The King also paid appreciative visits to Aldershot which both men much enjoyed, and the Smith-Dorriens were on dining terms with the Prince and Princess of Wales and other members of the Royal Family. On the one occasion that Queen Alexandra accompanied the King they insisted on seeing the Smith-Dorrien children. Gren and Peter were admitted to the room full of people and to their parents' consternation, Gren (who was to die a Brigadier at Anzio leaving a reputation for personal valour with which his father would have been well pleased) demanded loudly to know which was the King: the Queen, as always, was equal to the situation and patting him on the back assured him that his Monarch was "that stout old gentleman over there."

Smith-Dorrien received at this time a letter, carefully preserved, from a gentleman bearing the honoured name of Picton writing from an address in Brisbane who claimed not merely kinship but the right to the title of Earl of Dorrien and St Mary's. Sir Horace, whose interest in the genealogy of his family is shown by his careful compilation later in life of a most formidable family tree, was interested and returned a courteous answer though he did not accept the invitation to have the title transferred by some unspecified means to himself in exchange for a cash offer.

His preference for compulsory service which had already got him into trouble with the Press led him to seek membership of Lord Roberts's National Service League but the wise old man wrote to say that as the only general on the active list to be a member was Gaselee, who had relieved the Pekin Legations in 1900, he would do better not to join. Sir Horace took the hint.

In 1909 a Mr Maguire, a barrister who had been a lecturer at the Staff College in the eighties, published a condensed edition of Clausewitz which began with a dedication in the shape of an open letter to Sir Horace:

> It is now more than twenty years since I had the pleasure of working through with you the campaigns which the late General Sir E. Hamley selected as examples of the truth and force of the principles of strategy. Your presence as a student in our class was encouraging, your progress was rapid and your subsequent success has been complete ... but it is not altogether because you are in command of a great British Military Centre or because of your services in the field or because of your admirable system of Military Training and of your efforts to promote the progress of your subordinates in tactical skill that you deserve our highest esteem. We respect you especially because you have shaken off the trammels of a stupefying and degrading system of discipline falsely so-called. You despise the miserable anachronism which would treat the officers, non-commissioned officers and privates of our Army as either knaves or fools or mere machines. You think that men who can be trusted with our Imperial Greatness in the stress of battle can be trusted to look after themselves in everyday life. Your greatest service has been to teach our soldiers to respect themselves as men.

He concludes by applying to his former pupil, deservedly if with no great richness of imagination, the full text of Chaucer's "parfit gentil knight." One could wish to know whether the previous incumbent of Aldershot read it. His reaction would have been interesting.

Foch and Huguet came to visit Smith-Dorrien and they got on well, for Sir Horace spoke fairly good French at the time (though with more dash than accuracy); also came Russian, American, Japanese, and Turkish officers and his old friend Sir Evelyn Wood who was one of the most welcome of them all. (It is of the gallant old gentleman that the story is told of how, wandering one morning into his usual bathroom and finding it occupied by, unmistakably, a lady he rose instantly to the occasion by saying, "I beg your pardon, General" and bowing out. The lady herself told the story at breakfast so it must be true.) Another figure from the past was no less than the Empress Eugenie to whom Sir Horace had had to break the news of the death of her son nearly forty years before, and whom he was to meet again in Gibraltar fourteen years later when she was still a sprightly ninety-four. The Empress, at this time a mere eighty, was interested in everything and was particularly taken at the moment with the wish to fly in one of Mr Cody's new aeroplanes at Farnborough Common—to the horror of her suite who could not persuade her to give up the idea. They implored Lady Smith-Dorrien to use her influence on Sir Horace to find insuperable difficulties to the adventure which somehow he did. Mr Cody crashed the machine and killed himself soon afterwards.

Sir Horace did not interest himself in politics and indeed boasted that he could spot a politician a mile off. His staff had a drill for the situation; when the chief for no obvious reason shouted suddenly for horses it meant that he had scented one and was off. Any faint stirring of interest he might have felt in politicians was put to rest on the occasion when he was obliged to lunch a member of the Cabinet and thought to persuade him to disgorge a miserable £100,000 to equip the Army with the new Vickers machine gun as it was more efficient than the existing Maxim and half its weight. To his surprise the great man jeeringly accused him of being afraid of the Germans and observed knowledgeably that he had habitually watched the German Army at its training and that it was quite certain that if they ever went to war the Germans would provide the most monumental examples of crass cowardice the world had ever seen. Against this penetrating judgment there was little for Sir Horace to say.

In July 1909 Smith-Dorrien was bereaved by the loss of his beloved mother and had a long drive from the middle of an inspection by the Duke of Connaught which brought him to her bedside just before the end. She was a formidable old lady in the true Victorian style—all her five youngest daughters died spinsters as they were never allowed out of the sight of her keen eye—but he adored her and her death was a great grief to him. Another gap was caused in the same year by the death of his favourite sister, Mrs Tyrwhitt-Drake. The following March he met the King for the last time at Biarritz and noticed how ill he was looking: only five weeks later while on a refresher musketry course at Hythe (not a thing that all general officers considered necessary for their professional education) he learnt of the King's death and rode sadly in the funeral procession.

In 1911 he dined with the new King at Buckingham Palace and was gratified to learn that he was to be ADC General for the Indian tour and the Delhi Durbar (where the explosion of temper which Fortescue mentioned was to occur); did he tell the King of those caged tigers, now nearly fifty years ago?

Aldershot was not all hard work and hard entertaining for he found plenty of time for hunting and shooting which together with squash and golf kept him in the hard physical condition he enjoyed to the end of his life. He shared his wife's enthusiasm for gardening though he was still uninterested in any of the arts. But he was now over fifty and after his tenure had expired it was not easy to see what the Army had left to offer him. The lights were beginning to dim in Europe and he was not going to be too far off when they went out so he declined the offer to succeed Lord Methuen in the South African Command but accepted the Southern Command at home on his return from India.

He had done much for Aldershot which in its turn had done

much for him. He was no longer just one more general but a power in the land, very near to the top of the tree and on familiar terms with the greatest. Events were moving to a climax in the world outside. What part, if any, was he going to play in them?

CHAPTER FOURTEEN

By the time Smith-Dorrien's tenure of Aldershot was ending, the real possibility of war with Germany and alliance with France was in the forefront of the minds of most men who troubled themselves to think about it. The realization had been slow in coming and was reached with reluctance, for although the old ally of Waterloo had not endeared herself by her brutal treatment of France in 1871, (nor the Kaiser's notorious telegram to Kruger, or the overt challenge to the supremacy of the Royal Navy, or a multitude of incidents from the German naval showing-off before the American Squadron at Manila in 1898, to Count Waldersee's exhibitionism in China at the behest of his Imperial master), these things could be dismissed as minor irritants; the mistress of the seas could afford to regard them as no more than the uncouth behaviour of an upstart empire.

When all was said and done, was not the Kaiser the old Queen's grandson, and had he not comported himself so well at her death? Supreme war lord he styled himself, but was it really likely that he would in any circumstances make war on his own Uncle Bertie?

On the other hand, the French were no friends to England. True, they had been our partners in the last European war but that seemed something of an aberration. Certainly they had not behaved amicably to us since the naval incident in the Gulf of Siam in 1893 and Fashoda was a recent and painful memory. They had made common cause with Germany against us on behalf of ex-Presidents Kruger and Steyn and had supplied the Boers with their excellent artillery, unconcealed best wishes, and a number of volunteers. Why should peaceful, prosperous England shed blood for such people?

Sir Edward Grey, the Foreign Secretary, early learned what he described as the rough side of German friendship (a less urbane man might have justly called it blackmail). The agreement between the Powers for the administration of Egypt made unison essential, so when, as over the Turkish railway concession, the German government wished to clear competitors—particularly British competitors—from the market, nothing could be simpler than a threat of withdrawal of support in Cairo. Their unscrupulous demands having been met, the halter round Sir Edward's neck, as he called it, was relaxed again. The Kaiser's constant public flexing of his muscles over Venezuela and Morocco—whatever he might have protested about his love of peace in private—compelled British support for the French at the Algeciras Conference in 1906 on the heels of which came the first hesitant, back-door approaches to a military understanding between the two armies—if not the two governments.

The two original participants of this understanding were men who would quickly have been disowned by either side if the matter had leaked out and become an embarrassment. On the British side was Charles à Court Repington, sometime Colonel in the Rifle Brigade and veteran of the Atbara, Fashoda, and Buller's campaign in Natal who had been compelled to send in his papers in consequence of an indiscretion (some considered it as something worse) involving the wife of a well-known diplomat. Repington loved the Army second only to the lady and knew probably more about the French Army than any man outside it as for nearly five years in the 1890's he had been employed in the French section of the Intelligence Department, attended French Army manœuvres regularly, and there made many friends. In his book *The Military Resources of France* (an Intelligence publication) he spoke of the graduates of the Ècole de Guerre as "nowhere surpassed for professional knowledge" and expressed his admiration for the several arms of the service, save for their cavalry for which he had but modified rapture. The German

Army, of which he knew far less, he sadly under-rated except for its unique staff organization. The officer who brought Repington's career as a soldier to an end was a brother rifleman named H. H. Wilson, then a major and shortly to become Commandant of the Staff College, who treacherously revealed to the Army Council a written undertaking never to see the lady again given by Repington to two brother officers and which he had failed to honour. This resulted in Repington having to resign his commission. Fortunately for himself Repington was able to start a new career as a military correspondent and his articles on the Russo-Japanese war, published by *The Times*, gave him an international reputation. Though sometimes less than fair in his judgments of men, his thought was always ahead of his time and there was in him the material, if not of a great commander, certainly of an outstanding Chief of Staff. He was much influenced by Wilkinson's *The Brains of an Army* (1890) and was a passionate advocate of the adoption of the German Great General Staff system which Wilkinson had expounded in that work.

The French emissary, who appears to have been the initiator of the talks, was Major Huguet the Military Attaché, a personal friend of Repington, and a man greatly liked and trusted by those British officers with whom he came into contact (such as Sir James Grierson) and consequently regarded by his own countrymen as more English than French. He won Kitchener's heart, having learnt by chance of his part in the war of 1870, by obtaining for him the campaign medal and a letter of gratitude from his government. As his book *Britain and the War* (1928) bears the sub-title *A French Indictment* one supposes that he found his Anglophile views not unalterable. It appears that this achieved its reward for he eventually became a general, and his assessment of the characteristics of the islanders stirs ancient memories of Etienne Gerard. Huguet was a small dandified man, very close to what the English believed to be a typical Frenchman for he was voluble and interlarded his English with a stream of "Zs". Huguet told Grierson in December 1905 of French fears of an attack by Germany which Grierson passed on to the government. But it was after an article in *The Times* by Repington on 27th December that Huguet dined with him and let himself go on the subject. Repington at once wrote to Sir Edward Grey and to Admiral Sir John Fisher and through these intermediaries together with Lord Esher there was sent to the French government an official questionnaire as to the French position on possible joint military action. Throughout January 1906 Huguet, with the blessing of M. Roûvier the Prime Minister, was very busy. The matter passed to the Imperial General Staff, itself only one year old, and out of the private sphere on 15th January when Grierson was instructed to open official conversations—each side well understanding that neither assumed any obligation to the other. Grey did not find it necessary to bring this to the notice of the Cabinet, which apart from Campbell-Bannerman the Prime Minister and Haldane, remained in ignorance of the talks for the next five years.

1906 saw not only the beginning of these staff talks but also the final acceptance of General von Schlieffen whose famous plan, which even though watered down by Moltke in spite of its author's modifications in 1911, was to bring the empire wholeheartedly into the war by its violation of Belgian neutrality.

For the next four years nothing happened to disturb the vague understandings between the two staffs, save that their existence was kept secret. Wilson's successor, General Ewart, showed no desire to place a British element on the left of the French line, and avoided any commitment, however slight, to such a policy and in this incurred Huguet's displeasure to the extent of earning the adjective "timorous". But below the level of their chief, junior officers continued with the work, though more slowly than before.

In 1910 Henry Wilson, Repington's enemy, became Director of Military Operations at the War Office. Wilson bears no likeness to any other soldier of note. He had not seen, and continued never to see, any great amount of service commanding troops in action save for a short time in 1916 when he showed himself an incompetent corps commander. An Irishman with a strong bent for intrigue, he had a brain which has been variously described from superlative to third rate, but he shared with Repington an enthusiasm for all things French. Perhaps his closest friend was Ferdinand Foch then Commandant of the Ècole de Guerre with whom he was on Christian name terms (a much rarer thing with French generals than with British) and with whom he enjoyed the singular pastime of changing hats. Wilson had travelled extensively in France (particularly over the battle-fields of 1870) and on one occasion, as he records, laid touchingly at the feet of the unattractive statue of France at Mars-la-Tour a piece of map showing the proposed concentration areas of the BEF. He does not relate what subsequently became of it. As Commandant of the Staff College he had observed on a number of occasions that, "There is no military problem to which the answer is six divisions and a cavalry division". But that is precisely what could be provided and no military plan existed to place it anywhere but in some unidentified locality on the left of the French Armies. The French plans were, and remained until the outbreak of war, totally unknown to the British and if Wilson knew through his friendship with Foch of the existence of the grotesque Plan XVII he kept silence. The Royal Navy knew nothing of it and, until the arrival of Churchill at the Admiralty, it hugged to itself a private and mildly lunatic plan for a landing in the Baltic based on the experience it had gained 150 years ago under the conditions of the Seven Years' War. So that was the situation. If a war came and Britain found herself committed to the French side, the bulk of the Regular Army was to be immediately dispatched under guard of the Navy to an unknown place in north-east France to do it knew not what.

The British Army had not come conspicuously well out of the Boer War (to the unconcealed pleasure of French and German alike) and was lightly regarded by its potential Ally not merely by reason of its small size, but also for the official French view that it was antiquated, fit only for police duties or minor colonial expeditions and could never be of the slightest use to France. Huguet shared this opinion but soon altered his view as he was perhaps the first outsider to see that the Boer War had been a very real school of instruction. He admired the Army's new equipment, particularly and strangely for a Frenchman, its artillery. He began seriously to study how many men could be put into uniform in a continental war. The figure he reached was 150,000 but probably not all could be put into the field until the 30th day after mobilization: later he checked this number with the then DMO, General Grierson, who told him that his arithmetic was accurate enough but the times for mobilization and transport were much shorter than his estimate. Grierson, incidentally, was not only one of the official successors to Repington but also a former attaché at Berlin known to the Kaiser and the greatest authority in England on the German Army. Thus fortified, Huguet went with his encouraging news to his Ambassador, Paul Cambon, who believed the maximum figure to be no more than 30,000, and in consequence of this came the authority from the President du Conseil for the official discussions of which we know. The Kaiser's opinion of his Uncle Bertie's Army endures in the single lapidary adjective, "contemptible."

CHAPTER FIFTEEN

THE Smith-Dorriens greatly enjoyed Salisbury. As a military command it was less high-powered than Aldershot since it embraced only one Regular division—the 3rd—under the very adequate command of Sir Henry Rawlinson. At Salisbury, too, Sir Horace made his first close acquaintance with the Territorial Force; as we have already seen, he was agreeably surprised by what he found and proved a firm friend of the new force. He found the atmosphere of a cathedral city relaxing and it gave him all the opportunities he could wish of pursuing his sporting activities and cultivating his comparatively new role as a family man. Although now well past fifty he was happy in the company of his young sons and spared no pains in training them early to horse and gun; for their part they adored him although they were not exempt from an occasional burst of the Smith-Dorrien temper. At Harnham Cliff he had for the first time, a home and not merely a set of quarters, and there the family received an unexpected accretion.

Sir Power Palmer (Kitchener's immediate predecessor as Commander-in-Chief India) was step-uncle to Lady Smith-Dorrien in addition to having been one of the most agreeable and sympathetic General Officers under whom Smith-Dorrien had served. On his sudden death his two young daughters were left not merely orphaned but homeless and the Smith-Dorriens adopted them into their own household. It was a successful arrangement and they soon settled down and were accepted by the boys as their sisters.

12 Spy's view of the G.O.C.-in-C., Aldershot 1911.

13 *Royal visit to Aldershot—'Wully' Robertson behind the Queen.*

14 *Southern Command—Sir Horace presents the Army Cup to the 2nd Bn Sherwood Foresters.*

In 1912 he was promoted to the rank of full general and was thus on the penultimate branch of the tree. The only serving Field Marshal was Sir John French who together with Seely had been forced out of office as a result of the hubbub over the Curragh affair and was again unemployed. He bothered Sir Horace no more at Salisbury than he had done at Aldershot but took himself to Deal Castle, of which he had recently been appointed Captain, to nurse his further grievance without forgetting his old ones. Sir Charles Douglas, a sensible if undistinguished man, succeeded him as CIGS.

Smith-Dorrien was not a military innovator; his past had made him as conservative as most of his contemporaries. But he had a better idea of the pattern of future warfare than most. In addition to the Aldershot reforms which had permeated the Army, he was a powerful advocate of that neglected but war-winning engine, the machine gun. Remember that at a stage in his professional career, when most men would have deemed such a thing beneath their dignity, he had returned to Hythe (then at the peak of its reputation under Sir Charles Monro) and had learnt all there was to know about the handling of the weapon including its organization in units and the official thoughts behind its use. These he found sadly wanting. There was a machine gun section of two guns, (still the old Maxims) to a battalion of infantry or regiment of cavalry. The doctrine of *Field Service Regulations 1900 Part II* was: "The massing of machine guns is likely to attract hostile artillery fire. For this reason it is usually better to employ them in pairs in support of the particular body of troops to which they belong. When an overwhelming fire on a particular point is required it can be provided by concentrating the fire of dispersed pairs of guns. The guns of two or more units may, if required, be placed under the command of a specially selected officer and employed as a special reserve of fire in the hands of a brigade commander." *Infantry Training, 1911* deprecates the practice on the grounds that concealment and control are difficult and "the positions suitable for a number of sections in attack are often difficult to find at effective and close ranges and the combined movements of a number of sections is only possible under such conditions when the ground is very favourable." The massed machine gun battalions of 1917–18 would have found this diverting. Strangely enough it is *Cavalry Training 1907* which most nearly contains the true doctrine. "During the cavalry fight they will usually be massed under one commander but may be employed in pairs when necessary."

Sir Horace, as we have already seen, was trying hard to get the improved Vickers gun adopted into the service; Rawlinson tells us that Smith-Dorrien was also an advocate of the Brigade Machine Gun Company. In this very important matter he saw the future development of the "concentrated essence of infantry" more clearly than any of his contemporaries and the Machine Gun Corps of 1916 could with justice claim him as a god-parent. Machine gun officers of 1912 were rarely selected by their colonels because they were the brightest or most able of subalterns, but usually because it was a rather menial job that nobody fitted for real infantry or cavalry work would want. Fortunately the gun itself made a sufficient impression on its reluctant handmaidens and they formed a small band of zealots—as von Kluck was shortly to learn. Sir Horace's other demand had been met and every man up to and including the rank of sergeant carried a serviceable entrenching tool, a weapon second in importance only to the rifle but for so long overlooked. Like Wellington before him his gift was not in soaring imagination but in strong common sense and practicality. In 1913 he was created GCB— the last honour he was to recieve though his finest service to his King and Country still lay ahead of him.

Better to understand August 1914 we must make a brief digression. Henry Wilson had been Commandant of the Staff College between Rawlinson and Robertson. At the end of his tenure Smith-Dorrien, who had a high opinion of his ability, offered him one of his brigades at Aldershot but Wilson was not permitted to accept as he was already earmarked for the post of Director of Military Operations at the War Office, a job for which he was in every way better suited than as a commander of troops. It now fell to him to do all the staff work for the despatch to France of the Expeditionary Force—those "six divisions and a cavalry division" which provided the answer to no military problem. The next three years were Wilson's finest—if one forgets the tricky part he played in the Curragh affair. From the moment of his return to the War Office work started again with a certainty, a speed, and a decision hitherto unknown.

The dates of the English (the word is Huguet's) mobilization timetable were changed to coincide with the date by which the concentration of forces in France had to be effected; the Zone of Assembly was definitely fixed (with alternative zones as in the French plan): the stages of mobilization were brought forward in accordance with the new timetable; rail transport in England, ports of disembarkation, shipping dispositions, camps, rationing, organization of French interpreters, a double cypher for use between the two Armies, and a thousand other details were worked out. The County Territorial Associations on their own had registered 120,000 horses to be commandeered on embodiment. Railway transport tables in France were produced in collaboration with the French staff and the Companies of the Nord and l'Etat—a matter of great delicacy. The newly-formed MI-5 of Colonel Kell ran to earth nearly all the German espionage network in this country and with quiet efficiency prepared to strangle them the moment the word came. Not for nothing were the French convinced that Wilson was our only general and in their jargon code they spoke of the coming BEF as l'Armée W. For all this, and notwithstanding all that he may have done later, the memory of Sir Henry Wilson deserves his country's gratitude. When he was killed in 1922 outside his house at Eaton Place, ironically enough by two Irish gunmen, men forgot much of his double-dealing and intrigue and remembered only these, his best years.

At the same time the young Winston Churchill and the old Jackie Fisher were doing as much for the Navy. Thanks to these men, and to a host of others in lesser stations, the BEF was able to reach France safely and the machinery of mobilization and concentration was to run on well-oiled wheels. Churchill was certainly an admirer of Wilson for he records his pleasure when the latter relieved Robertson as CIGS in 1918, speaking of his superior intellect and loyalty even while acknowledging his odd mannerisms. Disliked by Kitchener and Haig, loathed by Robertson, the Goughs (John Gough refused to speak to him again after the Curragh), and by Pétain, distrusted by Spears as vindictive, but admired by Foch and Churchill, Wilson remains an enigma to this day. Like French, his best work had been done before the BEF sailed. From then on, notwithstanding that he rose to Field Marshal and the professional head of the Army, his influence was almost wholly for the bad. Wilson was wildly wrong in his judgment of great affairs ("We shall be in Elsenborn in three weeks"). After the battle of the Marne he hypocritically called for the Territorial divisions which he had done his best to ridicule out of existence, ("Kitchener's projected 25 Divisions are the laughing-stock of every soldier in Europe"); he was malignant in all things (he even accused his old Chief, Lord Roberts, who came to France in 1914 to see his beloved Indian troops—and incidentally to die there—of doing it "to qualify for a medal"). Nonetheless, his excellent staff work during this time deserves a recognition that his defects of character should not obscure.

Many years ago, old Bismarck in retirement had told Herr Ballin, the German millionaire industrialist and friend of the Kaiser, that when the great European war came it would begin with "some damned foolish thing in the Balkans." On 28th June it began. Archduke Franz Ferdinand, morganatically married to the Countess Sophie Chotek, took the opportunity of carrying out an inspection of troops in Bosnia in his military capacity (his wife's rank was deemed by the House of Habsburg so to disparage his own that she could not appear publicly with him on State occasions). At Sarajevo they were assassinated by the Serbian conspirator Gavrilo Princip. As Bosnia had only been annexed by Austria Hungary six years previously, condign punishment was bound to follow. Count Berchtold, the Austrian minister, grossly over-played his hand but this is perhaps understandable; it had long been the Austrian tradition always to be on the losing side—at any rate since the last siege of Vienna by the Turks had been raised by the Polish King John Sobieski. This is not to say that Austria lacked good soldiers; it was merely their continual misfortune always to encounter better. Archduke Charles had defeated Napoleon himself at Aspern-Essling, but had soon afterwards been annihilated at Wagram. Benedek had not done badly at Nachod and Konnigratz and might have done better still had he faced any other general than Moltke. For all that Conrad von Hotzendorf, the Austrian Chief-of-Staff, has been described by competent judges as the best strategist of his generation. And certainly the individual Austrian soldier lacked nothing in bravery or skill; the regular regiments justly claimed unbroken descent from the victorious army of Wallenstein and their military bands—Strauss trained—were the best in Europe. So, though few yet knew it, were their great siege mortars, unknown elsewhere and shortly to pulverise Liege and Namur. With such a long tradition of defeat it would be pleasant for Austria to find an antagonist against whom she could not lose; such a one appeared to be Serbia, the step-child of the hated Turk who had made Vienna for so many centuries a beleaguered frontier town. And so, after the failures of diplomacy, the guns of the Austrian monitors in the Danube opened on Belgrade. Inevitably the wheels began to turn. There was general mobilization, with streams of reservists leaving their homes in France, Germany, Russia, Austria, Serbia, and elsewhere; stiff boots, creased uniforms that had long lain on shelves in thousands of Quartermaster's stores, rifles covered in grease were thrust into hands which received them with varying degrees of enthusiasm; kepis, pickelhauben, caps, and helmets of many kinds were pulled on to heads. Trains steamed out to the frontiers, enriched by inscriptions like "Nach Paris" or "À Berlin" and indecipherable graffiti in Cyrillic script presumably bearing similar messages; rising over it, prayers and hymns thundered from the cathedrals and churches of western Christendom demanding a blessing on the armies of the worshippers as opposed to those of other worshippers across the border.

What would England do? Legally, she was committed to do nothing. The staff talks initiated so long ago by Huguet and Repington had been on a clear "without prejudice" basis, but there were two questions to which France justly demanded a straight answer: first, in French eyes, it was essential to keep open the sea route from Oran to Marseilles so that the Colonial

Army, France's only counterweight to the numerical superiority of Germany, could pass unhindered to its place in the line. If the French Navy were to be employed on this duty (by no means a sinecure as the large Austrian fleet could strike from its bases in the Adriatic in addition to anything Italy might do) the French Channel coast would lie naked under the guns of the High Seas Fleet. Would the Royal Navy watch idly while the coast towns from Dunkirk to Brest were shattered? Second, what of Belgium? The independence of Belgium was largely the creation of Palmerston and Talleyrand less than a century ago. Treaties apart, would Britain out of self-interest see the Low Countries in enemy hands and do nothing to eject the invader? Minds returned to 1870 and the Punch cartoon of Britannia, like a well-fed Valkyrie, one hand protectively on the shoulder of a smaller and milder version of herself (labelled, helpfully, "Belgium") the other on a half-drawn sword, over a caption of "Let us hope they leave you in peace, dear friend, but if they do not. . . ."

None knew the answer to these questions and few had less idea than the British cabinet itself. A Liberal administration which had opposed the Boer War, and which included men who had narrowly escaped man-handling from crowds as pro-Boers, was at least immune from any suspicion of the jingoism by which old men still remembered Palmerston. And of their number only one had ever seen a battle and that was of moderate dimensions in comparison with what could be expected in a conflict between the great powers of Europe. Three issues were at point; the possibility of a German naval bombardment of the French coast, the violation of Belgium, and the violation of Luxemburg. Sir Edward Grey, the man on whose shoulders lay the burden of advising the cabinet, had one overmastering fear. If Britain kept out, was it to be said that we had allowed France and Russia to involve themselves in a war relying on British help and that when it was too late had callously abandoned them to their fate? There had been an exchange of letters on this subject between Grey and Cambon in 1912 which made it plain that no obligation was assumed, and although the French Armies were deployed as they would have been had no island to the north existed, the fact remained that the French fleet was in the Mediterranean and nothing could stand between the fine new German battleships and the French north and west coasts but the Royal Navy. Grey was an austere man with a strong sense of honour. No man would have the right to accuse England of treachery if he could prevent it; with little hesitation he gave Cambon the assurance that if the Kaiser's fleet were to attempt to steam into the Narrow Seas the King's ships would bar the way. As soon as this information was sent to Berlin the German government undertook not to attack the coasts provided Britain remained neutral and thus the naval point ceased to have validity.

Germany declared war on Russia on 1st August. France, as Russia's ally, could not remain neutral especially as the greatest concentration of military power the world had yet seen was advancing on her. Five French armies lay on the eastern frontier from Belfort to a point north-east of Mezieres with their attention concentrated mainly on the centre of the line in face of which lay the Grand Duchy of Luxemburg. Plainly one of the combatants must sooner or later invade the other and the lawyer's question of obligations must precede the soldier's appreciation of military necessity. Our duty to Luxemburg was different from that which we owed to Belgium. It had been debated in Parliament in 1867 and the conclusions had been made clear both by Lord Derby and his Foreign Secretary, Lord Clarendon. In the 1831 Treaty there was a guarantee by the powers that Luxemburg was the possession of the King of Holland, not in his capacity as monarch, but as Grand Duke of Luxemburg. In 1839, by a separate treaty, the five powers bound themselves severally to maintain the integrity and neutrality of Belgium—but the guarantee to Luxemburg was a joint one. Thus while Britain had a right to take up the cudgels if Luxemburg were invaded, she had no duty to do so except in concert with her co-signatories; if the land invaded were Belgium, her contractual duty was to bring all her force to bear to carry out her obligations quite irrespective of the acts or omissions of her partners. The old debates were mulled over and the plainer it became that Luxemburg involved no automatic *casus belli*, so by contrast the inescapable duty of defending Belgium stood out in relief. No man could explain this away on any ground, even though some years previously it had been mooted that the treaty was out of date, but to the credit of the Cabinet no voice was raised to attempt to justify an evasion of this pledge.

From the German point of view this was so exasperating that Bethmann-Hollweg, the Imperial Chancellor, on the 29th July made to the British Ambassador in Berlin the proposal, that if Britain stood aside now, at the end of the war Germany would make no territorial demands on France, and that when hostilities ended Belgium would be restored. The French colonies were not included in this generous offer. In his answer to Sir Edward Goschen, our Ambassador at Berlin, the Foreign Secretary described this proposition as a disgrace from which the good name of the country would never recover but he continued even then in his powerful efforts to maintain peace. In this he had the aid of the German Ambassador in London, Prince Lichnowsky, a charming, popular and honourable man who hated the idea of a European War and who was kept quite in the dark by his own government as to its true intentions. Sir Edward had suggested a conference of ambassadors, an expedient which had done good service over the Bosnian annexations of 1912–13, but as he ruefully observed, certain continental circles held the view that he took too much on himself.

In truth, the ambassadors never had a chance to begin with. They all were men of the strictest personal honour, but the ambassadors of the central powers were cynically manipulated by their governments to obtain the time needed to complete mobilization. What did Lichnowsky know of the great 420 mm mortars made in the Skoda works, the mightiest artillery pieces ever—designed not for any defensive purposes, but to pulverize Brialmont's inexpugnable fortresses at Liege and Namur? It is certain that he knew nothing. His last talk with Churchill in which the latter used the phrase "My dear friend, let us not go to war" ended in tears and Lichnowsky was a man incapable of hypocrisy.

On 3rd August, Sir Edward Grey spoke in the House. After he was seated again, but before the House rose, there was brought to him a communication from the Belgian Embassy in London, saying that Germany had proposed a friendly neutrality on the part of Belgium to allow free passage to German troops; in default of an affirmative answer within twelve hours she would be treated as an enemy. The Belgians had replied that to accept such a proposal would be to sacrifice the honour of their nation and that aggression would be repelled by all possible means. This Grey read to the silent House; the ultimatum was sent to Berlin and at midnight on 4th August, war came to Britain.

In France, all were conscious of their relative weakness but none knew its full extent. There was no general desire for *revanche* for men remembered the last time the cry of "à Berlin" had been heard in the streets of Paris and what the end had been. They would fight if they must but only for the defence of the motherland and not for any selfish purpose. To avoid any suggestion of provocation the French armies had been pulled back ten kilometres from the frontier (giving up a number of prepared positions in the process) and all flying over Germany had been forbidden since 30th July. On the following day had come the news of the simultaneous mobilizations of Austria and Russia and the German ultimatum to the latter. Everywhere doubt gnawed about the probable action of the British. President Poincaré had made a personal appeal to the King and that constitutional monarch, whatever his private wishes, could not but return an answer that was regarded as evasive. When midnight of the 4th came there was a general relief and a very particular one on the part of the distraught Huguet.

What the French, rather surprisingly, did not know was the terrible power of their enemy. The Prussian system of compulsory service had produced enormous numbers of men surplus to the immediate requirements of the active army. These reserves —the sons of the men whom old Sir Colin Campbell had once called "verra good militia"—had been quietly and efficiently organized into reserve formations of a size and quality undreamt of outside Germany. The word "reserve" was at this point of time a loaded one in Britain and France. No Army, of course, can mobilize and take the field without filling its ranks with reservists, and in Britain the short service system of seven years with the colours and five on the reserve had produced a reasonable adequacy of well-trained men sufficient to bring a small expeditionary force up to its war establishment. Nevertheless a man who had for several years been engaged in a civilian occupation and become accustomed to regular hours and meals, a bed, a family, and above all light shoes, could not immediately be the physical equal of a serving soldier (quite apart from the many changes in training and war material). The only other immediate reserve was Haldane's Territorial Force, enlisted for home defence only, imperfectly equipped and trained and for all their intelligence and enthusiasm unfit to meet a European conscript army. The French with their shorter period of service could call up proportionately more men but of far less military capability. The greater German birth rate over the last generation added to their superior methods of training had given them an immense initial advantage for the only redress of the balance, the French Colonial troops, were far away and of mixed quality. In Belgium the Army had long been lightly regarded and the price was now to be paid for years of neglect; their best asset was King Albert, a truly heroic figure. The Russians, as usual, were something of a mystery to their Allies. The general belief was that their limitless manpower must of necessity ultimately prove irresistible in the east.

In the event, the German system placed at Moltke's disposal no less than thirty-four corps of two divisions each in the first six weeks of the war, with another four corps available soon after. Into Belgium there debouched some two million German fighting troops of high quality of whom 700,000 were serving conscripts and the remainder reservists. To withstand them, the French could muster at the outbreak of war only 1,300,000 troops—about the same number that were with the Colours before mobilization. True the French summoned to arms another 1,200,000 but these new drafts were quite unorganized and served only to choke the depots and increase the ration strength. The northernmost French Army, the Vth (commanded by General Lanrezac the pride of the theoretical soldiers) disposed some quarter of a million men with its centre on Mezieres. Long conscious of their numerical inferiority the French had paid great attention to their field artillery and built their plans around the famous and excellent light field piece—the Soixante Quinze. In doing so, however, they had neglected the heavier weapons in which the Germans excelled and for this they were shortly to suffer.

At their head was the rather unsoldierly-looking figure of General Joffre, "le Grandpère" to his Army. A heavily-built, slow-moving engineer he had been appointed to the supreme command only the previous year on the removal of General Michel. (Michel had outraged orthodox opinion by his strategic plan for an offensive-defensive. He did not accept the official view that "Le Reserve, c'est zero." Concerned by the possibility of a German attack west of the Meuse, Michel planned to stand on the defensive in the east and deploy the bulk of his armies on the Belgian frontier. In order to achieve this increase of front it would be necessary to use reserve regiments in the line. The proposal to use second-rate troops to manœuvre—as opposed to manning fixed defences—encountered such virulent opposition that Michel was forced to resign. How different things might have been if he had had his way is an interesting speculation.) Joffre owed his appointment to his former chief in Madagascar, General Gallieni, who relied on him not to be controversial, for since the Dreyfus affair the Army had been restive and in need of a sedative. Certainly the new C-in-C was outwardly phlegmatic; devoted to the pleasures of the table as a good Frenchman should be and believed to be as slow of wit as of movement, he was tranquillity personified, though possessed of a controlled capacity for rage very near to Smith-Dorrien's. To compensate for the inadequacy of his military education, Joffre was provided with General de Castelnau as Chief-of-Staff, the famous "booted Friar", a member of the old aristocracy and a practising Roman Catholic (religious views are of great importance in France). De Castelnau was a true disciple of Grandmaison and champion of the offensive, but was succeeded later by Berthelot when he himself was given command of the IVth Army. History has been less than just to Joffre, dwelling on his mistakes—which were undoubtedly terrible—but denying him, or at best detracting from, his great achievement which saved the Allies from losing the war at its outset. However under, but not because of, Joffre, Plan XVII was launched.

It is fortunate for posterity that the initial mistakes were not confined to one side. In Germany Moltke on his own initiative and to his eventual undoing had tampered with Schlieffen's plan. From the tremendous invading force poised to wheel through Belgium he had stripped seven divisions before battle was seriously joined and a little later, after the first encounter and worried by Rennenkampf's early successes in the east, he detached a further four divisions by rail to East Prussia. The seven divisions did little but invest Maubeuge and Givet, the other four arriving after Tannenberg contributed nothing on either front, but their absence may have cost his country its carefully-planned victory.

But it is time to return to England. The fleet had already disappeared into the northern mists to its war station, mile upon mile of great ships moving silently to Scapa Flow in the Orkneys. At Aldershot notices appeared in messes requiring officers to pay their mess bills before leaving, and on 5th August every Commanding Officer received a file of documents containing orders for the entraining of his unit. Within forty-eight hours 350 troop trains arrived at Southampton (the King inspected most before leaving) and thousands of lorries, still in their civilian dress advertising commodities ranging from corsets to whisky, converged on the docks. From every post-office in the country went telegrams to individual reservists recalling ex-regulars from factory, shop, and field. The Royal Proclamation embodying the Territorial Force appeared everywhere and four infantry divisions (two had been retained for a time so as not to empty the island entirely of regulars) and a cavalry division were crammed into the waiting transports, great liners to small tramps, and swiftly carried across the Channel under naval escort. The great majority sailed to Rouen where, in sight of the ruins of the castle of King Richard the Lionheart and to a roar of cheering from the delighted Normans, some 80,000 Englishmen marched to their rest camps—the first soldiers of their race to arrive in France as friends. None remained in these agreeable places for more than a couple of days before moving by train or road towards Belgium. The Expeditionary Force comprised I Corps, formerly known as Aldershot Command, being the

First and Second Divisions under Sir Douglas Haig with its complete regular staff and services, and the IInd Corps (the Third Division from Southern Command and the Fifth from Cork) under Sir James Grierson, who had outwitted Haig at the 1912 manœuvres. The Cavalry Division embarked in its separate brigades, the 3rd coming from Dublin under Major-General E. H. H. Allenby. (Allenby's natural lack of equability was not lessened by the loss of his best set of false teeth in the post a few days before and added to his cares was the worry that his wife might not obtain full compensation for their loss.)

At home in London Sir John French had been privately informed by the CIGS on 30th July that if an Expeditionary Force were to be dispatched he would command it. This was a surprise to French for he had had long talks with Churchill walking along Deal sea front in which he made it clear that he no longer expected the command, for he had had no military employment since his resignation in 1912. Moreover no one knew whether Britain would go to war or not, or what would happen if she did. On the morning of the 5th a body remarkable in modern history was convened by Asquith at Number 10. It bore the description of the Council of War. Most of the cabinet, save for the pacifiers who had dropped away, were there and among others included in the invitation were Lord Roberts, Kitchener (snatched back from a train at Dover to become Secretary of State for War), Sir Charles Douglas (CIGS), Ian Hamilton, Haig, Grierson, Henry Wilson, and Sir John himself. The CIGS, the professional head of the Army and responsible for all advice given to the Government on military affairs, was hopelessly outranked and silenced. Two important decisions were taken —to keep the 4th and 6th Divisions at home for the time being and to accept the arrangements made some time before to concentrate between Maubeuge and Le Cateau. Kitchener, Hamilton, and Haig both opposed this believing quite rightly that the area was too far north and that Amiens would be more suitable. The general opinion of the Council of War was that this would certainly be a short war, though Kitchener with his memories of 1870 was sure the Germans would go through the French "like partridges" and that the empire must organize itself at once to put into the field Armies reckoned in millions.

Sir John's Headquarters were established in the Hotel Metropole. His Chief-of-Staff was General Sir Archibald Murray (a good officer but lacking in physical and moral strength), and the unprecedented office of Sub-Chief (perhaps as a gesture to the French) was occupied by Henry Wilson. General Macready was head of "A" Branch, "Wully" Robertson was head of Q, and the talented Macdonogh was Director of Intelligence. The French government sent a mission led, to the surprise of nobody, by Huguet and on 14th August the party embarked for Boulogne in the destroyer *Sentinel*. As he regarded Napoleon's column on the heights overlooking the town, Sir John concluded that the Emperor would rejoice to see this friendly invasion of Englishmen prepared to sacrifice their lives to save France from destruction. This not unreasonable musing was revealed to posterity in Sir John's post-war book and drew from Huguet the sour comment, "This explains exactly the feeling of the great majority of the English. They did not understand yet that the help they were bringing us was in fact the best possible insurance for themselves and was the best proof of their own security."

But the mood of the staff was happy and optimistic. A number of officers had told Huguet during the awful days of waiting that if England had not gone to war they would for very shame have refused ever to set foot in France again. Huguet too was still a happy man. On his way to Le Cateau in the warm dark of the summer night his car was stopped by the time-honoured challenge of a British sentry: "Halt. Who goes there?" "For the first time since France and England were, this challenge was being heard on our soil not defiantly as from an enemy, but as a symbol of unity and concord. My heart was filled with joy." Sir John too was in exalted mood; was he not a Field Marshal commanding his country's only Army bringing succour to a hard-pressed friend? Surely it was to this that everything which had gone before in his life had always pointed. His business was to drive the Germans from Belgium. His instructions from Kitchener, now firmly *civilian* Secretary of State for all his seniority and badges of rank, emphasized that his command was independent and he would in no sense come under command of a foreign general. But how was he to start? Field Marshal or not, the fact remained that he disposed in all only about 100,000 men compared to the quarter of a million of Lanrezac, his nearest neighbour. And what were the Belgians doing? Sir John went to Paris to find out, met the President and his Ministers, arranged to meet Joffre the following day, and dined quietly with his Military Secretary at the Ritz. Apart from some polyglot banter about another Waterloo, neither party learned anything of the great events then going on at the front.

The Vth Army was facing north-east between Namur and Sedan ready to advance across the Ardennes, this disposition being founded upon the certainty of GQG that the German Army could not muster enough men to hold off the Russians, invest Liège and Namur, and still mount an attack west of the Meuse. No inkling of the existence of the mobilized reserve corps, nor of the fact that the German troops on the Russian front consisted only of three active and one reserve division, a cavalry division, and some second line troops, had ever penetrated to the Deuxième Bureau. Almost less credible would have been the suggestion that the resistance of Liège and Namur could be counted in hours. The Meuse itself remained a formidable obstacle and its left bank was very rugged country so it seemed unlikely that anything more serious than cavalry raids would take place.

Lanrezac had never believed this. A few days before the war he had sent a written appreciation to GQG in which he said he expected to see a wide sweep through Belgium (though in a conversation a few months earlier with the Governor of Maubeuge he admitted that he did not expect the Germans to cross the Sambre). On 11th August with Joffre's approval, he re-fused his left flank moving his best Corps—the First, under the formidable Franchet d'Esperey—to Givet with instructions to hold the passages of the Meuse. This was certainly an improvement in disposition but the path of the German armies was still clear and unmolested.

In a train between Rouen and Amiens, Lieutenant-General Sir James Grierson, GOC II Corps, died of a heart attack. The following morning Sir Horace Smith-Dorrien (who had been dispirited to see the Army march away without him) arrived at the War Office in response to a telegram and was shown at once to the presence of Lord Kitchener. Kitchener's first words to his old friend were that he had grave doubts as to the wisdom of selecting him to replace Grierson because he had just been told by the CIGS that "for some years past Sir John French had shown great jealousy of and personal animosity towards Smith-Dorrien and that the latter would be put in an impossible position." Sir Charles had also said that this was well known throughout the Army. Sir Horace replied that for his part he held no such feelings and he felt sure that by loyally serving Sir John he could overcome his dislike. On the strength of this Lord Kitchener confirmed the appointment even though Sir John had specifically asked for Sir Herbert Plumer, now virtually unemployed at Northern Command. With this unpromising beginning Sir Horace packed his war kit for the eighth time and sailed for France.

MAP OF COUNTRY FROM MONS TO PARIS

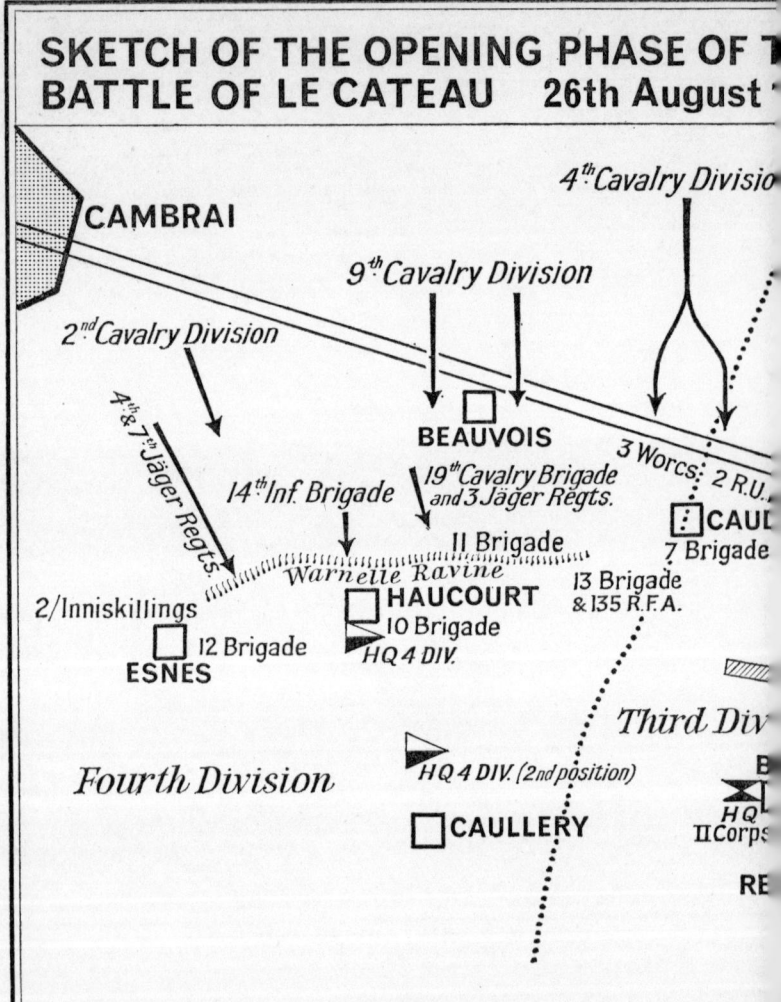

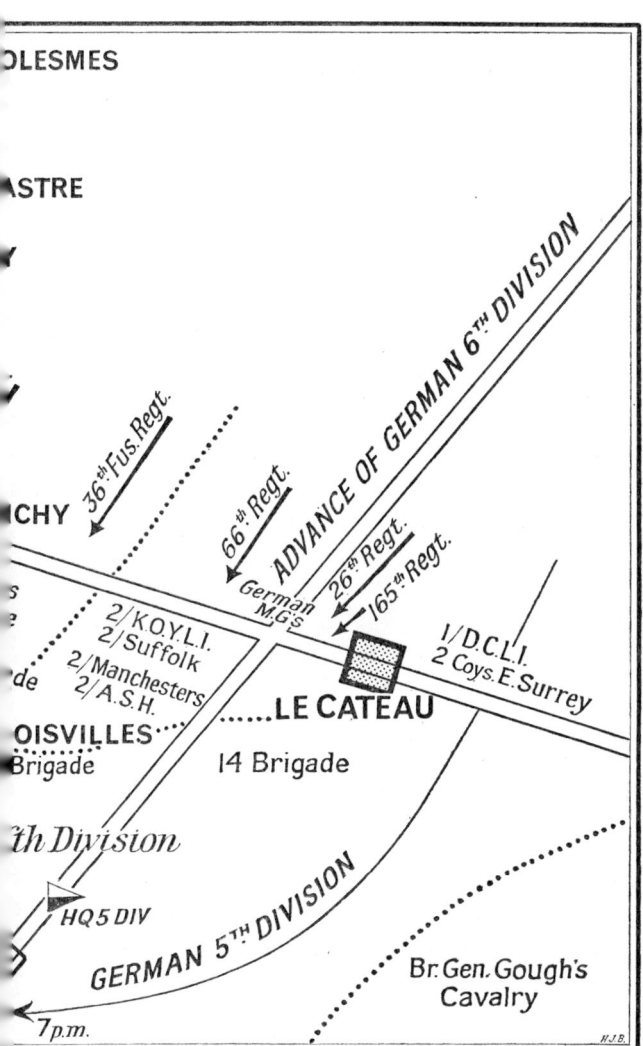

CHAPTER SIXTEEN

The Second Army Corps was less well staffed and equipped than its sister corps. I Corps had all its old Aldershot staff—men trained to the work and accustomed to working with each other. II Corps had a staff composed of such officers as were left over when the demands of I Corps had been satisfied. In addition to this, II Corps was short of an important portion of its artillery, some medical units, and some field companies RE. The physical condition of many of the reservists was poor nor was their discipline always what could be wished. To this disagreeable fact Sir John seems to have closed a blind eye when in his book, *1914*, he asserts their physical condition was good and daily improving.

Sir Horace with a small personal entourage arrived at Bavai, the Corps HQ, on the 20th and after a short meeting with his new staff motored back to Le Cateau to meet his C-in-C. He was not very cordially received but this was not unexpected. Each knew not merely that Sir John did not want Sir Horace and had asked for Plumer, but that the other was well aware of the fact. Sir Horace began by telling Sir John that the King had requested to be kept directly informed of everything pertaining to the II Corps and that this must involve writing a special diary. Sir Horace could not do this without the C-in-C's consent though this could be withheld only if Sir John was prepared to defy his Sovereign. Sir John gave his consent but it can have added little to his visitor's popularity that he must be regarded as a potential talebearer. Fortunately for the C-in-C's blood pressure he did not know that the King had already asked Haig by word of mouth for his opinion of the C-in-C and had received the reply that, "from my experience with Sir John in South Africa he will certainly do his utmost loyally to carry out any orders which the Government might give him. I have grave doubts, however, whether his temper is sufficiently even or his military knowledge sufficiently thorough to enable him to discharge properly the very difficult duties which will devolve upon him during the coming operations with Allies on the Continent." Haig, too, was keeping a diary to which he confided that his old Chief's military ideas in South Africa had shocked him enough, that he knew French to be unfit for high command and for good measure that his Chief-of-Staff, Murray, was an old woman lacking the backbone necessary to stand up to his Chief's dreadful temper. Of the Sub-Chief he commented later "He seems to acquire a more evil look each time I see him." It was against this further background that the strained meeting took place.

Once again Sir Horace knew no more than his horse-holder of what was going on. He had been kept in complete ignorance, in spite of the high commands he had held, of all the plans for the Expeditionary Force and he was not much the wiser when his meeting with French ended. Apparently II Corps was the left wing of the BEF which in turn was itself on the left of the French armies. The Corps was to move forward next day to the Mons-Condé Canal which would serve as a staging post for an advance into Belgium, by pivoting slightly on its right. He was given no information as to the dispositions of the enemy forces nor did he know what troops, if any, were covering his own left flank. There was no wireless communication between GHQ and either Corps HQ (the only sets in France were used for some inscrutable reason for signals between GHQ and the Cavalry Division; it would be hard to have contrived a more futile role for them). Smith-Dorrien must depend on motor-cycle DR's or officers covering long distances by motor, except when the railway company's telephone happened to be available. (Wireless, it should be added, was in regular use, both in telegraphy and telephony, by the Germans and the Russians.) The one point that was clear to him was that the BEF was on the offensive, as every man in it well knew and approved. There was no thought in any mind of a defensive battle, let alone a retreat, and the vast masses of transport were closed up well forward. On 21st August Sir Horace formally assumed command and next day the corps moved to the line of the canal.

Now let us return to the 17th and see what had happened at the meeting between the Field-Marshal Commanding-in-Chief the British Expeditionary Force and the General Officer Commanding-in-Chief the French Vth Army, his immediate neighbour and to whose plans he must, like it or not, conform.

General Lanrezac was at this time the brightest star in the French Army and was well aware of the fact. He was generally regarded as a man wedded to the Grandmaison doctrine and impatiently waiting the opportunity to hurl himself at the enemy's throat though his outward appearance gave little indication of the tiger believed to be lurking within. Even by the standards of the French service, where distinctions of rank mean more than one would expect in a republican society, he was regarded as unapproachable and ill-tempered. He was a large man endowed with a belly testifying to many years devotion to duty at the table and afflicted by the singular habit of hooking his pince-nez over his right ear. He suffered no-one gladly—fools and wise men alike. For the English his contempt was majestic. Lanrezac, however, was by no means a fool and was probably one of the most highly educated in a bookish way of all the Army Commanders of the day. He calls to mind the Chinese mandarin who,

"Never left his palace door
"But had grown blind, reading great books on War."

His command, known as the Army of Paris, comprehended some 300,000 men made up of four Army Corps, a Cavalry Corps, and five additional divisions, one of them cavalry. For his Chief-of-Staff he had General Hely d'Oissel, a tall, slim cavalryman of the old breed of *beau sabreur* who endured his chief's rudeness not only without rancour but with complete loyalty. Lanrezac knew very little of the English except that at long last they were going to cover his left flank—along with General d'Amades two divisions of Territorials and various kinds of armed policemen—all of them about the same degree of military worthlessness. In fact General Lanrezac was a very worried man who had no intention of attacking anyone at all if he could help it, but this information he kept strictly to himself for if it had become known he would have been on the first train to Limoges, the town which had the same significance to the French Army of 1914 as had Stellenbosch to the British some years earlier. General Ruffey, lately commanding the Third Army was already on his way to Limoges.

As early as 31st July Lanrezac had expressed to Joffre the view that the Germans might make a much wider sweep through Belgium than was believed at GQG though he did not expect them to go north of Namur. The great fortress designed by Brialmont at the end of the last century was still believed impregnable to an Army which had no time for cumbersome heavy artillery. On 11th August Lanrezac obtained permission to move Franchet d'Esperey's Corps to a position between Givet and Namur to cover the passages of the Meuse and in this he showed a better grasp of the situation than did his superiors. But it was still far short of reality. Liège was battered into submission by the great mortars on the 14th and he was oblivious to the fact that a blow was coming from the north and that very soon. The awakening was not far off for on the same day the Deuxième Bureau produced an intelligence summary predicating the presence of four German Army Corps and two Cavalry Divisions between Luxemburg and Liège. There were more than twice that number but at last light was beginning to shine through the fogs of the Meuse. Lanrezac sensibly proposed shifting the line of his Army to the north rather than stay facing north-east, and permission was given on the 15th. As part of the change of plan he lost two Army Corps and two reserve divisions—all of which he knew well—and received in exchange two African Divisions, three reserve Divisions, and XVIII Corps from the Second Army, all of them strangers. Plan XVII no longer existed and the function of the Army of Paris was now not to attack, but to place itself as best it could to meet the enemy on ground of the enemy's choosing. So far Lanrezac deserves great credit for willingness to depart from the Plan (one is reminded of General Trochu, Governor of Paris in 1870, who also had a Plan) but it is no wonder that he was a very worried man.

To Lanrezac's Headquarters at Rethel at 1000 on Monday 17th August came Field Marshal Sir John French; his force was now on a collision course with the German First Army, though Sir John did not yet know it. Clearly there was much to be said by both men and it was essential to the Allied cause that the interview must end with each fully in the confidence of the other. The security of Lanrezac's left flank was now in Sir John's care and with it the security of the entire French Army, indeed of France herself. The small victor of Colesberg and the portly Professor of the *Ècole de Guerre* walked together into Lanrezac's office. Lanrezac spoke no English, Sir John no French, though he did understand a little. Outside the room Spears and his companions made uneasy jokes that each was asking the other what had become of the penknife of the gardener's uncle. Huguet was greeted by Hely d'Oissel with "Well, here you are and just about time. If we are beaten it will be thanks to you!" Huguet was horrified. Here was a British Field Marshal rushing his Army forward ahead of its timetables to join in the fight and this was the comradely spirit with which its officers were greeted. But worse was to come. As the two grandees emerged and were joined by other senior officers Sir John stepped up to a map, adjusted his glasses, put his finger on a place name and with great daring stumbled out, "Mon General, est-ce que. . . ." Having thus exhausted his vocabulary he turned to Wilson and asked how to say in French "to cross the river." Suitably prompted he went on "Est-ce que les Allemands vont traverser la Meuse à—à. . . ." The name he sought was "Huy", an almost unpronounceable word to an English tongue requiring as it does a whistle over the "u". "Hoy" managed French at last in triumph. "What does he say, what does he say!" demanded Lanrezac impatiently. It was explained to him and back came the answer with a testy shrug of the shoulders, "Tell the Marshal that in my opinion the Germans have merely gone to the Meuse to catch the fish." Wilson watered this down to, "He says they will cross the river," but the tone and manner of delivery spoke for themselves. Probably nobody had ever spoken to Sir John French in such a way before. Lanrezac for all his great command was his junior in both rank and experience and it must have been interesting to the observers to watch Sir John's efforts to contain himself. He knew himself to have been deliberately insulted and by a foreign general of unsoldierly appearance at that. Twenty minutes or so after his arrival he took his leave. The memorandum handed to him by Joffre which gave the latter's appreciation of the enemy's situation on the previous evening was not discussed at all. Lanrezac also misunderstood the conversation on the subject of the employment of British cavalry, believing Sir John to have said that he refused to use it in its proper role but merely as a mobile reserve for his infantry. The meeting certainly was a long way from the first meeting of Marlborough and Prince Eugene outside the Lamb Inn at Gross Heppach. Lanrezac never returned the call.

It must have been a relief to the fuming Field Marshal to meet his new corps commander even if it was that object of his bitter jealousy—Smith-Dorrien. At least they were men bred in the same stable and he could unburden himself about the unmannerliness of this upstart, West Indian born, foreigner. It certainly rankled sufficiently for him to write loftily to Kitchener on 15th November that "au fond [observe how Sir John's mastery of the tongue had improved] they are a low lot and one always has to remember the class these French generals mostly come from."

When II Corps arrived at their assigned position on the line of the canal it furnished an outpost line of no less than twenty-one miles from Pommeroeul round the North of Mons to Givry where I Corps prolonged the line to the north-east for another seven miles. Sir Horace's own headquarters were established in the pleasant Château de la Roche at Sars-la-Bruyere (in the eighteenth century spelt Sart, hallowed ground on the edge of the old battlefield of Malplaquet and very near the site of the farmhouse where Wellington had rested on his way to Paris by the same Roman road after Waterloo). The cavalry were engaged in a private war around Binche with the German Horse.

The front of II Corps, including the dangerous salient of Mons, was impossibly long and vulnerable as Sir Horace pointed out at a conference on the following day. The C-in-C entirely agreed that it would be dangerous to hang on too long and accepted that it would be advisable to prepare a position across the gorge of the salient on which to fall back if need be and Major-General Hubert Hamilton, GOC 3rd Division, put this at once in hand. II Corps was still short of a significant portion of its artillery and some technical units; the ground on the enemy's side of the canal commanded its position from short ranges and was densely wooded and it was apparent to Sir Horace during his reconnaissance on the afternoon of the 23rd that it could not be held against serious attack. The rear position was no more encouraging and is thus described in the Official History, "The quadrangle Mons-Frameries-Dour-Boussu is practically one huge unsightly village, traversed by a vast number of devious cobbled roads which lead from no particular starting point to no particular destination and broken by pit heads and colossal slag heaps of ten to a hundred feet high. It is in fact a close and blind country such as no army had yet been called upon to fight in against a civilized enemy in a great campaign." The town of Mons being open to fire from north, east and west was quite indefensible but Sir Horace was unworried, for such news as he had officially received indicated that the enemy were in no great strength; he had no reason to question Sir John's expressed intention to move forward again next day and his precautions were no more than those which any experienced commander would take. What he did not know was that Lanrezac had been forced back and was already nine miles south of Mons and that a gap of a further nine miles existed between Haig's right and Lanrezac's left.

On the morning of 23rd August a conference took place in the Château (the fact being recorded by a plaque on the wall carefully preserved by the present owners) at which, Sir John claims in *1914*, that he told his commanders of the doubts which had arisen in his mind during the previous twenty-four hours and impressed on them the necessity of being prepared for any kind of move either in advance or retreat. Sir Horace, however, left the meeting firmly impressed with the idea that the Field-Marshal was full of optimism and that the canal position was merely a jumping off place for a further move into Belgium. Unfortunately for the Allied cause Sir John's state of mind, never very steady, was subject to dramatic and sudden falls and rises like the temperature of a patient with an intermittent fever. At one moment he was Sherman, brimming with optimism and ready to "Give 'em hell": an hour later he was McClellan, determined not to do anything beyond saving his Army. On 23rd August, whatever Sir John may have written five years later, Sherman was in the saddle. Unfortunately for his credibility he was to write of this day, "Up to this time there was no decided threat in any strength on Condé. Sir Horace, therefore, need not have feared an imminent turning movement and as regards his front he was nowhere threatened by anything more than cavalry supported by small bodies of infantry . . . every report I was now receiving at HQ pointed to the early necessity of a retirement of the British forces in view of the general strategic situation and I did not therefore deem it desirable to interfere with the Second Corps Commander." The "cavalry supported by small parties of infantry" was composed in fact of two complete German Army Corps and two cavalry divisions, with two more corps and the 3rd German Cavalry Division near at hand. The Cavalry Division, shadowed by a Zeppelin, had drawn off to the left of II Corps around Quiévrain to guard the flank and arrived in position between midnight and 0300, leaving Chetwode's 5th Brigade well away from "the Bull" around Binche. Lanrezac was under attack by the Guard Corps and the Guard Cavalry Division and his centre was giving way to such an extent that at 2300 he swallowed his pride and sent an SOS to the despised English asking them to attack the flank of the German columns advancing from the Sambre. This was asking the impossible but Sir John did agree to remain on the canal for twenty-four hours, and at Sir Horace's insistence the 2nd Division of I Corps was ordered to take over that part of II Corps' front which lay east of Mons. By now it was too late.

The fog of war was not confined to one side only for General Alexander von Kluck, Commanding the German First Army (of which the corps attacking Lanrezac formed a part) was blissfully unaware that the English had even arrived in France until he had word of an English cavalry squadron in a scrimmage near Mons late on the 22nd; he was, however, expecting them to arrive in strength on his flank on the 23rd having detrained at Tournai.

The fact of the matter was that II Corps was in its impossible position on the canal, with the 3rd Division of Hubert Hamilton (the same Hubert Hamilton who had brought Smith-Dorrien Kitchener's order to take his 19th Brigade across the flooded Modder River fourteen years ago) on the right, the 5th Division of Sir Charles Fergusson to its left, and the 19th Brigade (constituted differently from its namesake in South Africa and no longer carrying the Smith-Dorrien racing colours on its flag though it had again been thrown together from line of communications units) on the extreme left. Between 19 Brigade and the sea at Dunkirk were two French Territorial Divisions, the 81st and 82nd later to be joined by the 84th, about whose dispositions little was known—their orders were to form "a barrage against cavalry". On the right, Haig's I Corps prolonged the line around the Mons salient to the Sambre north-east of Maubeuge, including that same Saint Ghislain that Marlborough had stormed on 11th September 1709. Rough entrenchments had been thrown up on the 22nd but were still uncompleted and the position was particularly difficult on the front of the 5th Division where the land was a wilderness of deep ditches, straggling buildings, and high slag heaps which proved useless as points of vantage for each was either dominated by another slag heap or was too hot for observers to climb it. The deployment of II Corps over its absurdly long front was so thin as to be little more than an outpost line manned by a chain of small groups, with most of its field guns well forward.

Soon after dawn it became apparent that the German First Army had wheeled from east to south and was directly opposite the Mons salient. To the good townsfolk of Mons it was just another Sunday; it was true that newspaper reports of battles were eagerly discussed in the cafés but it was as sure as fate that the Germans could never approach their city for the great fortresses of Liège and Namur would interdict any movement into Flanders. The trains were running as usual, the church bells pealed their call for the faithful to come and worship, and life continued its usual placidity as it had done with hardly an interruption since Marlborough had passed that way.

At 0530 Sir John conferred with his corps commanders at Sir Horace's HQ leaving the latter full of confidence in spite of the fact that his line was twenty-one miles long and was dominated by hostile positions at point blank range beyond the canal. Though the C-in-C gave orders—rather superfluously—for the outpost line to be strengthened and the canal bridges prepared for demolition, no word was spoken of the possibility of retreat. This is hard to understand for late the previous night French had been told by Spears, arriving exhausted from Fifth Army HQ at Mettet, that that Army far from intending to attack had been driven back ten miles, and that both his flanks were now in the air. Soon afterwards Sir John informed Gough and Forestier-Walker, the two Chiefs-of-Staff, and Vaughan, the Chief-of-Staff of the Cavalry Division, that the French were not going to advance. At that meeting all questions had been forbidden and before it was dismissed a French staff officer had arrived with Lanrezac's request for an attack on the German flank. The battle of Charleroi had almost ended.

By 0900 the first shells began to fall thickly along the line of the Royal Fusiliers and the Middlesex of the 3rd Division and soon the infantry attack of the IXth Corps came in, spreading round the curve of the salient from Obourg to Nimy, coming first in heavy masses. If the British fire discipline had been good at Isandhlwana and Omdurman it was superb now: Royal Irish, Royal Fusiliers, and Middlesex warmed to their work with rifle and Maxim which broke up this attack with great loss. By 1100 another Corps, the IIIrd, appeared to the west of the Salient and were twice driven back in the same fashion. Hythe deserves a battle honour of its own for this splendid demonstration of the power of the rifle in trained hands. In the area of 13 Brigade the entire regiment of Brandenburg Grenadiers—Germany's best

—attacked the 1st Battalion the Queen's Own Royal West Kent Regiment and a half company of the King's Own Scottish Borderers and were temporarily halted with the aid of the four eighteen-pounders of the 120th Battery RA, whose guns had to be withdrawn at noon.

All through the afternoon the attack continued along the canal with similar results, except at Obourg, where the Salient was penetrated. The German Foot were shot flat by the old regiments of the British line whenever they attempted to fight their way through. The mental processes of the C-in-C are set out in his own dictated telephone message given verbally by Macdonogh to Spears at 1510 hours for transmission to Lanrezac:

> I am prepared to fulfil the role assigned to me when the Fifth Army advances to the attack. In the meantime I hold an advanced defensive position extending from Condé on the left through Mons and Erquellings where I connect with the 2 Reserve Divisions South of the Sambre. I am now much in advance of the line held by the Fifth Army and feel my position to be as far forward as circumstances will allow, particularly in view of the fact that I am not properly prepared to take offensive action until tomorrow morning as I have previously informed you. I do not understand from your wire that the XVIIIth Corps has been engaged and they stand on my inner flank.

Nobody had told Sir John that his Army had been engaged in an epic battle for the last six hours. When he came to write his book Sir John sadly prevaricated in trying to ante-date this message to the previous day, but the facts are dead against him. The message is even more cryptic in that he had already made known his decision of the previous night, to stand fast for twenty-four hours and had also informed Huguet that unless aerial reconnaissance early next day revealed very large forces on his front and unless his left flank was threatened, he would attack the German flank as Lanrezac had asked. The most probable explanation of this extraordinary behaviour is that Wilson in one of his more remarkable errors of judgment wanted to attack and had talked his Chief round. Smith-Dorrien and Haig might have expressed another view but they knew pretty well what forces were ranged against them; Wilson would not be parted from his happy delusion (inspired by GQG) that the Germans consisted of no more than one corps, two at most, and a cavalry division. At this time the right of Haig's Corps and the left of Lanrezac's XVIII Corps were separated by a full day's march with only Sordet's Cavalry Division patrolling in some fashion between them.

While ladies and gentlemen in England were taking their tea and indeed until the hour when most would dine, Wilson was busily drawing up orders for an attack on the 24th by II Corps, 19 Brigade, and the Cavalry Division to the north-east of Mons. This work of fantasy was brought to an end about 2000 by a wire from Joffre saying that there were two and a half corps opposite Smith-Dorrien alone. Three hours later news arrived that Lanrezac was falling back all along the line. The truth was that the BEF was being attacked by the five corps and a cavalry corps of von Kluck's First German Army, with VII Corps of von Bülow's Second Army in case these were not enough. Against Smith-Dorrien were ranged the IX, III, and IV Corps—six Divisions complete and prepared in every detail. Lanrezac was prepared to leave his unloved Ally in the lurch if by doing so he could escape blame for himself and was even at pains to put about the suggestion that it was the BEF which had retired first. After perusal of Joffre's wire Sir John issued at 2040 (although the Army did not yet use the twenty-four hour clock) the following order to II Corps. "I will stand the attack on the ground now occupied by the troops. You will therefore strengthen your position by every possible means during the night".

Back on the canal, the 3rd Division after a tremendous battle had retired on Frameries. Seeing the probability of a gap opening between his divisions, having no reserves, and realizing the futility of trying to communicate with his far-distant chief, Smith-Dorrien personally jumped into a motor at about 1900 (just at the time Wilson was working out his orders for the attack) and drove to Haig's HQ to borrow Haking's 5th Brigade, only three miles away, to plug the hole. Haig backed him up splendidly and the crisis passed thanks largely to Shaw's 9th Brigade which had already driven the Germans back before 5th Brigade arrived.

At 1915, immediately before his dash to Haig, Sir Horace sent to GHQ this message: "Third Division report at 6.47 p.m. the Germans are in front of his main position and are not attacking at present, they are, however, working round 3rd Division on my left flank. If it would appear there is a danger of my centre being pierced I can see no course but to order a general retirement on Bavai position. Have I your permission to adopt this course if it appears necessary?" Shaw, Haking, and their tired troops had removed the condition upon which the request turned, but in his book French presented merely the end of the message in order to create the impression that his pusillanimous corps commander was ready to fly without cause. Both Murray and Forestier-Walker, Smith-Dorrien's Chief-of-Staff, scout the idea that there was ever any such thought in his mind, and with the knowledge of French we have already gained it is certain that the Field Marshal was activated by sheer malice.

By nightfall the withdrawal to Hamilton's position across the gorge of the salient was complete. The Corps's front which had nowhere been pierced was shortened to about twelve miles and the soldiers holding it, despite about 1,500 casualties were in high spirits and knew themselves better men than their enemies. 1st Corps had not been seriously engaged and as we have seen there were now four brigades of cavalry—troops as good with the rifle in dismounted action as any infantry but numerically smaller, unit for unit, for some men had to mind the horses. It would be an exaggeration to say that "all they thought of was to dismount and start shooting"; the sword and lance were now of far less use than the Short Magazine Lee-Enfield rifle but the British Cavalry, thanks to the adoption of Smith-Dorrien's Aldershot doctrines, were incomparably more serviceable than either their enemy's or their Ally's.

The BEF had, against all the rules in all the books and contrary to everything taught in the Staff Colleges of continental Europe, carried out one of the most perfect disengaging actions yet recorded. In a wretched, unprepared position, outnumbered threefold and outgunned by an even greater ratio, they had hammered their enemy to a standstill and gained a precious twenty-four hours while he licked his wounds. The weight of the Ger-

15 In attendance on President Poincaré and the Prince of Wales, Portsmouth June 1913.

16 Off parade—with Lady Smith-Dorrien and Gren, 1912.

man attack, be it remembered, had fallen on the weaker and less perfectly organized of the two corps and it cannot be wondered that, even though they had been forced to yield an untenable position and move back for a few miles the men of II Corps were still confident. In all this they owed nothing to their own GHQ, thirty-five miles away from the battlefield. Sir John's only contribution to the matter was to write—of the afternoon of the 23rd—"The 3rd Division was now effecting a retirement South of the Canal to a line running West through Nouvelles [the name itself is an irony] and this movement had the inevitable result of bringing back the 5th Division and handing over the bridges of the Canal to the German Cavalry." This was, of course, nonsense and in the event it was only a matter of a few hours before Sir John himself was issuing orders for a retreat to Bavai. Sherman was dismounting to give place to McClellan, but it would have been far better for his Army if he had trusted the information given by his corps commander and issued his orders at 1930 instead of nearly midnight.

The order to retire reached Smith-Dorrien at 0300; with any reasonable signal arrangements it should not have been necessary for the order to be carried by hand over thirty-five miles of roads now choked with refugees in addition to the Army's own transport—100,000 men and their animals eat a lot of food in one day. Remember too that all the first and second line transport, with its multitude of horses and mules, was piled up near at hand waiting for the order to advance (which never came). This made all rearward movement difficult as a result of the inevitable traffic jams on indifferent roads. Even allowing for Sir John's hours of celebration (coinciding, by the way, with those occupied by Wilson in drawing his attack orders) wireless or even line telephony could have saved many precious hours.

At dawn on the 24th the Germans returned to the attack. Haig and Smith-Dorrien, having received nothing in the shape of a proper operation order for a withdrawal, made their own arrangements with each other. All day long the two Divisions fell slowly back, fighting every foot of the way, leapfrogging unit through unit and formation through formation, the one bearing the attack while the other marched rearwards to a new position from which the process could be repeated. De Lisle's 2nd Cavalry Brigade (whose Durham Light Infantry had long ago been the only foot regiment to win the Polo Cup in India) charged the German masses in fine style to take the weight off the left flank of the 5th Division but proved to be another gallant failure. This was no running fight and the units concerned remained homogeneous throughout the day. But midnight saw them back on the line Maubeuge-Bavai-Wargnies, tired, hungry but still indomitable. The only black spots were again communications failures; two regiments of the 5th Division (the Duke of Wellington's and the Cheshires) never received the order to retire and clung to their positions until they were over-run, the former losing 400 men. The Cheshires fared even worse, being completely surrounded and only two officers and 200 men remained to tell what happened to them. (Entirely by accident, however, their sacrifice did much to save the corps for the Dukes held no less than six German battalions at bay for a long time and after the surrounding of the Cheshires the whole German force had been hammered to a standstill and pursued no more after about 1500.) The day's fighting had cost Sir Horace's corps about 2,000 casualties, the bulk of them this time coming from the 5th Division. Something of the strain on commanders and staff can be judged from the fact that Hamilton's GSOI, Colonel Boileau, broke down completely and shot himself.

On the following day, 25th August, the retreat continued all along the line, the French Fifth Army falling steadily back through the thickly-wooded hills of the Ardennes, its artillery virtually intact but its infantry much thinned out by casualties. Lanrezac, being one of those men who must find a scapegoat when he himself was at fault, issued a formal instruction that his retreat had been caused solely by the delay of the IVth Army and the BEF in coming up—a thoroughly unjust charge, as he well knew, but apparently he considered the fabrication to be good for the morale of his own men. At the beginning of the day the two reserve divisions of Valabrègue, immediately to the right of Haig's corps, had fallen back to the south of Maubeuge though its so-called fortress (it had ceased to be one in fact a century before) was still untaken. General D'Amade had received two more reserve divisions sent from Paris to Arras and he now had some 80,000 men, plus the 25,000 strong garrison of Lille, to hold the seventy miles from a point near Douai to the sea but their exact dispositions were unknown and they were not first-line troops. This information Sir John had gained after a visit the previous day to General Sordet commanding a French Cavalry Corps at Avesnes. German cavalry was known to be as far west as Tournai and not too much should be expected of d'Amade's elderly Territorials. Cambrai, was said to be firmly held.

Sir John admits that he considered the possibility of immuring the BEF in Maubeuge, like Bazaine in Metz, but remembered Hamley's advice against it—likening such a commander to a man who when his ship is sinking lays hold of the anchor. It is a measure of French's military genius that he even contemplated so preposterous an idea. He took the only possible decision, the French XVIIIth Corps being already ten miles behind him, to continue the retreat for fifteen more miles to a position around Le Cateau. At the same time he telegraphed to Kitchener that "I think that immediate attention should be given to the defence of Havre".

It was not an easy matter to move the two corps tidily for at Bavai the Roman road running south-west to north-east crosses another ancient highway, the Chaussée Brunehaut which leads from south-east to north-west; in the southern angle lies the great Forêt de Mormal, nine miles long and three or four miles wide. There is no north-south road through the forest though several run east-west and the River Sambre winds along its eastern side. Though Joffre had intended that the BEF should keep to the west of it, the fact remained that the forest was to form a dividing block between the two corps as they continued to move south—I Corps by way of Maroilles and Landrecies and II Corps direct on Solesmes and Le Cateau. The order was issued at 2015 on the 24th. Sir Horace had been at GHQ, still at Bavai, at 1800 and described his situation to the Field Marshal from whom, not unnaturally, he sought orders for his future movements. He was told baldly that he could do as he liked and that Haig would be starting at 0500.

> I remonstrated saying that unless we moved early it would be a case of that day over again, when orders had been issued too late to avoid the enemy coming to close grips. He asked me what I proposed. I replied that I wished to start off my impedimenta (which would have rested many hours) soon after mid-night followed by troops at such times as would ensure my rearguard being clear of the Jenlain-Bavai road by 5 a.m. Sir John French concurred, remarking that Sir D. Haig could still do as he intended. Sir A. Murray the Chief of Staff was working at a table in the room and I went across and told him that it was essential that we should move as an Army, and implored him to get the Chief to issue an Army Order saying that the whole force would move as I suggested.

The order described above then appeared: Sir John in his book (p. 78) claims that he issued the orders at about 1500 but again this is palpably false. Sir Horace went to see him three hours later, after all, because he was entirely without instructions and we have seen that only by bullying Murray (though he speaks of "imploring" this is something that would not have come naturally to him) that any written orders appeared at all. (Its text is in the Official History at Appendix XIII.) Sir John would vastly have preferred not to be troubled to issue orders at all but to leave it to his subordinate commanders to work things out for themselves. Not since Burnside at Petersburg had a commander so abdicated his functions; Hamilton would never have done this but Sir John was sixty-two now and feeling his years. Besides, he had had a late night last night thanks to Spears and his depressing news. In fact I Corps was late in starting and reached no further than Landrecies where there was a spirited night action. This was the one day when Haig fell below his normal high standard, the result perhaps of a violent belly-ache treated by his DMS Colonel Ryan, with "something they give elephants." In any event, the night attack (beaten off mainly by the Coldstream Guards) caught him in an unguarded position and for the only time in his life he was guilty of the use of a dramatic phrase, "If we're caught, by God we'll sell our lives dearly." Such language can only have been produced by great stress; his back was not yet to the wall. There was, however, a gap of no less than eight miles between the two corps that night. Smith-Dorrien, understandably, permits himself the wry comment, "It would be interesting if he had told us in his book why the gap occurred and I cannot help feeling that had my Corps been the one to fail to carry out his orders the matter would not have been passed over in silence. Had there been no gap, in other words, had I Corps been in line with II Corps on the Le Cateau position on the night of the 25th and had the C-in-C remained near enough to the front to handle the two Corps a much more favourable state of affairs should have resulted." Sir Horace had never lent his Chief £2,000. Yet the gruelling march had achieved its purpose, preventing for the moment the full weight of enemy envelopment. Von Bülow commented, "The I German Army had, on the 24th, with its centre and left wing attacked with great success the British to the West of Maubeuge. On the 25th it should have continued its attack with a view to the envelopment of their left flank. But the enemy escaped by a retreat so well executed that, in spite of the brilliant marches made by the corps of the I Army it was not possible to obtain a definite success against the British." More British troops were on the way. General D'Oyly Snow's 4th Division, consisting of eleven battalions with one brigade of field artillery had crossed the Channel, arrived unmolested at Le Cateau station on the 24th, and were ordered to move forward at once to Solesmes to assist the retirement of II Corps, withdrawing to its left when the time came.

Sir Horace began his rearward movement early, as he had wished, only to find Sordet's Cavalry Corps blocking all the roads as it moved from east to west; this wasted a full hour and caused explosions of impotent rage from harrassed staff officers. The move back began at 0100 on the 26th, the same moment at which the 4th Division was moving forward to Solesmes.

The 5th Division, after a brush with the Germans about Breaugies and another near Bavai, marched along the Roman road at the forest edge without serious molestation; farther west, the 3rd Division (the two had neatly changed places the previous day to avoid the town of Maubeuge) became involved in a running fight during which the German advanced troops were practically in contact with their rearguard by nightfall. The day was stifling and men and horses were in the last stages of exhaustion. Many of the reservists, still only three weeks or less from civilian life, had been issued with boots too small for them and the march was described by a participant as "stumbling more like robots than living soldiers, unconscious of everything about them, but still moving under the magic influence of discipline and regimental pride. Marching, they were hardly awake: halted, whether sitting or standing, they were instantly asleep." Many of these troops had been for two days and nights without sleep or food, fighting and marching for most of that time but they somehow always managed to find enough reserve of will-power to turn about and drive off one more attack. At about 1700 the light began to thicken and rain fell in torrents. Soaked, exhausted, famished, but still intact, the bulk of the 3rd Division marched into their billets around Le Cateau, the 5th having arrived a couple of hours earlier. Their rearguard—the 7th Brigade—the newly-arrived 4th Division, and about half the Cavalry Division were still engaged or in contact with the enemy around Solesmes, but the Germans were now keeping a respectful distance from the terrible British musketry and shrapnel. Night closed in as exhausted men, khaki and field-grey alike, composed themselves for such sleep as they could get, but iron-hard, constricting boots had to remain on swollen, blistered feet for once off they would never be got on again. That night Smith-Dorrien's men lay almost on the site of the lines of Ne Plus Ultra where their forefathers had fought 203 years ago almost to the day when John Churchill, First Duke of Marlborough, had forced this supposedly impregnable place. When the sun rose next morning it would be the anniversary of Crécy. The scene was set for a battle worthy to be spoken of in the same breath as these victories of the island's past Armies.

CHAPTER SEVENTEEN

On the evening of the 25th at 1800, Sir Horace received a private note from Wilson telling him that the retreat was to be continued on the following day and three hours later definite orders to this effect reached him at his new HQ at Bertry, a village about five miles south-west of Le Cateau, in the middle of II Corps' line. In obedience, but with strong misgivings, Smith-Dorrien caused appropriate orders to be issued at 2215—orders in the nature of a warning only and not to be acted upon except at his specific behest. No communication with GHQ was now possible as it had decamped to St Quentin, a further twenty-six miles away along a road filled with refugees and masses of military transport. Sir John French cannot have been unaware that the situation on his left was deteriorating but he played no part in the coming battle at all, except by keeping well out of the way and going into retreat of another kind. Perhaps this was the most valuable contribution he could have made, for the state of affairs by nightfall was one for which Hamley provides no recipe.

Sir Horace was now completely on his own. He could, of course, comply to the letter with his orders, in which case blame for the disaster which must follow would rest squarely with the C-in-C (and many a General would have done precisely this). Happily for the Army and his country, Sir Horace was a man of moral courage as well as personal valour; such a course never entered his head. It has been said that Admiral Jellicoe was the one man who could have lost the war in an afternoon; there was one moment of time in August 1914 when another man by taking a wrong decision could have lost the war as quickly. The English should always be thankful that the decision lay in the hands and able brain of General Sir Horace Smith-Dorrien.

All through the 25th his divisions had marched and dug and fought (and remember again that half these men were reservists who should never have been committed to battle at all without at least a few weeks' re-training. The Fifth Division in particular had suffered from the scorching heat of the days for the great beeches, oaks, and hornbeams of the Forêt de Mormal, a forest which had existed since Roman times, had prevented any relieving breezes from reaching the marching column. Moreover, this was Wednesday and these men had been fighting and marching since the previous Saturday. This extract from the War Diary of the 1/DCLI is typical of the infantry units' experiences.

"Outpost duty on and defence of Mons Canal from 4 p.m. 22nd to 11 p.m. 23rd August. No rest on night 23/24; rations failed on 23rd Aug. Outpost duty again on night 24/25 Aug: neither officers nor men had eaten anything since 11 a.m. on that day. At 5 a.m. 25 August retirement continued, the Battalion furnishing the rear party until 2 p.m. Le Cateau was reached at 6.30 p.m. The men were then served out with rations. The battalion was formed up ready to march again at 6.25 a.m. on 26th Aug."

The lack of rest and of food,[1] the constant digging, the marching on blistered, aching feet clamped in clumsy ammunition boots, the webbing cutting into the shoulders (each man carried fifty-nine pounds of kit excluding his blanket), the smell of sweat soaked khaki serge, and above all the utter bewilderment are things that can only be understood by those who have undergone the like experience. Not since Sir John Moore's retreat to Corunna in 1808 had British troops been called on to endure such a combination of torments and, like Moore's men, this Army did not fail to rise to the situation.

The leading troops reached their bivouacs (no billets to-night)

[1] Changes of plan had for the moment disrupted the supply organization.

at about 1700 but it was nearer to midnight when the last columns of fours staggered in. To complete their misery a thunderstorm burst on them at about 1900 flooding the roads and making them dangerous for the transport. North of Le Cateau there is a steep gradient running into the town which the deluge had turned into a water-chute down which skidded, three abreast, guns, limbers, baggage wagons, and ambulances, the whole surrounded by myriads of refugees using every kind of man and animal-drawn vehicle, and screaming with panic in the rain and thunder.

At Solesmes, six miles to the north, the 4th Division were already drawing their first blood in a rearguard action. The cavalry, too, had managed to keep von Kluck at a respectful distance during the day but with dusk came a serious attack. The best short account of it is a letter from Allenby to Smith-Dorrien some weeks later:

> On the 25th August I had the task of covering the rear of the Army in its Western flank during the retirement on Le Cateau. Towards nightfall a fierce attack was made on the Cavalry Division under my command and a gap was opened between the rear and flank guards. The rear of the IInd Army Corps was then passing through the town of Solesmes, a defile, and the situation became precarious. I had at the time only one regiment of cavalry to fill the gap. Riding to the rear of the column I met Brigadier-General McCracken and gave him the situation. Brigadier-General McCracken at once rose to the occasion. He collected what troops were near to hand and led them to a position whence they could cover the column entering the defile. At the same time he stopped and brought into action a Brigade of RFA and a Howitzer battery. This ready initiative checked the enemy but they brought several batteries into action under whose cover their infantry resumed the attack. Until after dark Brigadier-General McCracken maintained his stand under severe gun and rifle fire and did not retire until the rear of the column was in safety. He then withdrew skilfully and with comparatively few casualties. I consider that his ready and daring handling of the rearguard averted a mishap which might have been a disaster. I am glad to be able to bring his action to your notice as I think it deserves recognition.

Not even Sir John French who from the calm of St Quentin came to the conclusion (later to appear in his book) that Allenby with a cavalry brigade had saved McCracken could prevent the latter's immediate promotion. But then Sir John always got on with Allenby—probably mercifully—for if he had treated Allenby as he did Smith-Dorrien it might have ended, as did a similar quarrel between the American Generals Nelson and Davis, in shooting! The names of McCracken's Regiments ought not to be omitted; they were 3rd Battalion the Worcestershire Regiment; 2nd Battalion, the South Lancashire Regiment (PWV's); and the 1st Battalion, the Wiltshire Regiment.

Sir John, before taking his departure, asserted that "I had late in the evening of the 25th visited several units of II Corps in their bivouacs and though tired indeed they did not strike me as worn-out troops—by the break of day on the 26th the 5th Division on the right had secured several hours rest . . . the 7th Brigade had only just arrived in cantonments at 10 or 11 p.m. after a heavy day's march and some severe fighting but they could in an emergency have marched at dawn. The 4th Division on the left of II Corps was comparatively fresh." Sir Horace could find no trace that the C-in-C had visited any of his units; "I have endeavoured without success to ascertain what units the Field-Marshal actually visited: Official Reports show that beyond a few Supply Units which had started in the small hours there were not until late in the evening, any troops in the bivouacs and billets they occupied that night. I myself arrived in the town of Le Cateau at 3.30 p.m. and at once sought for the C-in-C. He was not to be found either at GHQ office, or at the Château he had been living in and no one knew when he had left or where he had gone to, not even the Chief of the Staff, Sir Archibald Murray, who was still there: the GHQ was in the process of being moved to St Quentin and it was generally believed that Sir John had gone in the direction of that place." Comment on this highly idiosyncratic method of exercising high command seems unlikely to be helpful.

These were the hours at which II Corps reached their bivouacs that night, sunset being at 1900 hours.

- Fifth Division: Head reached Le Cateau 1500, tail after dark as the bivouacs were from three-quarters of a mile to two miles beyond the town it would be about right to add one and a half to two hours before units were settled for the night. One and a half battalions were sent back to occupy high ground to the east of the town in the vain hope of making contact with the absent I Corps. Like everyone else they had to entrench themselves and got little, if any, rest. 28th Brigade RFA, which had been on rearguard, reached Reumont at 2330. The divisional ammunition column did not arrive until the morning of the 26th.
- Third Division: The main columns reached their bivouac area about 1830 except, as we know, 7th Brigade and also 2nd Battalion The Royal Irish Rifles, part of the South Lancashires and 41 Battery RFA who reached Maurois at 0400 and rejoined their division about 0800. They had been cut off by floods of refugees and French Territorials. Total casualties for the three days, excluding stragglers, 2054.
- Fourth Division: Had been sent out under GHQ orders to the neighbourhood of Briastre to cover the retirement of the Cavalry Division, 3rd Division, and 19th Brigade with orders to remain out until all were through. In fact owing to the amount of Cavalry Division transport passing through Viesly, the movement of the rearguard was delayed until after midnight—three Brigades only got to their positions between 0330 and 0530 hours.

General Snow with the 10th Brigade (amongst whom was Second Lieutenant B. L. Montgomery of the Royal Warwicks) reached Caudry about midnight finding the 11th Brigade there waiting for orders. The 12th Brigade was somewhere (he knew not where) on the Le Cateau-Cambrai road. Owing to the darkness they halted until dawn, Snow himself riding to Haucourt, having left orders with his brigadiers to retire to the high ground to the north as soon as there was enough light to see. He left at about 0230 and the move started about an hour and a half later although the darkness was succeeded by heavy mist. When the rear of 10th Brigade had cleared Viesly, Snow's GSO2 found the head of his division and its commander in the middle of a muddy field having taken a wrong turning. A French guide was found who led them off with the transport in front. Whether by acident or design the guide took them in the wrong direction—further north to Cattenières. As the darkness lifted it was found that only the transport had followed and the brigade had made its own way through Ligny to Haucourt where it arrived at about 0400, the brigadier (Haldane) having narrowly escaped capture. This brigade remained in divisional reserve, Hunter-Weston's 11th taking ground north of Ligny and beyond the Warnelle stream, with Wilson's 12th prolonging the line leftwards to the Moulin d'Esnes. Esnes itself was barricaded by Sordet's cavalry. As the brigades reached their destinations they came under heavy shellfire from the direction of the Cambrai road and were forced to extend, luckily more or less on the position where they were required. "Comparatively fresh" seems hardly an apt description even though we are not told of the standard of comparison. Sir Horace's order for a retirement reached Divisional HQ (although strictly speaking the Division was not under his command) but for lack of time it was not repeated to brigades.

The Artillery position of the corps was this:

Third Division	XXIII Brigade RFA Three Batteries (107, 108, and 109) eighteen-pounders.
	XL Brigade RFA Three Batteries (6, 23, and 49) eighteen-pounders.
	XLII Brigade RFA Three Batteries (29, 41, and 45) eighteen-pounders.
	XXX (Hows.) RFA Three Batteries (128, 129, and 130) 4·5 Howitzers.
	48th Heavy Battery RGA, four sixty-pounders, Divisional Ammunition Column.
Total:	fifty-four eighteen-pounders, eighteen 4·5 Howitzers, four sixty-pounders. Seventy-six pieces.
Fifth Division	XV Brigade RFA Three Batteries (11, 52, and 80) eighteen-pounders.
	XXVII Brigade RFA Three Batteries (119, 120, and 121) eighteen-pounders.
	XXVIII Brigade RFA Three Batteries (122, 123, and 124) eighteen-pounders.

	VIII (Hows.) Brigade RFA Three Batteries (37, 61, and 65) 4·5 Howitzers. 108th Heavy Battery RGA, four sixty-pounders, Divisional Ammunition Column.
Total:	fifty-two eighteen-pounders, (two had been lost on 23 August), eighteen 4·5 Howitzers, four sixty-pounders. Seventy-four pieces.
Fourth Division	XIV Brigade RFA Three Batteries (39, 68, and 88) eighteen-pounders. XXIX Brigade RFA Three Batteries (125, 126, and 127) eighteen-pounders. XXXIII Brigade RFA Three Batteries (27, 134, and 135) eighteen-pounders. XXXVII Hows, RFA Three Batteries (31, 35, and 55) 4·5 Howitzers. (The sixty-pounders and Divisional Ammunition Column had not yet arrived.)
Total:	fifty-four eighteen-pounders, eighteen 4·5 Howitzers. Seventy-two pieces.
Cavalry Division	III RHA (D and E Batteries) thirteen-pounders. VII RHA (I and L Batteries) thirteen-pounders.
Total	twenty-four thirteen-pounders.

The RHA contained neither reservists nor remounts having been made up to strength by other RHA batteries. Each brigade was accompanied by its ammunition column.

At two o'clock in the dark of the summer night there arrived at Bertry the massive figure of the GOC Cavalry Division and his GSO1, Colonel John Vaughan, with disquieting news. They of necessity had the most up-to-date intelligence both of the movements of the enemy and of the condition of the troops of the British Divisions and so important were their tidings that an immediate conference was convened of the available senior officers, Hamilton of the 3rd Division, with Maurice, his GSO2, Forestier-Walker, and the cavalrymen. There was no spokesman for either 4th or 5th Divisions nor anyone from the CRA but it simply could not be helped. Allenby had seen enough of the 5th Division with his own eyes to be able to speak about its condition.

Allenby's addition to Smith-Dorrien's knowledge was that at 2300, just after he had received GHQ's order to continue the retreat, Colonel Ansell of the 5th Dragoon Guards had reported to him that although the 4th Division had withdrawn successfully from the high ground north of Viesly overlooking Solesmes, the enemy were now in possession of it. These enemy troops, the leading element of IV Corps, could with the coming of daylight dominate the positions from which both 3rd and 4th Divisions would be moving and with his weakness in cavalry (only the 4th Cavalry Brigade was available and that close to exhaustion) Allenby had no means of holding them off. The Bull therefore expressed the view that unless the retreat could begin before the end of the night the enemy would be upon them. It was not necessary to point the obvious, that with the IIIrd Corps, the IVth Corps, and von der Marwitz' Cavalry Corps attacking them—odds of about three and a half to one—Sir Horace's Divisions must be routed before breakfast-time. He asked Hamilton if his division could move at once and received the reply that units were still coming in and he could not form up and move before 0900. All present knew the 5th Division to be in no better condition and Allenby could not but add that his Cavalry Brigades were so scattered and exhausted that little assistance could be expected from any of them. The front of II Corps was already pinched in by the Forêt de Mormal to the east and the pressure of von der Marwitz to the west. The only crumb of comfort was that Sordet's Cavalry Corps was known to be moving across the rear westwards, but they were as burnt-out as everyone else. D'Amade's Territorials were understood to be somewhere around Cambrai, some six miles away, but little was known of their dispositions and there was no direct contact with them anywhere.

This was the moment to which the whole of Smith-Dorrien's previous life had been directed and the decision now to be taken must be his alone. Though not an over-imaginative man, he saw the situation plainly. If II Corps were smashed nothing could save Haig; with the BEF destroyed, Lanrezac would be routed, both Paris and the Channel Ports would fall and it would be 1870 again, Worth, Sedan, and Metz together. If Smith-

Dorrien obeyed orders the best he could hope for would be to save some of his cavalry and infantry, though even this was doubtful for on the congested roads and in the last stages of exhaustion they could put up no serious resistance to German cavalry and lorried infantry. Certainly all his guns and transport would be lost and his name would go down in history as the man who had commanded the British Army which suffered the most humiliating defeat since Saratoga and Yorktown. The alternative was to disobey orders, a thing unnatural and utterly repugnant to an officer with forty years of discipline behind him. True, he had done it before—remember Colvile and the cavalry wounded—but this time he had a chief who loathed him and to whom it would be a joyous thing to see Smith-Dorrien broken by court-martial.

He had only one good card in his hand if he decided to disobey. Field Service Regulations could be prayed in aid if he succeeded but only then. So there remained the one thing, that British field commanders have drawn on generation after generation—the ability and determination of the subaltern, the sergeant, and the private soldier to get their generals out of a scrape. The British soldier is popularly supposed to yield pride of place to the French in the attack and in August 1914 this may have been true (though it would not remain so for long) but put him in some sort of trench with his SMLE and bountiful ammunition, plus a packet of Woodbines if possible, put nearby his gunner brother with his eighteen-pounders and field howitzers similarly supplied, and there is no soldier in the world—not even the Japanese—whom it is more difficult to budge. On this Sir Horace staked everything; he had always been a betting man and now he had another Shannon, another thoroughbred, who was to carry for a few hours the entire Allied cause. Sir Horace's mind was made up; this was not a council of war putting matters to a vote, it was a high Commander giving orders. They were prompt and definite. II Corps and attached troops (Allenby and his cavalry by their commander's own consent came under Sir Horace's orders and 4th Division and 19 Brigade were included as a matter of course) would accept battle where they stood. He buttoned his wife's picture into his tunic pocket, sent a long message by motor car to GHQ (where it arrived at 0500), and went personally to Fergusson at Troisvilles immediately after. There he learnt that the last of that General's rearguard, the Royal Irish Rifles were still coming in, dead on their feet.

At 0645 Sir John was on the telephone by the railway wire between St Quentin and Bertry, demanding speech with the corps commander. Sir Horace motored to the station and put through his call about a quarter of an hour later but the C-in-C had not waited for him and he could only speak to Henry Wilson. Wilson explained that the C-in-C did not wish a battle. Sir Horace was to get on with his retreat at once; Sedan was mentioned. Patiently explaining to this staff officer that the battle had already begun (the guns were clearly audible) and could not be switched off at will Smith-Dorrien went on to explain that he intended to deal von Kluck a smashing blow after which he would slip away in the dark. Wilson wished him luck and added that his was the first cheerful voice he had heard for three days. The scene at GHQ must have been a little depressing, Wilson himself being at the bottom of it for his Francophilia had been rudely shaken by the events of the last week. Sir John did not like Lanrezac and the whole BEF was alone, isolated, and imminently about to be destroyed. French had only one task now, to keep his Army in being, to refit and fight another day somewhere else. Now this idiot infantry general was spoiling it all by not running away as he had been bidden. It would be another Sedan all right, Sir John knew all about that for he had been a midshipman at the time, and he would be blamed for it. But he would see that this charge-stopping, piquet-removing man who thought of nothing but machine guns and getting cavalry—his cavalry—out of their saddles and into holes in the ground should suffer for it. Disobey orders, would he? Sir John would see about that; for a start he moved his headquarters back another thirty-five miles to Noyon and told no one

The battle of Le Cateau had started on the left of the 4th Division the previous night when a troop of horse and half a dozen lorry loads of Jager had come within thirty yards of the Inniskillings near Esnes under cover of darkness. They were driven off by rifle fire and by 0330—during the normal pre-dawn

17 On the Eve of War—a picture postcard of 1914.

18 *The Shadow: 'Mons'—a still from a film made in 1924 in which Sir Horace played the part of himself.*

19 *The Substance: 'Mons'—The Cameronians at La-Ferté-sous-Jouarre, September 1914.*

Imperial War

"Stand-to"—the rest of 12 Brigade arrived (Essex, Lancashire Fusiliers, and King's Own) and dug in on the plateau north-west of the hamlet. The western flank for which the Germans had been probing now existed. An officer of the King's Own recalls that at dawn they formed up in close column facing the enemy, piled arms, and lay down their equipment, spending ten minutes checking its alignment. The brigadier (Wilson) rode up to the CO and a few minutes later they were told to remain where they were as breakfast would shortly be up. None had eaten since the previous day. It was cheerfully bandied about that French cavalry were out in front and the enemy could not possibly worry them for at least three hours. Some cavalry indeed trotted up to about 500 yards from them, had a good look round and trotted away again. A subaltern who spoke up and said that he was quite sure the uniforms were not French was crushingly reminded that he was very young. The cavalry returned quite peaceably, this time with vehicles, the sound of iron-shod wheels on pavé could be plainly heard and the cry went up "Here come the cookers." As men bustled about getting out their mess tins the machine guns of the supposed French opened up with long bursts. The corn had just been taken from the field and the stream of bullets four feet from the ground cut the stooks off at the top. Though it lasted only a couple of minutes 400 casualties were caused mostly among one company which was moving off in fours. The colonel fell at the first burst, dead, and the senior major swiftly had arms unpiled and attacked. The cavalry drew off but some of the worse wounded, left in Haucourt church, fell later into enemy hands. There were no Field Ambulances with the 4th Division. Von Kluck himself, holding a different view of the function of commanders, arrived at Solesmes during the night to direct the battle and to out-flank Smith-Dorrien if he could. The artillery of the 4th Division was concentrated under its CRA more than in the other two divisions largely because of the manner of the division's arrival, but the absence of the big sixty-pounders, the only British weapon at this time capable of a counter-battery role, was very much felt. The German guns by dawn were ranged in an arc all along the corps front and the 5·9 howitzers, a weapon which the British of 1914 regarded with the distaste which those of the next generation were to feel for the eighty-eight, had things very much their own way.

On the right, in and around Le Cateau itself, lay the 19th Brigade with the addition of the 59th Field Company RE fighting as infantry who came under attack soon after it was light by the left column of IV Corps. These were roughly handled and passed on the news to von Kluck that the British did not seem to be retiring. In fact the brigade, which had spent the night in the goods yard and main square of Le Cateau, had received no orders and continued in column of route to Reumont where they were turned about and constituted the corps reserve. The right of IV Corps were similarly treated by the left hand brigade (the 7th) of the 3rd Division at Caudry, where the German 4th Cavalry Division appeared. Of the other formations involved, the 9th Brigade at Inchy received the order to stand fast from Allenby personally at about 0330. The other two brigades of Hamilton's Division around Caudry and Audencourt apparently received no orders but conformed with their neighbours, 15th Brigade received it at 0500, and 13th and 14th Brigades were reached an hour or so later, though no orders ever filtered through to the one and a half battalions (DCLI and two companies East Surreys) to the east of Le Cateau itself. They were already formed up in column of route in a street on the east side of the town at about 0600 when they came under attack by the German 72nd Regiment. They were turned about and doubled smartly to the high ground north-east of the railway sation where they dug themselves in and beat off all attacks until about 1600 when after their relief by the 1st Cavalry Brigade they withdrew in good order down the Roman road to Maurois. Von Kluck must have been aware of the big gap between Smith-Dorrien's right and Haig's left and also that Cambrai was held by the French so he should have had a pretty good idea of where II Corps front began and ended. His numerical superiority in guns was considerable and he had learnt that the BEF, even in retreat, had a sting in its tail so like a sensible man he began the frontal attack with his artillery, followed by the envelopment of both flanks. His intention was to pin Smith-Dorrien to the ground with his IVth and IInd Cavalry Corps, envelop his right with the IIIrd, and his left with his IInd and IVth Reserve Corps. The bombardment opened at about 0600 and spread and thickened as each corps came up and added its contribution. Luckily for the British the soil here is fairly light—loam varying from a few inches to several feet in depth over the underlying chalk, and it was not too difficult to dig reasonable cover. The villages along the front, Troisvilles, Audencourt, Caudry, Ligny, and Esnes all stand on a ridge forming the main position, in gently undulating cornland, ridge succeeding ridge at intervals sufficient to give good fields of fire, though each affording the attackers the advantage of much dead ground. From any spot on the battlefield one can see not less than half a dozen church spires, invaluable observation posts and each a splendid aiming point for the 5·9s. The British Army had not yet fully learned that the fortified village of Marlborough's and Wellington's times was now an unfortified shell trap.

The Royal Regiment performed prodigies on that day, attack after attack being broken up by rapid and accurate shrapnel, though they took heavy casualties from the searching 5·9s, their fire sometimes directed by aircraft and from the German field artillery and machine guns. On the right, in the 5th Division area, the situation was most dangerous for the difficulty of finding good gun positions there was insuperable and the gunners came under fire from both north and east simultaneously. Many of the guns were in the open and drew on themselves salvo after salvo of heavy metal, but to their eternal honour no serviceable gun ever lacked a team, the casualties being replaced over and over again by a dwindling band of gunners, drivers, and oddments. They were also hampered by the fact that their eighteen-pounders all had the old spring recuperator (later to be replaced by compressed air) which had a habit of giving out after much firing and necessitating the pushing back of the barrel by hand after each discharge.

The main business of artillery is, of course, to beat up the infantry of the other side and throughout the morning as the sun rose and dispelled the mist this was not neglected. The main weight of the attack of the German infantry of IV Corps fell upon the two left hand Brigades of the 5th Division and the right hands ones, (8th and 9th) of the 3rd between Caudry and Le Cateau itself. Marwitz, who had missed the educational experience of being on the wrong end of the rifles of the BEF at Mons, was keeping up his pressure further to the west. The 7th Brigade in Caudry will be remembered as yesterday's rearguard which had fought at Solesmes and arrived where they now fought very late last night and "on their chinstraps". Later on, Caudry became a small salient as the pressure of the IVth Reserve Corps aided by nine machine guns from the Cambrai road pushed the 4th Division line back along the Warnelle stream, and it seemed a target for every German battery, salvo upon salvo bursting in black smoke and flame amongst McCracken's men already half dead with fatigue of previous days. Attack after infantry attack came in but each time shaking fingers crammed chargers-full of cartridges into magazines, left hands adjusted sights and right fore-fingers and thumbs worked bolt and trigger. Attack after infantry attack drew off leaving their dead and wounded behind them. Eyes might be bleared with lack of sleep but they could still align the tip of the foresight on one field grey figure after another. At about 1345, as the result of an order issued under a misapprehension, the brigade and all its guns withdrew from the village but one of Hamilton's ADC's, Crichton, collected as many as he could and led them back to hold the position until the order to withdraw arrived at about 1530. The 8th Brigade lost all its brigade transport to shell and machine gun fire.

At about 1300 Sir Horace decided that von Kluck had been hammered enough to enable the retreat to continue and so the order went out. This was as hard a decision to make as the previous one for if Smith-Dorrien miscalculated, he was done. He may well have remembered Hector MacDonald at Omdurman, parrying beautifully blows from two directions, and he himself had learned a lot about withdrawals from the tribesmen of the Tirah Valley and from the example of Christiaan de Wet. He needed no Hamley to advise him, for he was always swift to sense the moment to move or to stand. He timed it to perfection though communications were so bad that it took one and a half hours to get the order to the first battalion, and as luck would have it the IIIrd German Corps arrived on the battlefield at the same moment to hurl itself at the battered 5th Division and 19th Brigade from east and south working down the valley of the Selle as the left of IV Corps tried its luck again from the north. There comes a breaking point at which men can endure no more and the reservists of the 5th Division had reached it. They were being battered by the great shells; some forty of their own small guns were out of action and they could stand no more. They had been under continuous fire since about 0600 and the Argylls and the Manchesters of 19th Brigade had taken heavy casualties in their forward move from Reumont to help out the Suffolks and 15th Brigade RFA who were being hammered by German guns on the high ground east of the Selle. No orders had reached them and at about 0600 the officer commanding the 15th Brigade RFA had told his batteries, "We will fight it out here and there will be no retreat." By 1330 only five guns were left firing and the howitzers had run out of ammunition. Away to the left things were better. Hunter-Weston's 11th Brigade had been four times forced out of Ligny and each time had retaken it under his personal leadership. The 8th, 9th, and 15th Brigades were having no great difficulty in holding their positions and the 12th (the left flank brigade) though it had been compelled to yield some ground was very much in command of the situation. At about 1430 the 5th Division began to crumble. There was no panic, no "sauve qui peut"—not even "nous sommes trahis"—they just walked calmly away smoking their pipes like a crowd leaving a race meeting, covered by the fire of one devoted Howitzer Battery (the 61st) and one sixty-pounder of 108 Battery firing lyddite as its stock of shrapnel was exhausted, and the Suffolks, the Argylls and the Manchesters. As the Suffolks and the Manchesters were overwhelmed the flank of the KOYLI became exposed. No orders to retire reached them but somehow they managed to cling on until 1630 when resistance ceased. The Suffolks of 14th Brigade had been actually retiring in artillery formation when the order to stand reached them. Their position, not of their choosing, did not lend itself to defence and their casualties exceeded 700. The KOYLI were surrounded on three sides and under fire of field guns brought to within 900 yards. For the last hour they realized that they were alone but rebuffed efforts to send in a flag of truce and ignored the British "Cease Fire" blown on German bugles. Suddenly the whole countryside along the front and as far as the eye could reach from right to left was alive with Germans. Desperately Major Yate and Captain Keppel called on the men to charge. The next moment they were struggling in the hands of Germans who had come up behind them. Some men were bayoneted but, to the honour of the German soldier, most of the unwounded were made prisoners and the wounded were respected. How the end came on the right is described by Colonel Stevens, the CO of XV Brigade:

> About 2.40 some cheering was heard on our right, about 300 yards away and over the crest. About 5 minutes afterwards we heard "Stand fast" and "Cease fire" sounded and whistles blown. Then it was shouted down from the right, "You are firing on friends." All firing stopped at once. On standing upright and looking just over the crest we found everyone standing up and the firing line being rounded up by Germans. The position was lost, considerable numbers of the enemy being round our right and right rear. All 26 guns out of 52, 123 and 124 batteries had to be abandoned because the casualties in horses had been such that none remained to pull them away.

The end came too for 52 RFA, the old Bengal Rocket Troop. Silenced except for two flank guns served entirely by wounded (Captain Barber Starkey who with a wounded sergeant had kept one gun firing to the end died of his wounds a few days later) at about 1445 when the flank was overwhelmed by the German 26th Infantry Regiment. Only dead and wounded men lay around the guns they had served so well.

> Lieut. Longman, of one of the 5th Division reserve units recalls it this way: Then I saw a sight I hope never to see again. Our line of retreat was down two roads which converged on a village about a mile behind the position. Down these roads came a mob—men from any Regiment there, guns, riderless horses, limbers packed with wounded quite unattended and lying on each other, jostling over ruts etc.

It was not a rout, only complete confusion. This was the German's chance. One battery of artillery sent forward, or one squadron of cavalry, would have turned this rabble into a complete rout and the whole Army would have been cut up piece-meal.

Meanwhile we were the only Regiment I saw in any order. We had not been engaged and had only lost 1 officer and about 30 men: we had also had a hot meal so that we were in good condition. We went back in a succession of extended lines in absolute order and formed up behind a farmhouse near where the roads met. Here we waited in mass while the rest of the Army streamed past. It was a most trying half-hour. It seemed inevitable that they would follow up and then the jam in the village would have been indescribable—I have since heard that they had sustained fearful losses, and also a Division of French cavalry was covering our retreat. When the rabble had got past we moved off. Marching at attention, arms sloped, fours dressed etc. through the village: 7 p.m. moved off again and marched till 1 a.m.

The other two divisions, which had been in very heavy fighting all day, disliked the order to retire as they felt that they were holding their own and giving the enemy as good as they got, but of course they obeyed. Their retirement, performed as an operation of war, was as perfect as could be desired. There was no disorder, no lack of discipline, everything worked like a machine. The only small lapse came when from time to time infantrymen, marching at ease be it understood, dropped for a moment from the ranks to pat the hot barrels of the guns and to give a cheer for "their" gunners. The march discipline of the Royal Regiment, wounded men bringing their guns out of action as if after a field day in the Long Valley, brought a lump into many a throat. It was a fine day to be a British soldier and a particularly fine one to be a Gunner. As to the commander, Major A. F. Becke, the Secretary of the Historical Section of the Committee of Imperial Defence writing in 1919 says, "Both his generalship and his character rose far superior to the critical occasion. For that August day as the fierce fight swayed and surged he remained the master—both of himself and of the situation and in his eager grip the sword bit deep into the German host." 52 Battery had fired no less than 1,100 rounds, the most in any day since a six gun battery of muzzle-loading nine-pounders had fired almost the same number at Waterloo. Field Artillery Training Section 146 lays down that "to support infantry and to enable it to effect its purpose the artillery must willingly sacrifice itself." For neither the first nor the last time in its long history the Royal Regiment had carried out its orders. No need to ask where *Fas Et Gloria* led on the 26th August 1914. 37 Brigade alone won three Victoria Crosses.

There had been some bad moments during the battle, the worst of them being at about 1600, after the retirement had started, for gunfire to the left of the 4th Division could have meant that the IVth Reserve Corps or Von der Marwitz Cavalry had succeeded in working their way round to the west, where only the French Territorials around Cambrai—not one of them under forty and long away from any form of military service—stood between the BEF and the sea. As it happened, the French Territorials manfully stood their ground all day against von Gronau's 22nd Reserve Division but no-one was yet aware of it. Smith-Dorrien mounted and rode to a nearby hill from which, though nothing could be seen, he could plainly identify the distinctive crack of the Soixante-quinze. Sordet had come round with his tired horsemen and was standing guard over the flank. The French cavalry may have dressed in the fashion of Ruritania, carried an absurd rabbit-carbine, been shocking bad horsemasters (the sore backs of their horses could be smelt from afar as they hardly ever dismounted), and had the unsoldierly habit of carrying bundles of forage lashed to the guns themselves, but their gun was the powerful, rapid firing seventy-five and they knew how to use it.

CHAPTER EIGHTEEN

Sir Horace had good reason to feel well pleased with the day's work. Von Kluck, who was a generous enemy, admitted later that he had tried all he knew to out-flank him and had failed; "If I had succeeded, the war would have been won." The outcome of delaying actions such as this are not susceptible to description as victory or defeat. The Germans were masters of the field but were unable to pursue and could do no more than count their dead and lick their wounds. No German troops had been treated like this since the French had so rudely received the Prussian Guard at St Privat in 1870. The invincible army had now had its Magersfontein and the spirits of the bowmen of Crécy must have rejoiced that the blood of their sons ran as fiercely as ever. The terrible island infantry, lightly regarded for the last half-century, had rocked the victors of Liége Charleroi and Namur and dropped them in their tracks. German casualty figures are not always reliable but the generally accepted number is about 9,000 very few of whom were prisoners.

The British bill was heavy too; nearly 8,000 men were casualties of whom 2,600 were prisoners, (the 4th Division alone losing over 3,000 men and thirty-six guns). The worst hit unit was the 1st Gordons of 8th Brigade who had lost their way in the moonless night, marched directly across the German front and somehow found themselves in the middle of a mass of troops which they took to be French. Fire was opened on them from all sides and though they made a fight of it the battalion ceased to exist within ten minutes. This disaster affected the Army in a manner out of proportion to the size of the casualty list and men would speak of it in hushed whispers, for the days had not yet come when the extinction of whole units and formations was a commonplace. By the Battle of the Aisne the Gordons were back in their place in the line, their ranks filled with sons and younger brothers seeking to avenge their honour. French, even when writing after the war when figures were available, claims the casualties to have been "at least 14,000 officers and men and 80 guns." It is hopeless to attempt to unravel the mental processes of this obsessed man. The blunt truth was that II Corps was still in being, weakened of course by the loss of one-fifth of its numbers and more than one-fifth of its guns, but full of fight. Even in the battered 5th Division no man had thrown away his rifle and all they would need before they could fight again was food, rest, and re-organization (not forgetting tobacco, a serious matter to a mainly pipe-smoking Army; one connoisseur, in fact, recommends dried tea leaves in preference to brown paper or the chopped-up seats of cane chairs). The gamble had been won. When time permitted Sir Horace expressed his gratitude in an Order of the Day, giving due credit to the soldiers of Sordet and d'Amade, but properly giving the honours of the day to IInd Corps.

Off went their leader to report himself to GHQ at St Quentin. Arriving in the deserted town and palpably lost, he was accosted by an ASC officer who knew him by sight and the following dialogue took place:

"Are you looking for GHQ, sir?"

"Yes."

"They are gone, sir."

"Gone! Where to?"

"To Noyon, sir."

Noyon is thirty-five miles from St Quentin. What Sir Horace said is again not recorded, but he motored on. He had held his command now for five days. Far to the east the battle of Tannenberg was about to begin.

Before Sir John had left St Quentin there had taken place the second and last meeting with Lanrezac, with Joffre himself present. It was an ill-tempered affair steeped in gloom for no news of the stand at Le Cateau had arrived and Joffre freely admitted his plans to be in disarray. Lanrezac was disagreeable because the British were in St Quentin where his left should have been so Joffre pacifically substituted La Fère. He told of the formation of his new sixth Army under Maunoury but of course no thought of an offensive battle on the Marne was in anyone's mind yet. The muted conversation was carried on as if a corpse were in the house and in this ungenial spirit it broke up. Huguet telegraphed GQG at 8.15 saying "Battle lost by British Army which seems to have lost all cohesion. It will demand considerable protection to enable it to re-constitute. GHQ to-night Noyon. Fuller details will follow". Poor Huguet. If only he had been there to see the fierce pride of the marching regiments he would have sung a different song. The moral is simply that headquarters, hopelessly and by their own fault out of touch with the fighting troops, have a tendency to morbidity

Von Kluck was not served much better. The Channel ports were his for the taking but his intelligence had told him that the British were based at Calais with their lines of communication through Lille and Cambrai. Being already across that railway he extended his right to prevent them from connecting up with these imaginary lines and thus lost his opportunity forever.

Before leaving St Quentin Sir Horace had managed to find Colonel MacInnes, the Director of Railways, from whom he demanded trains for his wounded and exhausted soldiers. McInnes replied that GHQ had ordered him to send all the trains away but he agreed to keep them until the General's return from Noyon. By both sides of the road D'Estrées-St Quentin Sir Horace had seen in the light of his headlamps mile upon mile of ammunition boxes obviously thrown wildly away. On entering the town he found an ammunition column and its CO clearing out with empty wagons. "The OC told me that some shots had been fired as he came along the road, he believed from Uhlans, and to save his men and horses he had ordered all ammunition to be thrown away and had galloped away and seemed very proud of it". Sir Horace, knowing there to have been no enemy patrols about, weighed into the suddenly deflated officer. The officer was subsequently court martialled and dismissed the service but he immediately enlisted in the ranks and "I hear proved himself one of our bravest soldiers". These are the sort of things that happen to the best of men in the nightmare conditions of their first experience of war before judgment has been matured by familiarity.

Sir Horace reached Noyon at about 0100, had the usual difficulty in locating the house which had the distinction of sheltering the C-in-C and learned that that warrior with all his staff were taking their well-earned rest, the journey having been tiring. Eventually the great man appeared in his night-shirt with the aspect of a Roman Senator untimely disturbed. Sir Horace, naturally in high fettle, gave a brief exegesis of what his Corps had done only to be upbraided for unseemly optimism. However, he extracted seven trains from his somnolescent superior and arrived at St Quentin station as dawn was breaking to put them to use. He established himself in the Mairie and went out to watch his exhausted men shambling in, turning off to the station those who could obviously march no farther.

It was here a little earlier that Sir Tom Bridges had the experience of getting worn out men onto their feet which forms a small piece of history. At 1800 his brigadier put him in charge of a commando—Bridges' word—of 150 cavalry drawn from his own 4th Dragoon Guards and the 5th Lancers, saying that "they were in a very tight corner and must fight it out and die like gentlemen." By way of bathos, the Maire had already announced his intention to surrender his city and had extracted a written undertaking from two incredibly foolish infantry colonels that they would fight no more, in order to save the place from bombardment. Their battalions had obediently piled arms in the railway station and were lying in disorder. The furious Bridges—he was then only a major—issued an ultimatum that if they had not moved off within half an hour he would leave no British soldier alive in St Quentin. They moved off. Both colonels were in due time cashiered but it is pleasant to record that one of them, Elkington, (Montgomery's CO) joined the French Foreign Legion as a private soldier and performed there such prodigies of valour that he was eventually reinstated in his rank. There comes a pitch of physical exhaustion when judgment is unseated.

Some hundreds of exhausted men were lying in the square unresponsive to kicks or threats. Bridges and his trumpeter equipped themselves from a toy-shop with a tin whistle and a drum—fortunately they were able to make quite a good fist of "The British Grenadiers"—and got them slowly to their feet. With the reinforcement of a couple of mouth organs he soon had them on the march again—a demonstration of the power of music allied with will-power. By the time the Germans entered St Quentin the garrison consisted of one British straggler, complete with rifle, who insisted on shooting it out until riddled by a machine gun. All day Thursday the retreat continued; but from now on there could be no further close pursuit and although the men would march in a state of automatism, tormented by thirst, sleeplessness, and hunger as during the four previous days, there would not now be the eternal turning about to fight a rearguard action several times a day. The stand at Le Cateau had achieved its object and the pursuers were now faint. It remained only to get scattered units together again, collect up the stragglers, feed them, and replenish their pouches and wagons for there to be an Army in being again. Regiments were down from 1,000 or so to a few hundred bearded and filthy men, many with puttees or bandages wrapped round sore feet that could no longer bear a boot, and trousers trimmed to the dimensions of football shorts to make the heat more bearable. But they were regiments still. Junior officers and NCOs exercised commands beyond their ranks, ammunition mules served as officer's chargers, and all bore in their eyes witness to the four days and nights of fighting and marching with little or no sleep. The widely spread—and not discouraged—rumour was that this was a strategic withdrawal which would soon end with an about turn and a pitched battle in which they would square accounts and still be on the Rhine by Christmas. Undoubtedly they were not a pretty Army, perhaps the filthiest since Lee's Army of Northern Virginia (whose path could be traced by its bloody footprints), but like Lee's Army they knew themselves better men than their opponents and wished nothing more than another great fight. Robertson, the QMG, had very sensibly thrown the supply system to the winds and had caused dumps of food, forage, and ammunition to be set up at every likely cross-roads for all comers to help themselves as they needed.

By and large the retirement was orderly though it may not have looked it to the eyes of those with little or no battle experience. During the 27th, the corps fell back south of the Somme to a line running through Nesle-Ham-Flavy, the hope being that on the following night it would reach the Oise and enjoy a decent rest of a few hours. GHQ by the way, had left Noyon to move into the more suitable lodging of a wing of Napoleon's palace at Compiègne. On the 28th more fuel was added to the fire of Sir John's wrath against his contumacious subordinate; not only had Smith-Dorrien disobeyed Sir John's order (an order that was by definition the quintessence of all military wisdom) but his Corps had not even been destroyed as it should have been. And now this same man was going to have the temerity to question still another order. It happened like this. Sir Horace, in accordance with his habit, was showing to his weary men that they had a General and that he was not on the point of shooting himself in despair (as poor Samsonov was doing at about the same moment in a wood near Tannenberg). In the process he encountered Hunter-Weston (Hunter-Bunter to the Army) commanding II Brigade who seemed unusually out of sorts; when asked the cause of his low spirits he replied "It's that order!" "What order?" Hunter-Weston, an old friend of Sir Horace, explained that he had received an order a short time before that all ammunition not absolutely essential, officers kits, and other impedimenta were to be unloaded and all transport was to carry troops rearward to its maximum capacity. This, of course, is the kind of decision that might have had to be taken if the battle of Le Cateau had ended as a disaster but as things were it smelt of panic and was certainly a stiff blow to morale. The matter of the officers' kits may seem a small thing but it must be remembered that in 1914 it was the officer's responsibility to provide himself with everything—even to his personal weapons. Hunter-Weston did not mince words in saying that the order had had a very damping effect on his men for it was clear that it would not have been issued were they not in a very tight place, whereas the enemy was now only in small parties and at a very respectful distance. Sir Horace at once sent a signal to the headquarters of his divisions to say that the order was to be disregarded; in the case of the 4th Division it was too late for the officers' belongings and other cargo had already been burnt. When Smith-Dorrien met the Field Marshal there came a quarrel of some magnitude. Sir Horace was convinced that the order had been issued by mistake (in fact, it had originated in one of those fortunately inimitable messages from Henry Wilson to the GOC 4th Division of the "Dear Snowball . . . yours Henry" kind). Sir John, with a pomp in direct ratio to his inches, said that it was his own order and that Smith-Dorrien took an optimistic view of the situation which Sir John could not accept. Sir Horace was not the man to bend under the superior philosophy of Compiègne, he understood far better than the other man the unnecessary increase in suffering brought about by the burning of spare clothes and boots and was not slow to say so. High words passed, though how high we shall never know. Sir Horace had the right of it, though the heart of the matter was that he had added to the score of his offence in the eyes of his chief who was becoming conscious of his own incompetence.

Just before this meeting the IInd Corps, coming south from Ham, had marched past the C-in-C to the great pride of their commander. Men who had been whistling and singing as they strode along sloped their arms on the whistle for "March to attention" and passed the Field-Marshal in fine style. Sir Horace was "very proud of their carriage" and reserves a special word for 15th Brigade RFA which had lost all but two guns and very many men; those who remained took those two guns past the C-in-C as if returning from a field day. Nevertheless, that imperceptive warrior was within a matter of hours of writing to Kitchener about the "shattered condition" of IInd Corps. It would have been more in the interest of historical truth to speak of the shattered condition of the Field-Marshal and most of his staff, for about the only man there earning his pay was the QMG, Wully Robertson (whom many a soldier had cause to bless for manna from Heaven, in the shape of biscuits, corned beef, boots, or even a clean shirt picked up by the roadside). Murray was a nice man and an honourable one but completely out of his depth now and in the throes of a *crise des nerfs*; Wilson, finding his adored French Army to have feet and legs of clay, was thinking in terms of a great entrenched camp at Boulogne; Macready, the cold-blooded and unattractive Adjutant-General, was devoid of employment in the absence of returns from dispersed formations. They must have been a genial family for the now panicky C-in-C who had, according to Huguet, already told General Robb, Inspector-General lines of communication of his intention to make a "definite and prolonged retreat due South passing by Paris to the East or West" and ordering him to take the necessary steps. French kept this entirely to himself (the silence being maintained in his book) and Kitchener only learnt of it on the 30th in a message direct from Robb. His force now boasted, in name at least, three corps for on the 29th arrived the agreeable General Pulteney and his staff to transform Snow's 4th Division and the masterless 19th Brigade into a new formation named the IIIrd Corps. An example of the complete lack of grip by GHQ is given by Hubert Gough, then commanding the 3rd Cavalry Brigade. With great difficulty he managed to get through on the telephone to Wilson on the 27th to ask for instructions. The helpful answer was "You are on the spot. Do as you like, old boy!"

The last three days of August were employed in continuous marching, still southwards though for most the 29th was a day of blessed rest, the Vth Army being now behind. Sir Horace, who had had four consecutive hours sleep for the first time in a week, was called that day to a conference at Compiègne with Haig and Allenby and amongst those present was General Joffre. There were many notes to be compared. Earlier in the day de Lisle's 2nd Cavalry Brigade had had quite a serious fight with German vanguards and two infantry brigades had been needed to help him out. The Royal Flying Corps had reported large columns of the enemy bearing down several miles away but the IInd Corps was blowing all the bridges over the Oise and falling back, still in great heat, to the line of the River Aisne.

20 First Ypres. French cavalry passing through 19th Bde, October 1914.

Imperial War M

21 First Ypres. Scots Guards marching down the Menin road, October 1914.

Imperial War [

22 First Ypres. Supply column in Flanders.

On the 29th Lanrezac at last moved to the attack of Guise, his first even moderately successful offensive action to date. The strike towards St Quentin had been a costly failure but away on the right the dashing Franchet d'Esperey had carried out a successful assault in the old style, placing himself and his staff, all mounted, at the head of the 2nd Brigade which, with Colours unfurled and the bands crashing out "La Marseillaise" and "Sambre et Meuse" charged as their great-grandfathers had charged at Iena and like them had the satisfaction of seeing the colour of the Prussian knapsack. It was only a partial victory but it did much to restore to the *pantalons rouges* their faith in themselves and to give the enemy a taste of the true mettle of the French soldier when properly led. The story has long persisted without denial that Franchet d'Esperey (soon to become "Desperate Frankie" to the British), catching sight of a lugubrious Brigadier named Pétain whom he had known before the war as a staff college lecturer, called out to him, "Eh bien, M.Le Professeur a l'école de guerre, que pensez-vous de ce mouvement ça?" Mercifully, perhaps Pétain's answer has not survived but in any event "Sambre et Meuse" has an effect on the *simple soldat* at least as emotive as Bridges' "British Grenadiers" had on their phlegmatic ally. The only remarkable thing about the movement was that, in defiance of all the rules, it came off.

At the very moment when these events were taking place on his right, Sir John opened his conference with his own senior commanders—Haig, Smith-Dorrien, Allenby, and Murray. Sir John was already in pessimistic mood for he had chosen to put his faith in an unofficial report that Lanrezac had failed in his attack towards St Quentin. His consultation with that officer and Joffre had done little to restore his drooping spirits, even though Wilson had had his own meeting with Berthelot, Joffre's Chief-of-Staff, and General Belin. Wilson had learned that Lanrezac was shortly to join the other dismissed generals at Limoges. He knew also of Joffre's frantic efforts to form his new Sixth Army under Maunoury for the defence of Paris and that he was entreated to remain in the field to maintain contact between this Army and Lanrezac but he had no mind to do so.

Sir Horace arrived at 1500 in no kindly frame of mind towards his inadequate chief. While it was true that he knew little of the situation outside his own corps area (save that the gap between Haig and himself had now narrowed to no more than a couple of miles), he was with good reason well satisfied with the result of his recent battle and far from despondent. His corps was quickly putting itself back into shape and his soldiers were only too anxious to measure swords again with von Kluck's men. The Commander-in-Chief's diary does not even record that a conference took place but it does say this:

"C-in-C proposed to retire to a safe locality in order to refit, which will take eight or ten days. Deficiencies in material very heavy, though Joffre anxious for us to maintain line north of line Compiègne-Soissons. Commander-in-Chief replied impossible."

The fact of the matter was that Sir John had already had his mind made up for him by his *eminence grise*, Henry Wilson. Smith-Dorrien ought to have been destroyed in consequence of his disobedience and, following the logical mental processes of Pooh-Bah, he therefore must have been destroyed. The fact that French had himself seen II Corps bloody but unbowed was quite beside the point. This could not possibly be the fault of the omniscient, omnicompetent Field-Marshal so where did the blame lie? Clearly with the contumacious Smith-Dorrien whose incapacity had brought the Army to this pass; this is how Sir John has recorded it:

> This [filling the gap between the Vth and VIth Armies] I had every intention of doing. I am bound to say I had to make this decision in the face of resistance from some of my subordinate commanders who took a depressed view as to the condition of their troops. When I discussed the situation at a meeting of British Commanders held at Compiegne, Sir Horace Smith-Dorrien expressed it as his opinion that the only course open to us was to retire to our base, thoroughly refit, re-embark, and try to land at some favourable point on the coast line. I refused to listen to what was the equivalent of a Counsel of Despair.

There is nothing to be gained by mincing words over this; the statement is a wicked, malicious lie. These are the comments, all contained in letters to Sir Horace, from the other generals present:

> Sir Douglas Haig, "As regards the question which you ask me, namely, can I remember your saying anything at Compiègne on the 29th August 1914 which was of the nature of a Counsel of Despair, or indeed anything which could have been twisted round to such a meaning? I can quite honestly say that I have no recollection of your having done such a thing."
>
> Sir Edmund Allenby, "I remember the conference at Compiègne but I have no recollection of your expressing an opinion to the effect that the only course open was to return to the base, re-embark and land elsewhere."
>
> Sir Archibald Murray, "I have not the least recollection of your urging at Compiègne on the 26th [*sic*] August a return to the base and re-embarkation. You are perfectly at liberty to make that statement, as also, that I have never known you in the least pessimistic, but on the contrary full of courage at all times."

It will not have been forgotten that less than twenty-four hours had passed since the affair of the "dumping kits" order in which Sir Horace had been accused by the same chief of excessive optimism and failure to appreciate the seriousness of the situation. On that occasion Sir Horace admitted to having been angry and to have spoken with some heat so it is merciful that he did not know before leaving the conference of the calumnies which were being prepared for him. Perhaps it is worth mentioning in concluding the account of this lamentable business that Sir Horace's own diary entry merely says, "I was sent for by Sir John French at Compiègne and found General Joffre there, also Generals Allenby and Haig. Joffre was under the impression that his attack that day had been successful and it was not until afterwards that we learned that it had failed." If accusations of cowardice and needless depression have to be made there is a target for them which is far more deserving than the commander of II Corps.

At 0445 the morning of the 30th, Huguet telegraphed GQG that he had seen Sir John and urged on him the desirability of changing his orders, particularly stressing the importance of a forward movement by I Corps. All he was able to obtain was an undertaking that the bridges would not be blown up and that Haig might be stopped after his short march and then turned about. Later in the morning Sir John's pendulum seems to have swung back, for when Spears and Duruy, the new head of Fifth Army Operations Section, visited him in the palace he had just returned from his daily horse exercise and was in good spirits. Sir John interviewed Spears alone, discourteously keeping Duruy waiting, and before the conversation had advanced very far the door was flung open and a senior artillery officer erupted into the room, sobbing out, "All the guns in the Division are lost." Murray, shaken out of his customary urbanity, seized the man by the arm, said sternly, "To my knowledge you have seven left" and turned him out. The conversation, about the condition of the Vth Army in general and Lanrezac in particular, was renewed and Duruy at last invited in, thus missing the edifying exhibition which had just ended. He made eloquently the point that his Army was already in a perilous position and that any further British retirement would expose both Allies to frightful danger. He was promised a decision later.

At 0735 Huguet was able to report to GQG that French had just given orders for the retreat to stop. I Corps was to maintain contact with Lanrezac's left at La Fere, and II Corps was to remain within ten kilometres of the Oise, behind which the Vth Army was retiring.

To Joffre's message of thanks the reply was given that the BEF could not take up a position in the front line for at least ten days for want of men and guns and Sir John could not therefore comply with Joffre's request to fill the gap between the two French Armies, namely the line Compiègne-Soissons. This, not surprisingly, caused Joffre the greatest alarm for the only inference to be drawn was that Sir John intended to have no part in the coming battle when the British would be most sorely needed. Worse was still to come. At 0300 on the 30th Huguet again telegraphed to the effect that French wished not merely to continue his retreat but to withdraw across the Seine to Mantes and Poissy to refit, thus shifting his base westwards from Amiens to Le Mans. This would have involved a march straight across that of the Sixth Army and was obviously impossible. Joffre suggested that the retreat be to the east of Paris behind the Marne between Meaux and Neuilly-sur-Marne, after which they could move by the south of the capital and then west. Sir John's intentions, though kept *in petto*, were manifested by his order on London for maps for the whole force as far as Angers, more than 150 miles south-west of Paris, and his discussion with the horrified Huguet of the merits of La Rochelle, far away on the Atlantic coast, as a base. Huguet was no more horrified than was the Secretary of State for War when he received Sir John's letter advising him of these decisions. Sir John made it plain that he had no confidence in his Allies and was not going to be tied to any French plan—rather than do that he and his Army would be spectators at the destruction of France. French's extensive military reading may or may not have covered the Duke of Ormonde's betrayal of Prince Eugene in 1712 which he was now prepared to emulate without even Ormonde's excuse that he did what he did on Cabinet instructions.

On the 31st the Fifth Army found itself menaced by a sudden thrust by Richtofen's 1st Cavalry Division. Richtofen's Division had crossed the Oise by the bridge at Bailly—left undestroyed by culpable negligence—and between the hours of breakfast and tea had ridden unopposed through Nampcel to Terny, just north of Soissons. Lanrezac's weary men were in no position to stop them and he sent an urgent appeal for help to GHQ. As usual, GHQ had obligingly disappeared. All that Huguet knew was that it had been at Dammartin at 1115 hours when his first message was sent off but now it was to be found neither there nor at Crépy-en-Valois (designated as advanced GHQ). Only the initiative of Spears using a combination of village postmistresses and *gendarmes* succeeded in getting to the telephone an officer of the South Irish Horse (Haig's Corps Cavalry) at Vauxbuin who managed to pass the message to his corps commander. Sir Douglas of his own initiative ordered the regiment to move at once to Venizel on the Aisne from where they held Richtofen from the western end of the Chemin des Dames until nightfall. This small unit played a considerable part not only in saving the

Fifth Army but in keeping Richtofen from the gap behind Lanrezac's left flank. Richtofen, fortunately, was not an enterprising commander; his horse-shoes were worn out so as it happened no great harm came of his advance. By the morning of 1st September the Fifth Army had with super-human efforts got itself to the south bank of the Aisne and relative safety. Even more important, Von Kluck, believing himself to have destroyed the BEF at Le Cateau, was now diverging from the plan and marching south-east. The players are now all waiting in the wings for the miracle of the Marne.

Let us return briefly to London to see the consequences of Sir John French's dejected messages (which by now had reached the Cabinet). This was the latest one:

My Dear Lord K.,
 Tonight a report has come in that the Fourth French Army has been driven back towards Rethel. This was the line which, as I explained to you in my wire this morning, was assigned to it in the new dispositions of General Joffre; and so the rumour that he was driven back may not be true, but still it is very disquieting. I feel most strongly the necessity for retaining in my hands complete independence of action, and power to retire on my base when circumstances render it necessary.
 I have been pressed very hard to remain, even in my shattered condition, in the fighting line, but I have absolutely refused to do it, and I hope you will approve the course I have taken. Not only is it in accordance with the spirit and letter of your instructions but it is dictated by common sense.

The wire referred to reads: "This morning I received an official communication that General Joffre has made a change in his plan of operations and now intends to take up a more backward position. . . . General Joffre appeared to me to be quite anxious that I should keep the position which I am now occupying north of the line Compiègne-Soissons. I have let him know plainly that in the present condition of my troops I shall be absolutely unable to remain in the front line, as he has now begun his retirement. I have decided to begin my retirement tomorrow in the morning, behind the Seine, in a south-westerly direction west of Paris. This means marching for some 8 days without fatiguing the troops at a considerable distance from the enemy. . . ."

Kitchener and the Cabinet, for once unanimous, were appalled by this plan, realizing that if Sir John were to have his way the War could be lost now. Kitchener sent a telegraph message pointing out the consequences of this decision which drew a long reply:

If the French go on with their present tactics which are practically to fall back right and left of me, usually without notice, and to abandon all idea of offensive operations, of course then the gap in the French line will remain, and the consequences must be borne by them. I can only state that it will be difficult for force under my command to withstand successfully in its present condition a strong attack by even one German Army Corps, and in the event of a pause in my retirement I must expect two Army Corps at least if not three. If owing to Russian pressure the withdrawal of the Germans turns out to be true, it will be easy for me to refit north of Paris; but this I cannot do while my rearguard is still engaged as it was up to last night. An effective offensive movement now appears to be open to the French, which will probably close the gap by uniting their inner flanks. But as they will not take such an opportunity I do not see why I should be called upon again to run the risk of absolute disaster in order a second time to save them. I do not think you understand the shattered condition of the Second Army Corps and how it paralyses my powers of offence. . . . Your second telegram of today. If the French Armies are driven south of their present position, I could engage not to go back further than a line drawn east and west through Nanteuil. I shall reach this position tomorrow and endeavour to re-fit there.

In reply to Kitchener's last wire (there is considerably more correspondence by telegraph than is set out here: the curious can find it all set out in Sir George Arthur's *Life of Kitchener* which first brought it to light, but be warned that it is mostly repetitive) Sir John signalled peevishly. "If you order it we will go up into the front line tomorrow and do our utmost, but I am convinced it would end in grave disaster to the French troops, for I could never extricate them as I did before." It must in charity be assumed that Sir John really believed himself to have achieved this feat.

Lord Kitchener, with full Cabinet approval, habited himself in the undress uniform of a Field-Marshal (the only Army rank that remains always on the Active List) and left post haste for Paris to interview the sender of these near-hysterical missives. On the same day a German aviator dropped over that city a message announcing the arrival of his country's Army in three days' time.

The government left hastily for Bordeaux, France's now traditional reserve capital, to the strains of "La Marseillaise" chanted by sardonic Parisians to new words:

> "Aux guerre, citoyens,
> Montez sur les wagons."

CHAPTER NINETEEN

KITCHENER knew perfectly well that a visit by him would offend his touchy subordinate and that his appearance in military guise would be construed as an insult and as an attempt to interfere with the executive rights and responsibilities of the C-in-C. Nevertheless the thing had to be done and he palliated it as best he could by leaving the choice of meeting-place to Sir John, who chose the neutral ground of the British Embassy in Paris. There can be little doubt that Kitchener came armed with plenipotentiary powers to remove Sir John at once if he judged it necessary and he would have done it with no more compunction than he had done with his friend Gatacre so long ago.

Although in an exchange of letters which passed soon afterwards between Churchill and French the former (in any attempt, successful as it turned out, to smooth ruffled plumage) said that the visit was intended only as an encouragement; the omnipotent Olympian was perfectly capable in this great crisis of removing the C-in-C and assuming temporarily the command himself, confident that the Cabinet could do no other than ratify his action *ex post facto*. No documentary evidence of the state of Kitchener's mind exists but all his past proclaims his capability of taking an action so extreme if he were to be confronted with the fact that the Commander-in-Chief steadfastly refused to take his place in the Allied line. It was within Kitchener's own lifetime that Sir Colin Campbell had said flatly that it were better for every man of the Queen's Guards to lie dead upon his face than that the enemy should see the colour of their knapsacks and this was a situation a thousandfold more desperate than Balaclava. Happily Kitchener's overwhelming force of character was to prove a sufficient sanction. Huguet was struck with the difference between the two men, Kitchener "calm, balanced, reflective, master of himself, conscious of the great and patriotic task he had come to perform: the other sour, impetuous, with congested face, sullen and ill-tempered in expression. The difference was striking; the one really looked the man and leader he was whilst the other looked on the contrary like nothing but a spoilt child upon whom Fortune had smiled prodigiously but who, the day she left him, seemed abandoned and forlorn."

Sir John must have known of his own insecure position and passed immediately to the offensive. He expressed furious resentment at Kitchener's arrival in uniform (though, in fact, this was his normal dress at the War Office) as being calculated to undermine his position with the Army and the two men then moved into a private room, alone. What exactly passed between them will never be known though it is fair to assume that Sir John blustered a good deal and was made aware that continued tenure of his command was conditional upon his reversing his intention of taking his Army out of the field and of leaving Joffre to fight his greatest battle unaided.

Kitchener was by far the stronger personality and was in a commanding position. Sir John expressed indignation at being taken away from his headquarters at a moment when his presence was badly needed, (though this did not seem to have worried him excessively in the recent past on those occasions when his own staff did not know of his whereabouts nor had it inhibited him from summoning the chief executive officers of his two corps to waste hours motoring through choked roads when their own commanders needed them most). None the less, other than making affronted noises, French could only obey the Cabinet's commands. His protestation that Kitchener's presence "as a soldier" would undermine his authority with the Army was a masterpiece of fatuity. All armies, not least the British, when they find themselves out-numbered and out-gunned tend to regard themselves as neglected by their people at home (the expression "Forgotten Army" has been heard since) and a visit from the man who above all others save the King himself epitomised the nation's determination to fight to the end could not have had other than a heartening effect. Sir John was good at spontaneous visits to the fighting men ("Oo's the old bloke?" was a familiar cry and his genuine little speeches went down well) and indeed this was the usual reason for his unpredictable absences, but he would brook no other performer stealing his show. The result of the interview is recorded in Kitchener's letter drafted that same evening:

My dear French,

After thinking over our conversation today I think I am giving the sense of it in the following telegram to the Government I have just sent. 'French's troops are now engaged in the fighting line where he will remain conforming to the movements of the French Army, though at the same time acting with caution to avoid being in any way unsupported at his flanks.'

I feel sure you will agree that the above represents the conclusions we came to; but in any case, until I can communicate with you further in answer to anything you may wish to tell me, please consider it as an instruction.

By being in the fighting line you of course understand I mean disposition of your troops in contact with, though possibly behind, the French as they were today; of course you will judge as regards their position in this respect.

I was very pleased to meet you today and hope all will go well and that Joffre and you will make the best plans possible for the future which you will, I hope, communicate to me. I leave the first thing tomorrow morning.

Yours very truly,
K.

I hope you will do your utmost to re-fit as soon as possible from the Lines of Communication, and put in men and horses necessary to refill units to their proper strength.

Later in the day Joffre received this letter from Millerand, the Minister of War:

My dear General,

I would have liked to talk to you over the direct wire concerning the enclosed note. It was drawn up in my presence by Field-Marshal Sir John French at the end of a conference lasting more than two hours following upon his arrival today in Paris. (Millerand and Viviani, the Premier, had been present at the Embassy for the conference.) I do not wish to infringe in any way upon your liberty of action, for that as well as your responsibility must continue to be complete; but I feel I should tell you that the Government is unanimous in wishing that you could find a way to accept Sir John's proposition. . . .

The proposition was that a line of defence along the Marne a few miles to the west and north-west of Paris should be dug, Sir John undertaking to hold his position around Nanteuil for as long as he could, provided that he ran no risk of lacking support if he were attacked.

Joffre, who was watching the long German arm reaching down to the east of Paris its centre and left heading now for Verdun, could hardly have been expected to show enthusiasm for the prospect of preparing a defensive position with its wings behind a river (which he would have to cross in order to attack); nor did he do so. The plan seemed hardly in harmony with Kitchener's telegram to the Cabinet for nothing could be less calculated to "conform to the movements of the French Army." Joffre had troubles enough of his own well away from the area of the BEF for he was skilfully co-ordinating the movements of the Third, Fourth, Fifth, and Sixth Armies while a dozen German Army Corps were moving south from Rethel towards the exhausted men of Sarrail (Ruffey's successor in command of the Third Army), Foch, and de Langle de Carey. Joffre did, however, find time to replace Lanrezac by Franchet d'Esperey and it may be remarked that he did it as an honourable and courteous gentleman should, personally visiting the victim, expressing appreciation of his past services and gently pointing out that he was exhausted and needed rest. (Sir John when his opportunity came ordered things differently.) Lanrezac's last recorded utterance was a quotation from an earlier Horace to the effect that happy is he who remains at home caressing the breast of his mistress instead of waging war. At this moment the weight on Joffre's shoulders was more than any mortal man could be expected to bear and it is to the eternal glory of the cooper's son from the slopes of the Pyrenees that he bore it as no other man of his generation could have done. True he had made dreadful miscalculations, and the tally of his mistakes was not yet complete, but in those days he held in his strong hand the sword of the Allies and showed himself a true *maître d'escrime*.

The part he had in mind for the BEF to play was of necessity a small one but it was vitally important and there was no understudy waiting in the wings. If the actor declined to perform the play would fail. French must not be allowed to drop out except at the price of the loss of the war and eternal, deserved infamy for the islanders. Galliéni, the Governor of Paris, who had once been Joffre's military superior, was feverishly strengthening and sharpening the sword of Maunoury whose Sixth Army now contained D'Amade's two reserve divisions, the 61st and 62nd, (not élite troops but by no means contemptible), the fresh and excellent 45th Division from North Africa, the IVth Corps from Sarrail's Third Army around Verdun, the VIIth Corps from Alsace (which had already brushed with von Kluck on the Somme before retreating on Paris), two unused reserve divisions, the 55th and 56th, a Moroccan Brigade, and Admiral Ron'arch's fine Marines. Day by day Maunoury was growing stronger, whereas von Kluck, well to the south-east and for the most part across the Marne, became more heavily involved. Another new Army, the Ninth, under the redoubtable Foch and consisting of eight infantry divisions and one of cavalry was conjured up between the Fourth and Fifth Armies centred on La Fère Champenoise to the south of the soon to be famous marshes of St Gond. Maunoury's task was to drive the Germans across the Oise while Franchet d'Esperey was to march north covered by Foch holding the centre. The BEF was to turn about and advance between the Fifth and Sixth Armies, attacking von Kluck on the Grand Morin astride Coulommiers and maintaining its objective regardless of what might be happening on either flank. From corps commanders to company cooks the British could have asked nothing better: unhappily it was not with them but with their unaccountable chief that Joffre had to do business. "Entrench Boulogne—fortify Le Havre—arrange harbour facilities at Saint Nazaire"—these were the great matters occupying French's mind. Wilson claims in his diary to have wanted to halt the retreat, Murray was almost *in extremis*, Wully Robertson was growling to himself and quietly doing very well in his charge of re-fitting but there was no strong mind for French to rely upon for reasoned judgment. French was more despondent than McClellan had ever been and was nearer in spirit to Medina Sidonia than to any commander of modern times, his obsession with Sedan and the dismal events of 1870 never far away.

He reached his HQ at Dammartin at about 1900, his feathers still much ruffled, but he was for the moment cheered by the news of the great feat of arms performed by "L" Battery RHA at Néry—perhaps the British cavalry's finest unaided victory of all time. Here was the vindication of their training in which the thirteen-pounder and the short rifle in the same hands that had sent the cavalry to the top of the Aldershot musketry returns taught von der Marwitz a bloody lesson. Néry was the cavalry's Le Cateau and there could be no question now of who were the best horse-soldiers in this war. Perhaps there was something to be said for this business of dismounting and starting to shoot after all, for Néry was a palpable victory which the C-in-C acknowledged by moving GHQ backwards again to Lagny in the small hours of 2nd September. There he received a letter of welcome from Galliéni which included a well meant if infelicitous remembrance that Galliéni had been in Madagascar during the South African War and had heard much there of his guest's exploits. If Denys Reitz and his exiled friends were the sources of information—as they probably were—one feels that Galliéni says too little or too much. The rear of GHQ arrived during the day at Melun, where Galliéni arrived on the 4th to find only Murray at home. To him Galliéni unburdened Joffre's plans for the attack and asked that the British fill the gap between the two French Armies. Murray naturally could give no such undertaking in spite of the pleasing news of the removal of Lanrezac. Sir John, less moved by his ally's grave embarrassment than by "some pressure on Haig", ordered a continuation of the retreat which, he said, facilitated the movements of reinforcements, supplies, and materials. Huguet also came in the night with dispatches and a staff officer from Joffre who told Sir John that the great attack had begun with the Sixth Army crossing over the Ourcq and asked on behalf of his chief that the BEF should do its duty. Later still came Maunoury in fine spirits saying that his cavalry had reported few Germans north or north-west of Paris, and announcing his intention to attack with all vigour and asking for Sir John's "best support". An odd coincidence, but these are the very words used by the 7th Earl of Cardigan at the opening of the charge at Balaclava to Lord George Paget: "I expect your best support, mind, Lord George, your best support." "You shall have it, my Lord," was Paget's reply. French's was of the same tenor and of equal lack of precise meaning. Whatever it may have been intended to convey, Joffre took it as an undertaking to comply with his plan and at 0915 Huguet telephoned to Franchet d'Esperey that French had agreed to take his place in the attack. Joffre sent a message that he would himself come to Melun at 1400 to express his thanks and reported fully to Millerand at the Ministry of War. Joffre arrived at the Château of Vaux-le-Pénil where the C-in-C was living, at the same moment as did Spears, sent by Franchet d'Esperey to find out what was going on.

Now came the most dramatic meeting of them all. Joffre, hatless and bowed, spoke in his low voice first to thank Sir John for having taken a decision upon which depended the fate of Europe. He explained lucidly the situation with the change in direction of the German line of advance and paying generous and merited tribute to the Squadrons of the RFC which had been his eyes. The short plump Field-Marshal bowed courteously but did not speak. He understood a little French (to the end of his life he could not so much as give directions to a taxi-driver to take him to his hotel) but he signed to his staff, all eager to translate, that he understood. Joffre explained what the Fifth and Sixth Armies had to do, he drew out the great tapestry of the battlefield, how the great and so-far victorious German columns were blinding on to their destruction if every soldier, French and British alike, would only do his duty. The next twenty-four hours would be decisive for the hour would not come again. Joffre spoke of his orders to his Frenchmen, how the time for retreat was over, and how those who could not advance must die where they stood. General Spears, an eye-witness, continues, "We saw the battlefield, the onward rush, the guns galloping up in the dust, the blinding flash; we heard the screech of bursting shells and under the torn blue sky we saw the men who had been ordered to stand their ground falling on the thirsty earth and staining it with dusty dark red patches. . . . British co-operation was demanded in words of exalted eloquence inspired by the feeling and the truth within the man. Everything the British could give, all they had, was asked for. Then turning full on Sir John with a feeling so intense as to be irresistible clasping both his own hands so as to hurt them, General Joffre said "Monsieur le Marechal, c'est la France qui vous supplie."

Sir John had understood enough, his strong emotions were touched but under their stress his slender stock of French failed him. With tears rolling down his cheeks he turned to the nearest French-speaking officer and said, "Damn it, I can't explain. Tell him that all men can do our fellows will do." Emotion and tears are not always discreditable to a man and for all his terrible defects Sir John French was never insincere. "Your best support" now had a definable meaning. Murray rather spoilt it by blurting out that the British could not possibly begin their advance before 0900 (Joffre had ordered it for 0600) but the weary Marshal only replied, "It cannot be helped. Let them start as soon as they can. I have the Marshal's word, that is enough for me." The staffs then got down to the detailed work of translating these noble sentiments into the cold prose of operation orders.

Just for these few jewelled days relations between Sir John and Sir Horace had blossomed; the former seemed to have learnt more about the consequence of the latter's disobedience at Le Cateau than he had formerly known. They met at Haig's HQ on the 4th and again when Sir John visited II Corps HQ on the 6th, the day that the battle of the Marne began, Sir John praising his subordinate by saying that the battle of Le Cateau had saved the whole situation and promised to say the same in his dispatches—which in due time he did. The order for the turn-about was well received throughout the Army, one beaming

23 The popular hero, 1915. The eulogy in Sir John French's Dispatch makes wry reading in conjunction with his later book.

24 *Peace. The General introduces David to the Calpe Hunt, Gibraltar December 1918.*

25 *Off parade again—Gibraltar 1920.*

brigadier saying "Why, it's better than Corunna. Moore had to take to his ships, he did not advance again." Many units leaving their billets on the morning of the 6th, did not know whether they would be trudging off towards the Atlantic, and bursts of spontaneous cheering were heard as the news spread. Sir Horace's Corps were still much knocked about for while the ranks had been re-filled in part by drafts from the depots, the precious guns, particularly in the 5th Division, could not be replaced. Most serious of all was the shortage of experienced officers for the casualties amongst the commissioned ranks had been disproportionately heavy (even though not nearly so bad as had been the case with the French).

The battle of the Marne raged for three days and nights over a front of 150 miles and its course is well known; this not being a history of the Great War is not the place in which to look for a detailed account of it. How Maunoury, Franchet d'Esperey, and Foch proved to a sceptical world that the French Army, routed in 1870, undermined by the Dreyfus affair, and weakened by its recent performances under indifferent leaders, was capable in this supreme crisis of producing chiefs in no way inferior to the Marshals of the Empire has been recorded over and over again. Like other Armies, the French Army has had its evil days since 1914 to some extent because the men who ought to have advanced in command as the years went by, died in swathes as subalterns and captains on the Couronne de Nancy, in the Marshes of St Gond, and on the wooded hills of the Argonne. It is well for those who feel impelled to criticize events which took place later, sometimes much later, to bear this in mind and to consider the villages, some half-deserted to this day, where the long, interminable lists of the names of the young men are spelt out in bronze and stone on countless ugly memorials. For all its emotional beginning the action of the BEF, though indispensable, was almost an anti-climax. Basically the German plan was to break the French centre somewhere near Nancy while the armies of the Crown Prince, Duke Albrecht of Würtemburg, and Von Hausen kept their right wing in chancery around Verdun. The broken pieces, including the notionally already broken BEF, could then be shepherded some to Paris, some to Verdun. Against the dispirited armies of even a week ago the plan could have worked but there were new and firmer grasps on the controls now. It was no longer a rabbit that was contemplating the snake, it was a mongoose. The sequence of events for a final German victory had to be first, the breaking of Foch; second, the holding off of the BEF to enable Von Kluck to outflank Maunoury to the north of Paris; third, the crushing of Maunoury's Sixth Army with the help of troops released by the recent fall of Maubeuge. Of these three desiderata the second was the most important for if necessary the attack on Foch could be broken off without fatal consequences.

On the morning of the 6th as Haig's Corps crossed the Grand Morin they observed a heavy column of German infantry marching south turn about and march away without firing a shot. This was not, as many were pleased to think, a manifestation of terror at the sight of khaki but Von Kluck's Second and Fourth Corps ordered away from the British front to join in the attack on Maunoury. In front of them now were only the three cavalry divisions of von der Marwitz. They did not cause undue delay and as the BEF advanced into the gap the cavalry had hastily created between the halves of Von Kluck's Army, the time he had available to defeat Maunoury became that much shortened (while his adversary grew steadily stronger as new units reached him). Now came the hour of Galliéni's taxis.

The BEF entered pillaged Coulommiers on the 7th, Smith-Dorrien taking up his abode for the night in the nearby Château de Faremoutiers ("very dirty, littered with debris and the remains of the breakfasts of the officers which we had to clean up"). There he records that two men had to be shot, one for plundering and the other for desertion. The man who had had the Aldershot piquets removed was no slack disciplinarian—nor did his men expect him to be.

Next day, still fighting against the German rearguard, by no means as formidable as they were to become in 1918, his corps headed for the south bank of the Marne where the bridges were still intact. On his left Pulteney's Corps had not fared so well for all the bridges on his front had been destroyed and the far side of the river was strongly held. Sir Horace rode over to see him for the left flank of his own Fifth Division was exposed to fire from the high ground around La Ferte. "Putty", as this likeable General was known by everybody, was in the course of saying that he could manage the business by himself when the C-in-C arrived in fine fettle—Sherman was firmly mounted now —and for perhaps the first time permitted himself openly to criticize Haig for being laggard. It still did not satisfy Huguet; "If a Foch or a Galliéni had been so placed, or even an energetic leader understanding the situation and willing to hustle his troops, the result would have been even more decisive."

Sir Horace now had his own aeroplane squadron, which pleased him greatly. "Real heroes", he called them, "they appear to have put the fear of God into the Germans' aeroplanes for they hunt them wherever they see them . . . but every time they go up they bring back quite invaluable and what always proves to be true information." This is where the traditional cavalry spirit had gone and it was to belong for the future, with the young pilots of the Maurice Farmans and B.E.2c's and their successors. What a long time ago Isandhlwana had been.

On the 10th Smith-Dorrien saw something new—the woods full of stragglers in field-grey. Over 1,000 prisoners were taken by his corps but his head was never in the clouds. While Wilson was bragging about being in Elsenborn in three weeks Sir Horace was patiently writing, "But I still realize that the main bodies of the German Corps in front of us may be in perfect order and that the people we are engaged with are strong rearguards who are sacrificing themselves to let their main bodies get far enough away for fresh operations against us." The King's congratulations on Le Cateau arrived that day and gave him great pleasure. As always he was at pains to see the congratulations passed on without delay to those who had earned them. (One of his nicknames in South Africa had been "Half Rations and Full Congratulations.") About two thousand prisoners were taken and many dead were counted by his corps the following day but this could not be called hard fighting. The weather, however, had broken now and the nights were cold and wet. Sir Horace complained that many men still had neither greatcoats, ground sheets, nor any change of clothing thanks to the panic order which had caused so much anger during the retreat and the needless shifting of 70,000 tons of stores from Le Havre to St Nazaire. Still no gun replacements had reached II Corps—all told they were forty-two pieces short—but so far as it affected Sir Horace the battle of the Marne had petered out and on 12th September the Army was on the line of another river whose name was to ornament many a Colour and to spell the end of the War of movement for a long time to come. The battle of the Aisne was about to open.

CHAPTER TWENTY

THE valley of the Aisne is one of the most beautiful and peaceful regions of northern France and very different from the ugly Pays du Borinage around Mons. From a high green plateau north of the river run green spurs like the fingers of a flattened hand, the tips towards the river, and across the wrist runs the ironically named Chemin des Dames—the carriage road made in the eighteenth century for two daughters of Louis XV. The middle-aged and sedentary can today climb gently for about 300 feet up any of the re-entrants, examine cursorily the dugouts and underground workings made by the Germans in later campaigns and consume sandwiches and coffee in the lee of a haystack standing where its predecessors have done since man first learned to plant corn. Nothing in this smiling countryside shows that its soil is enriched by more blood, French and British, than any part of the western front save the Ypres salient and Verdun. At Ypres the progress of fifty seedtimes and fifty harvests have concealed that which lies below the surface and only the ubiquitous cemeteries and the punctual and heart-wringing "Last Post" sounded nightly by Belgian volunteers as the traffic is stopped at the Menin Gate tell the great tale. Verdun is still a place of horror, from the hideous Ossuaire to the nature-abhorred parcels of land still poisoned by mustard gas upon which nothing will yet grow. The Aisne valley is pastoral, like something from an Aubusson or Savonnerie design, which proclaims an older France. It was opposite the Chemin des Dames that the advancing British arrived on 12th September, the gaps in their pitifully thinned ranks now in part filled by reinforcements from home. The sight of some of these incurred Sir Horace's displeasure for many were drunk with ten miles' marching to be done—still one should not be too censorious for it was the last opportunity for a lot of them.

The IInd Corps arrived on the river line without much trouble though the 3rd Division had to come to the help of Allenby whose cavalry had occupied Braisne and was being heavily counter-attacked. The German front had thickened now and this was no mere cavalry screen being driven in. Away to the left Pulteney's IIIrd Corps and Maunoury's Sixth Army were hotly engaged. So began the longest battle the British Army had fought for many years; from the 12th September to the 2nd October it lasted and it began with the Allies in a position of great danger. Sir Horace, like Haig, relied on reports from his young airmen. He knew them all and had seen their Maurice Farman "pushers" and B.E.2c's, with open cockpits, skids between the wheels, and smelling strongly of warm castor oil, taking off from their little airfields, cruising at a speed of about sixty mph and returning pregnant with news. He had heard the distant popping as aerial warfare began with the twelve-bore shotgun and the massive ·455 Webley and Scott revolver, had seen the cardboard boxes of steel arrows, named "Flechettes" and looking something between a cross-bow quarrel and a large dart, which were scattered over the enemy columns without, apparently, ever hurting anybody. Now what he needed to know above all things was the siting of the German battery positions but the summer rainstorms were lashing down and blinding the aviators. The river is, in places, about 100 yards wide, deep and unfordable, those bridges which were still capable of use being carefully registered by the German gunners and under steady fire. Much infantry had been ferried across by various means and clung as best they could to the finger tips of the wooded ridges but the river lay between them and their guns. From the increasing volume of the German fire it became plainer that far from being up against cavalry alone, they were engaged with the main German force. For the entire duration of the battle there was never a movement of more than half a mile each way, for this was a hard slogging match which ended the war of manœuvre. Thoughts of out-flanking or being out-flanked were now irrelevant for it was a matter of carrying the Chemin des Dames if one could or clinging on to what we already held north of the river should that prove impossible.

By the evening of the 13th all the infantry of the BEF were over the river and the rain had stopped though only for a time. The German intention to withdraw no more but to fight a bigger Le Cateau on ground of their choosing was becoming clearer from the weight and frequency of their counter-attacks and the fact that many of the shells now bursting amongst the British were of the heaviest calibre—bigger by far than the 5·9. Sir Horace, his corps in the centre, was ordered by GHQ to stand fast on his line while Haig tried to work round the right flank and Maunoury the left. Henry Wilson was still brimming with witless confidence that the Germans would soon be forced from France but Sir Horace, whose feet were firmer on the ground, was less sanguine. He was, however, a happy general, well pleased with his now experienced staff; "We are a very happy family and are thoroughly enjoying our campaigning together." How different, how very different, from the un-fraternal atmosphere at GHQ.

Now we begin to hear the dread words "trenches" and "wire". For the first time the Germans were falling back on prepared positions using their defenders' best friends and more than one attack petered out in face of them. On the 15th during an interval in the rainstorms Sir Horace spent a few hours in a hayrick on the high ground to the south of the river with General Wing (his CRA) and Hubert Hamilton (who had but a month to live). They had a splendid view of the entire battle and were under some shellfire which, if anything, Smith-Dorrien rather enjoyed. ("A shell, Sir. Very animating" as old Picton had said.) Wing then led him round the batteries where experts produced pieces of enemy projectiles which seemed to have come from siege guns. The Germans indeed intended to stay. The rain went on and on, attack was followed by counter-attack, the 2nd Queens in particular taking Troyon with a fine bayonet charge. There were, however, two matters of critical importance taking place of which no-one on the Allied side could yet have known. The brave King Albert I had made a sortie with the Belgian Field Army from Antwerp which cost him 8,000 casualties but kept the German command from sending help from that quarter to von Kluck. But two Army Corps, one from Alsace and another fresh from the taking of Maubeuge, were marching to his aid with a speed that would have won Marlborough's approval. Such was their pace that men fell out and died from sheer exhaustion as Marlborough's had done on the occasion when "the Duke requested that the infantry shall step out." As it happened their efforts were not in vain for they arrived with no more than two hours to spare at the very moment when von Kluck's line was bulging to the point of rupture.

During this period Sir Horace was shocked by another example of human depravity. Frenchmen, it seemed, existed in noticeable numbers who were willing to sell their country to the invader. One farmer with a telephone line direct to German HQ, was found, the richer by 50,000 francs as his reward for passing on all the information he could get about Allied movements. He, with fifteen others of the same mind, was summarily shot.

On the 24th Sir Horace's Corps was strengthened by the arrival of two six-inch howitzers—veterans of South Africa but still fit for service. Their deep note did much to hearten his outgunned men but it was a wretched day for him as the Foresters, of Haig's Corps, had been badly hammered in an attack on the German trenches losing five officers killed and nine wounded, the casualties among the men being still uncounted. So it went on day after day, the valley being a mass of bursting shells which happily made more noise than they caused hurt for the Army was now well entrenched. The First Lord of the Admiralty, finding maritime affairs insufficiently exciting, came to see the battle. Like Sir Horace he tried to cross the bridge at Vailly but the storm of shells rendered it impossible. Mr Churchill, who somehow always seemed to draw fire, was never a comfortable companion anywhere near a battlefield. The Swedish Minister, who was also visiting the front with a kindly gift of cigarettes for the British troops, fared worse for the blast from a German shell wrecked his car and killed his chauffeur. At least the troops did not suffer as they had done on the retreat from lack of food, for rations were now being distributed with comparative ease—neither side yet having the skill or the resources for harrying those whose business it was to move provisions from the railhead to the soldier.

By 2nd October a stalemate had arrived and it was plain that neither side was going to make any substantial rupture in the lines of the other. It had been a very near thing, for the British (reinforced by the last Regular Division—the 6th) were very nearly onto the Chemin des Dames when the two German corps arrived, dead beat but by no means useless. These were promptly formed into a new Seventh Army and the German line was now too strong to be broken by uphill charges supported by an indequate number of guns. For a time the Chemin des Dames was to have a period of relative tranquility. One result of the battles of the Marne and the Aisne had been that Moltke had received his quietus. The Supreme War Lord had never thought much of him ("your uncle would have given me a different answer") and now the great plan for the subjugation of France lay in ruins. He was replaced by the elegant von Falkenhayn whose reign was to last until the hammer broke in his hand on the anvil of Verdun.

Sir John now took stock of the situation. Wilson's three weeks were up and the Allies, far from being in Elsenborn, were bogged down with the BEF a long way from the French left wing and the Channel ports. Falkenhayn, with plenty of troops at his disposal, was obviously bound to have another try at carrying out a modified Schlieffen operation and the War was sure to move north again very soon. No British commander could ever be happy so far from Calais and Boulogne and if by any chance Falkenhayn were to risk all by invasion of the island he would find only Haldane's Territorials to stop him. The Force had profited greatly by its two month's concentrated training but as everyone knows Kitchener would have none of it, (he was never able or willing to distinguish between these elderly ex-conscripts and the fit young volunteers who had the misfortune to bear a similar title) and packed off many units to relieve the regular garrisons in India and elsewhere who were being hastily organized into new divisions, described as regular though their artillery was mainly drawn from the TF batteries.

Sir John rightly mooted to Joffre that the time had come for the BEF to return to its natural place nearer to the sea. Joffre, who was busy lengthening and thickening his own line seawards did not like leaving the Aisne too thinly held but he saw the force of Sir John's argument and eventually agreed. On horseback and by train the BEF left the Aisne never to return—except for the few divisions decimated after the March retreat of 1918 who had to undergo a second martyrdom under the worst of French Generals. Falkenhayn was also moving seawards and with a lull in the fighting elsewhere, there began what has gone down to history by the inapt name of "The Race to the Sea." Sir Horace summed up the situation: "I always regarded the conception and execution of this great flank move as providing the largest nail in the coffin of the enemy in the whole war. But for this I am unable to see how the Germans could have been stopped from seizing Calais and Boulogne—and it was only just in time." As indeed it was. By mid-October the IInd Corps found itself holding a line—a line on the map, be it understood—at the southern end of what was to become the Salient, from a point between Laventie and Aubers Ridge in the north to another near Givenchy on the La Bassée Canal in the south. On his right was Maistre's XXIst Corps, on his left Pulteney's IIIrd Corps (which now embraced the 6th Division) prolonging the line to Armentières, beyond them again the two Cavalry Divisions (the original division had been divided between Gough and De L'Isle) holding the sector north to Hollebeke. The 7th Division and 3rd Cavalry Division (collectively called IVth Corps) under Sir Henry Rawlinson had been landed at Ostend and after operations around Antwerp had joined the BEF from Ghent and had turned about between Hollebeke and Hooge, in front of Ypres itself and across the Menin Road. The 1st and 2nd Divisions did not arrive until the 20th. Between them and the sea, thirty miles away, were more French and Belgian troops including the excellent French Marines at Dixmude. Von der Marwitz had made a dash for the sea with his cavalry on the 11th but had been checked by de Mitry's horse and driven back by Allenby on the following day. The so-called line was very irregular and unfortified, a gap between Sir Horace and Pulteney being filled by French cavalry; the aspect here is one of utter flatness, such ridges as there are lying to the east, with the spires of the old and lovely city of Ypres visible from everywhere. Arable land this, with small woods dotted here and there, part of the old Duchy of Burgundy and renowned since the middle ages for the weaving of cloth. Ypres is a walled city, taken in hand by Vauban, with its moat facing to the east from which in the past the threat to its commercial serenity has come and in which direction the lion on the Menin Gate still fixes his gaze. To the German Army it was an article of faith that Ypres must be taken: on Armistice Day 1918 it was said with truth that no German soldier ever entered Ypres save as a prisoner. The price the Army paid for its right to this assertion may be read in the panel upon panel of English, Welsh, Scots, and Irish surnames with those from Canada, Australia, New Zealand and South-Africa upon the Menin Gate and on the countless rows of stones in the immaculately kept cemeteries.

The first round in this Herculean, four-year long fight was about to begin—it was to be the last fight of the British Regular Army. France too is entitled to an equal share in the glory of first Ypres for the Salient was not yet a British preserve and the red trousers and blue capotes of General D'Urbal's men were a conspicuous sight. It was to be a soldier's battle in the tradition of Oudenarde and Inkerman, fought to no plan but with units being pushed in to plug gaps as fast as they arrived and where the ultimate victor was General Wavell's Unknown Company Commander. Sir John has written of the plans he made with Foch for a combined offensive, and was confident that he was outflanking the German right, von der Marwitz's raid notwithstanding. Henry Wilson, who though nearly always wrong, was at least consistent in his errors, told his diary on the 13th, "We must push, push, push as there is nothing in front of us." Sherman was in the saddle again; Rawlinson, who had come under French's command on the 15th, was ordered to turn about and attack Menin. That level-headed General quietly did nothing of the kind which was as well. The 7th Division was commanded by General "Tommy" Capper, whom we last met as a company commander in Sir Horace's XIIth Sudanese riding up the Jebel Surgham at Omdurman, one of the bravest men who ever drew breath. If the order had come from Rawlinson he would have put himself at the head of the division and led it to ruin at the hands of the German artillerymen and machine gunners (anticipating his death in some such fashion three years later). Surprisingly, Sir John treated him mildly over it. All this time the British were still on the attack, small battles being fought all along the thirty-five mile front. It could not last as the Germans with their geographical and man-power advantages were pouring in troops, having no less than seven full corps in the line by the 20th, despite what the Sub-Chief of the General Staff believed. The cavalry spirit emanating from GHQ had produced the inevitable result that no digging took place. When the German attack broke on them the British had not merely no reserve line, they had not even a front line, nor had they any wire at all. Shallow waterlogged trenches, by no means continuous and usually overlooked from the higher German positions—even when they were not actually caught in enfilade—were the only fortifications between the enemy and the sea. There were none save local reserves for the length of front demanded the presence of every available man in the firing line. Over all fell the steady, drenching Flanders rain—the same rain which had made Marlborough's men curse and swear and which was to draw the self-same oaths from a later generation.

The 14th October was the saddest day of the campaign for Smith-Dorrien for it was then that his very old friend and trusted divisional commander, Hubert Hamilton was killed by a ball from a shrapnel shell. They buried him that night in the churchyard of the village of Lacouture near to where he had fallen, as many officers as could be collected from the firing line and all his staff marching in procession to the churchyard while the Germans attacked all along the line a mile or so away. "The rattle of machine-guns, musketry, and artillery fire made it very difficult to hear the Chaplain, the Rev. MacPherson, read the Service. Quite unmoved by the heavy fire, much of it over our heads at the time, the Chaplain read the funeral service beautifully. It was quite the most impressive funeral I have ever seen or am ever likely to see—and quite the most appropriate to the gallant soldier and fine leader we were laying in his last resting place. I fancy all were much moved by the scene—as I was myself." ["The river is in flood and so far as I have heard Paardeberg Drift, the only one available, is unfordable: but Lord Kitchener, knowing your resourcefulness is sure you will get across somehow."]

Between Hamilton's death and burial Sir John called, so he says, at IInd Corps HQ at Bethune. Sir Horace explained that he held a front of eight miles with his left in the air, that he had suffered another thousand casualties in the last two days, that some battalions were at less than half their war establishment and, above all, that the very heavy losses in highly trained officers and NCOs were making themselves felt in reduced efficiency. Sir John appeared to grasp this but five years were to pass before he informed the world that "he [Smith-Dorrien] was in one of those fits of deep depression which unfortunately visited him frequently. He complained that the IInd Corps had never got over what he described as the shock of Le Cateau and that the officers sent out to him to replace his tremendous losses were untrained and inexperienced and lastly he expressed himself convinced that there was no great fighting spirit throughout the troops he commanded. Even if, as I consider, his point of view was needlessly pessimistic, Smith-Dorrien was certainly confronted with a difficult task." It is only possible to comment in the same terms as have been used about the insanely defamatory statements made on the subject of the Compiègne. Forestier-Walker, who of all men should have known Sir Horace, scouts the accusation, pointing out also that his HQ were not in any case at Bethune. He says flatly that "I, who must have seen more of the General at that time than anyone else and have had far better opportunity of seeing him in such moods, if he did indulge in them, do most emphatically assert that from first to last of my intimate relationship with him I never saw him him in a mood which could possibly be described as one of deep depression. Things were often pretty desperate in those days which were the worst I have experienced in this war, but Sir Horace was throughout wonderful in concealing the anxiety which at times it was impossible that he could not but feel, and I owe much to him for his example in this particular." The kindest conclusion to draw is that by the time this nonsense was written Sir John's mind, never well-balanced, had become unhinged. Sir Horace's realistic and, as it turned out, accurate appreciation of the situation conflicted with French's (or more probably Wilson's) own appreciation during one of his Sherman periods and therefore must by definition be wrong and probably cowardly too. There is no accounting for how a man in so high a position could behave thus, or how a man capable of such behaviour could have been placed in so high a position.

The next day General McKenzie took over the 3rd Division and four days later Fergusson went home on promotion being succeeded by General Morland. To add to his difficulties his DAQMG, Rycroft, was thrown by his horse and rolled on.

Casualties (roughly 9,000 in the retreat and another 3,000 on the Aisne already) were now considerable, every day bringing its losses with little to show for them though a slow advance continued, McKenzie soon winning his spurs by taking one loopholed village after another with his guns right forward among the infantry. The corps was wheeling slightly to the right, old captured Boer Pom-poms, issued as anti-aircraft guns, coming in very useful for clearing out villages, but the gap which this necessarily opened up on the left became more and more exposed. The French cavalry which should have filled it lost their way and a handful of 19th Hussars had to do what they could to close it. By the 19th the conclusion could no longer be avoided that the Germans had increased greatly in strength and that the attackers would soon become the attacked. The divisional commanders wisely began to entrench where they happened to find themselves, especially around La Bassée where a factory was incorporated in the works.

At about this time, the front being to some extent stabilized, came the first flight of trippers to the back areas, a Member of Parliament unaccountably metamorphosed into a staff colonel being found "inspecting" hospitals, and a number of influential ladies who were conscious of no vocation to nurse but who wanted a little excitement wandering around and wasting people's time. Sir Horace, inclined to be strait-laced where ladies were concerned, thoroughly disapproved and was not slow to say so.

On the 21st the German tidal wave came sweeping in. With his now well-known acuity of mind Sir John tells us that on the same day all his worst forebodings as to the enemy's strength were realized. "Intercepted wireless messages established the certainty that the comparatively small German force which on the night of the 18th we judged to be between Ostend and Menin was now reinforced by no less than four Corps . . . although I looked for a great addition to the enemy's numbers within a few days from the 18th, the strength they actually reached astounded me. This taken with the speed in which they appeared in the field came like a veritable bolt from the blue. . . . All hope of any immediate offensive had now to be abandoned. It was now simply up to us to hold on like grim death to our positions by hard, resolute fighting until relief in some shape should come." This is an abject confession of incompetence for apart from the obvious military probability that in such a stroke lay the best German hope of victory, the fall of Antwerp only seventy-five miles away was well known to have released large bodies of troops from the 15th October onwards. Sir John's own highly competent Chief of Intelligence, Macdonogh, and Murray had already warned him of this. Four Army Corps do not suddenly materialize like a shoal of herring and the blame for the disadvantageous conditions under which the BEF had to fight one of the decisive battles of history must lay squarely on the shoulders of the C-in-C.

Now the terrible decision had to be made. Either the Channel Ports must be risked or the danger of losing touch with the French to the south must be accepted or, to put it another way, he must choose between letting go with his left hand or with his right. He took the brave decision, what Fortescue calls "the one great thing [he] did during his period of command on the Western Front", and tightened the grip of his left hand, using Haig's newly-arrived Corps to cover the city. The cavalry were to fight on foot (as no other cavalry in the world could do) and Pulteney and Smith-Dorrien must hang on, forever if need be, without hope of relief.

The full weight of the attack fell on Haig. If the Ist Corps had been spared during the retreat, the events of the next fortnight would do more than even the honours, and how they shot the German Army to a standstill, and how Douglas Haig accompanied by his staff (all as immaculate and unperturbed as at an Aldershot field day) rode slowly down the shell-lashed Menin Road, is no part of this story. Even Sir John had another moment of Sherman when in reply to an urgent call for help he observed that his only reserves were the sentries at his gates and if need be he would lead them into the battle and the last of the English would die fighting. He would have been as good as his word for with all his grievous faults Sir John was no Falstaff. He was a courageous soldier. Amongst the attackers were a number of reserve divisions made up almost entirely of young students and the undergraduates from famous German universities—the sons of Haldane's Göttingen contemporaries. Under the German system of conscription they were allowed to do their service as *ein jahr freiwilligers*—one year volunteers— because it was reckoned that their above-average intelligence and education enabled them to assimilate their military lessons more swiftly than the ordinary recruit. There is some deep-seated quirk in the Teutonic tribal memory, going back perhaps to the lost legion's of Varus, that demands a regular blood-sacrifice of the nation's youth and which in our own day produced the odious but formidable Hitler *Jugend*. These young men, all of the best officer-material, were not sufficiently trained to manoeuvre but came on in mass formations under the inspiration of the purest patriotism. Here and there where the line was at its weakest they broke through by sheer weight of numbers but always a battalion was found from some sector under less pressure to move in and drive them out. They advanced shoulder to shoulder, singing as they came, and above the thunder and rattle astonished British soldiers could hear snatches of "Die Wacht Am Rhein", the battle song of 1870. They were cut down like grass as had been the regiments of young French recruits at Blenheim, and the men who should have been the company commanders of 1916, and possibly the battalion commanders of the last battles, bled out their lives on that fearful plain. To this day in Germany men speak of it as *Der Kindermord Von Ypern*, the Massacre of the Innocents.

Though they escaped the worst of it, Pulteney and Smith-Dorrien were by no means spared. Attack after attack was driven back, counter-attack after counter-attack was launched and all the while Sir Horace with such labour as he could muster was digging a new and more defensible line a couple of miles to the rear. On the 22nd, the Eve of the Feast of Crispian, Conneau's cavalry on his left gave way but mercifully the gain was not exploited and on the following night the corps retired to the new position. The weather was beautiful again. Sir John sent some help to his dog-tired men in the shape of Indian troops, elements of the Lahore Division recently landed at Marseilles, and a battery of 4·7 guns. Neuve Chapelle changed hands more than once before being abandoned as a shell-trap. On the 28th General Willcocks, commanding the Indian Corps, came to give the heartening news that help was on the way and the brave Conneau called to say "that every French soldier under his command would die in support of me should they be required to do so; he is a fine fellow." McKenzie was forced home with appendicitis on the 29th and Wing, the CRA who had shared his haystack on the Aisne, replaced him. The roar of the cannonade continued from Givenchy to Ypres but nowhere did the line break. Every man knew the stakes and though they had marched, fought, and dug for ten terrible weeks their discipline held and their musketry and gunnery never failed. Surely there was never an Army such as this.

On the 31st October, II Corps was relieved by the Indian Corps but still there was no rest. Many of II Corps' veterans had to return to the line to stiffen the inexperienced Indians, others were rushed north to help the cavalry at Messines, and the remaining battalions went still further north to fill the emptied ranks of I Corps. Though no longer under Sir Horace's command they were there at the crisis when von Fabeck, sixfold stronger in infantry, launched his all-out attack south of Ypres with the object of isolating Haig and then destroying him. Fabeck penetrated the British line in those places which for want of men lacked defenders, but never could he break through.

General Dubois, commanding the IXth Corps proved himself as true a friend as Conneau and never refused a call for help.

The 31st was the day of crisis. "The line that stood between the British Empire and ruin was composed of tired, haggard and unshaven men, unwashed, plastered with mud, many in little more than rags", the Official History says, the Army's answer to Mahan's "far-distant storm-beaten ships upon which the Grand Army never looked stood between it and the dominion of the world." The onslaught started at Messines where the 9th Lancers were almost wiped out. Here on Hallowe'en took place the charge of the London Scottish, the Territorial battalion affiliated to those same Gordon Highlanders lost at Le Cateau. In their kilts of hodden grey and with their old-fashioned long rifles they cleared the north of the village. Haldane's Territorials had drawn and shed their first blood—no entry appears in Henry Wilson's diary. The press rather over-did the publicity, but that was not the fault of the Scottish nor does it detract from their first feat of arms.

At Gheluvelt, on the Menin Road, the steadfast Queens were reduced to two officers and twelve men, the Loyal North Lancashires to one officer and fifteen men. Here at noon came the climax of the battle. The village passed to the Germans, there were no reserves of any kind left and the main road to Ypres was opened. The situation was saved, and possibly the battle also, by the irresistible charge of three companies of the Worcesters, men from the lovely Vale of Evesham who, under the command of Major Hankey took the bayonet to the German garrison and put them to flight, losing 100 men in the process. General Lomax, commanding the Ist Division was killed with six of his staff officers by a shell which struck his HQ at Hooge Château, a warning not to use buildings marked conspicuously on maps. At nightfall the 1st and 7th Divisions had lost three-quarters of their complement, but the worst was now over. The 7th, 9th, and 15th Brigades of II Corps were formed into a composite division under Wing and transferred to Haig's command, and a number of unbrigaded territorial battalions now moved into the line alongside their Regular brethren.

Attacks, though not of the same magnitude, continued from the

2nd to the 9th November, and the bombardment did not slacken. On the British side artillery ammunition was beginning to run low. On 11th November the last German wave crashed in, twelve divisions on a nine mile front from Messines to the British left north of the Menin Road with diversions all along the rest of the line from La Bassée to the sea. At 0900 after an artillery barrage of two and a half hours, twenty-five Prussian battalions—about 17,500 men—advanced down either side of the Menin Road. The Scots Guards, Black Watch, and Camerons—less than 800 rifles—the Duke of Wellington's Regiment, the Royal Fusiliers, the Northumberland Fusiliers, the Lincolns, the Oxfordshire and Buckinghamshire Light Infantry, and the ubiquitous RFA smashed them. North of the road, by Nonne Boschen, the attackers broke through to the very gun line and were cast back by the eighteen-pounders firing over open sights at point blank range. A captured German officer, being led past the reeking batteries, enquired what lay behind them. "Divisional Headquarters" he was told. "God Almighty," he replied with feeling. Though attacks continued for some days the battle was won and over. The Prussian Guard had measured swords with what had once been Aldershot Command and had been roundly beaten. In the course of the battle there appeared in the British line twenty-three names new amongst the old county regiments but well respected in the Territorial Force: the Honourable Artillery Company, the oldest military body in the land, with a legitimate pedigree going as far back as Henry VIII, the Artists Rifles, formed by a group of Victorian painters during the invasion scare of 1859, Queen Victoria's Rifles, the Queen's Westminsters and Hertfordshires, the men of the general's own county being prominent amongst them. They now had three solid months post-mobilization training behind them and, provided that they were initiated with some care, were in every way fit to take the field. They soon won golden opinions from everyone including the critical Huguet. A new near-regular division also arrived (the 8th, made up of troops released from garrison duty overseas). The Channel ports were now safe, both sides grievously hurt, and the Flemish winter with its icy Siberian winds was closing in. The Armies sank to the ground in whatever places the chances of the battle had forced upon them and began to put down their roots.

Sir Horace had no part in these great events for after handing over to Wilcocks on 31st October he had not a single unit under his command. After a couple of days pheasant-shooting around Hazebrouck he had a visit from Sir John who, with unusual affability, suggested that Sir Horace and his staff might like a few days' home leave. While the Old Harrovian doubtless remembered a tag beginning *Timeo Daneos* he jumped at the opportunity. He was fifty-six now and for ten endless weeks had carried an almost insupportable burden and he had never enjoyed perfect health. He makes no complaint in his diary of his neuralgia, but, deprived of sleep as he had been and enduring the strain of five major battles, it must have plagued him. He had a couple of days in London with his wife, reported to the King and to Kitchener, and was back in France by the 14th, collecting up his scattered command and taking over the sector in front of Kemmel Hill. On the day of the famous Christmas truce the BEF was re-organized into two full Armies, the First under Sir Douglas Haig and under Smith-Dorrien the Second consisting of his old corps now commanded by the experienced Fergusson, Pulteney's IIIrd Corps and, a little later on, a new Vth Corps under that splendid General, for all his Blimp-ish aspect, Sir Herbert Plumer. "His coming was a great joy to me for he was an old friend of mine and would be sure to be a delightful person to deal with: and this proved to be the case." There was no sort of animosity between Sir John's choice for Grierson's successor and his supplanter. The two generals thought similarly, had much in common, and each liked and respected the other. Plumer, too, had had experience of the baseness that can affect men holding high public office. In 1905 he had been Quartermaster General when Arnold Forster was Secretary of State for War and was known to share his views on certain aspects of the proposed re-organization of the regular Army reserve system. When the Conservative government was turned out of office after the general election a lying rumour was insinuated that he was wedded so closely to the out-going administration that he would not be as assiduous to his duties under its successors (who were of a different mind about the scheme). Haldane, without making any inquiry of Plumer, dismissed him from office and he was relegated to half-pay at a time when his son had just entered Eton and his two daughters were being educated in Paris. Lady Plumer observed with understandable bitterness that whereas she had to give her servants a month's notice, her husband had had less than a week's. He felt the blow terribly but behaved with the utmost restraint and dignity, as his friend was to do in the very near future.

A piece of typical malice towards Smith-Dorrien came in the translation of his excellent Chief-of-Staff, Forestier-Walker, who was summarily removed under the pretence that a new division at home was waiting for him to assume its command. On arrival in England he found this to be quite untrue and was kept kicking his heels for a month at the time when his services were urgently needed by the Second Army. His successor was Major-General George Milne, later to be with Franchet d'Esperey joint victor of the overlooked Salonika campaign, the first to break through the ring held by the central powers. This would have been Sir John's chance to rid himself of the depressed, despairing, delinquent of Le Cateau had he wished to take it. The fact that he did not is of itself eloquent. There were no operations worthy of the name for the next six weeks and everybody's attention was directed to improving the defences and making the trenches more or less habitable. The II Corps had by now incurred over 11,000 casualties in the Ypres battle and over 26,500 since the war began. The number of fallen officers was dreadful. The BEF had suffered losses at Ypres alone of 2,368 officers. The French do not distinguish losses between battles in quite the same way but theirs must have been comparable. No man knows exactly how many German troops were lost but the generally accepted figure is about 130,000.

Another branch of Sir Horace's family was represented by his nephew Eddy, the ADC of South African days, who was staff captain to the 9th Brigade at Kemmel. His contribution, most serviceable if undramatic, was to set up there a vast carpenter's shop turning out wooden troughs and tubs, cut in two and with a seat across them, which were sent to the trenches as fast as they could be made. Braziers too were collected up in large numbers in an attempt to keep men dry and in such pursuits was Sir Horace engaged from his HQ at Bailleul during the lull. He inspected every unit in his command and by common consent his visits were a heartening experience to his men who felt for him the respectful affection which their sons reserved for Alexander and Slim.

Sir John, meanwhile, was not without his troubles. On 1st November, during the climax of the battle a secret conference had taken place at Dunkirk, now safe behind the Belgian inundations. Sir John was for obvious reasons excused attendance and Kitchener, who had by now lost whatever shreds of confidence he had in French after the Paris meeting, was alone with Poincaré, Joffre, and Foch (Joffre's deputy in Flanders). What passed is uncertain but Wilson insisted that Kitchener had offered to replace French by Sir Ian Hamilton, at present commanding home forces. Foch is said to have repeated this to his crony Wilson who swiftly and untruthfully asserted that Hamilton was capable of the impossible feat of speaking less French than could Sir John. The Frenchmen, preferring the devil they knew, held themselves out as perfectly satisfied with the C-in-C but of course Wilson at once carried the story to his chief who exploded in paroxysms of grief and rage. He sent his ADC Captain F. E. Guest, to visit Asquith personally with the result that Kitchener in cabinet denied indignantly the whole story. Asquith, probably rightly, wrote it down to Wilson's innate talent for mischief-making and in concert with Kitchener blocked Wilson's promotion when Murray relinquished his appointment in January 1915. The fact remains that Wilson got the story from Foch, an honourable man with no vested interest, and Huguet asserts it dogmatically, so it must be that Kitchener had said *something*, even if it improved with transmission. Relations between the two Field Marshals, never cordial, were now abysmal and Sir John never again felt secure in his exalted post. But for Wilson's deception he might have been ousted then and the command placed in more capable hands; "might have been" are the saddest words in the language.

CHAPTER TWENTY-ONE

SIR HORACE now stood at the peak of his military career. Even his arch enemy had paid him these tributes in his Official Dispatches dated respectively 7th September and 8th October:

> I cannot close this brief account of this glorious stand of the British troops, without putting on record my deep appreciation of the valuable services rendered by General Sir Horace Smith-Dorrien. I say without hesitation that the saving of the left wing of the Army under my command on the morning of the 26th August could never have been accomplished unless a Commander of rare and unusual coolness intrepidity and determination had been present to personally conduct the operation . . . it is impossible for me to speak too highly of the skill evinced by the two Generals commanding Army Corps. . . . I further wish to bring forward the names of the following Officers who have rendered valuable services. General Sir Horace Smith-Dorrien and Lieut. General Sir Douglas Haig I have already mentioned in the present and former dispatches for particularly marked and distinguished service in critical situations—since the commencement of the campaign they have carried out all my orders and instructions with the utmost ability.

This is the official record, enshrined for all time in the archives of the Army and there will be found few, now or previously, who would wish to quarrel with it. From now on, however, nothing that Sir Horace could do would please his exigent chief. The French honoured Sir Horace as he deserved, for on 11th January in company with Haig he was decorated with the Grand Cross of the Legion of Honour, including a hairy kiss on both cheeks, by the President of the Republic in his tasteful campaigning kit of blue peaked cap, reefer jacket, shamefully ill-fitting blue breeches, and chauffeur's leggings.

In January, Murray succumbed to influenza and had to go home. He had been a good staff officer though quite incapable of standing up to the ugly rages of his chief. Spears recalls an occasion when he visited him in an hotel to find him poring over a map on the floor of his bedroom clad only in his underwear and periodically withdrawing from the war as the chambermaid popped in and out. Wilson was confident of succeeding to an assignment for which he felt himself ordained by providence but his treachery on the 1st November had cooked his goose with both Asquith and Kitchener. The post was offered to Wully Robertson who did not fancy it but felt it his duty to accept. This must have been particularly galling to Wilson who had for long been motoring around various headquarters usurping Murray's functions and behaving as if he were the master of the British Army. Wully's elephantine memory had not forgotten Wilson's attempt to twist him over the matter of the Staff College furniture and he was now in a position to get some of his own back. He was not a vengeful man but he would have been more than human and certainly untrue to his reputation if he neglected an opportunity to make the supreme object of his contempt and loathing realize his relatively lowly position. At least there was now a substantial buffer between Sir John and Sir Horace but it was not enough, for trouble now began in earnest. It started with the arrival of Plumer's Corps. One of his Divisions, the 27th, had been scraped up from garrisons in the Caribbean and Hong Kong who were sent after several miserable winter months in a wet, muddy tented camp near Winchester to St Eloi, the unhealthiest place on the entire western front where the trenches, just taken over from the French, were poorly constructed and water-logged and the Germans unusually pugnacious. The weather was vile and by mid-January over 1,000 men were in hospital. To add to their troubles they had been issued with boots so ill-made that the heels came off and the nails went through. Sir John, looking as always for someone he could blame, and furious because he could not now redeem his promise to Foch to take over more line, brutally put this inevitable consequence down to bad staff work by Second Army. Sir Horace wrote a placatory letter pointing out a few unpalatable truths and again Sir John erupted. On 10th March began the attack by I Corps on Neuve Chapelle where a great opportunity was lost by Sir John's inept disposition of his reserves. The Second Army's role was to mount an attack on Hill Seventy-five, opposite Mount Kemmel, to interdict the movement of German reserves to Haig's front. The attack was a costly failure because shortage of artillery shells reduced the preliminary bombardment to inadequacy and the German wire remained wholly undamaged. The Wiltshires and the Worcesters lost twenty-eight officers and 343 other ranks to no purpose. Sir John's rage fell upon the Army commander because the latter would not agree that the want of success was due to the lack of fighting spirit of his troops. Sir Horace wrote his wife on 13th March,

> My attack on Hill 75 failed—and Sir John is furious in consequence—not that that is unusual for he appears now to live in a state of unreasonable fury. I don't mind, but it would make things easier if one had not such a wild beast to deal with. 7 p.m. I have seen Sir John again and he had recovered his equilibrium. Fancy if every time an operation did not attain the success I hoped I was to rant and roar at my Generals. In this case I was just as disappointed as Sir J., but I sent a telegram to Generals and troops thanking them for their efforts and regretting the casualties.

Sir John's behaviour was now infamous: "If the Germans exploded a mine or captured a trench, or if a small local enterprise on one of my brigade fronts was not completely successful, it was all my fault and yet he would argue that I did not set my mind sufficiently on the higher duties of Command of an Army but worried too much about petty details and interfered too much with Corps Commanders.

I told him in reply that the role he had allotted to my Army was to spread out on a large front (about three times as long as the First Army) with a view to holding the enemy, thus leaving me only sufficient troops for small local reserves, but that my plans for a big offensive on any part of my front were all matured and could be put into execution whenever he gave me sufficient troops for the purpose. I invited him to give me a few concrete examples of my shortcomings so that I might rectify them but this he said he could not do as he was merely telling me his impressions. On one occasion because 'I had allowed the Germans to open a sudden burst of artillery fire' and follow it by an infantry attack at St. Eloi on the 14th March he personally abused me and my Army in no unmeasured terms and said he was considering whether it would be possible for us to complete the campaign together."

General Snow's view of this nonsense appears in a letter written to Sir Horace in 1921: "I was amused to read . . . that Sir John accused you of allowing the Germans to open that burst of fire on the 27th Division at St. Eloi on March 14th. I hate rows as much as anyone and quite understand your feelings when you say that you do not suppose that your defence will ever be published but I think the world ought some day to be told the truth, not to show that Sir J. is not telling the truth but as a matter of History."

On 7th April came another wound, for the IIIrd Corps was removed from his command save for administrative purposes. Sir John would show his obstreperous subordinate that only one man in the BEF matured plans for big offensives. Within his Army things were not so bad. Milne proved "a tower of strength" (he was to be a post-war CIGS), the South Midlands Territorial Division arrived and impressed him greatly and the 1st Canadian Division, including his old South African friends, the Royal Canadians, followed them. He now had an Army of nine divisions, the price for which was the taking over of five more miles of line from the French.

On 15th April he wrote in his diary of a new and hideous threat to the line. Prisoners taken by the French were speaking freely of batteries of enormous tubes of asphyxiating gas, sixteen of them to every forty metres, and one prisoner produced a wad of wool and a container of oxygen to be used for their own protection. All that was needed was a favourable wind. No 6 Squadron RFC was sent off to search for them but could find nothing suspicious and although the information was widely disseminated no precautions could be taken for lack of knowledge of the nature of the asphyxiant. To distract attention the Germans now turned their huge siege pieces on Ypres and began its systematic destruction. On 21st April the ancient Cloth Hall, the pride of many generations, disappeared in smoke and rubble. Next day the gas was poured onto the French six miles to the north, aircraft reporting that it looked as if the whole of their trenches were in flames. While Sir Horace was in Ypres a terrific bombardment opened both on the French and the Canadian left. Sir Horace told Plumer to try to restore the situation with the reserve Canadian brigade, the way to Ypres being now open and somehow the thing was done, a new front being made to face north between St Julien and the Canal. The French were in chaos, their Senegalese having run away clutching at their throats, and all their guns were abandoned. No effective counter-attack, the only remedy, was possible but during the 23rd a scratch force of several battalions under Colonel Geddes of The Buffs, de L'Isle's 1st Cavalry Division, and the 13th Brigade was flung together. The attack began in thick mist almost unsupported by artillery and made little progress though its spirit can be judged from its losses. Seventy-three officers and 2,346 other ranks. By a merciful dispensation of providence the Germans did not realize the extent of the damage they had done and confined their attack to the Canadians and 28th Division between St Julien and the Menin Road. The Canadians in four days fighting lost 200 officers and 5,000 other ranks but their stand was heroic and they yielded no ground. The beautiful memorial garden near St Julien reminds us of their courage. On 26th April the Allied attack was renewed by the Lahore Division and General Putz's French troops. The French made some headway before the gas was turned on, it falling this time on the Indian troops. The Indians suffered heavily but again the attack petered out. That evening Sir Horace wrote a long letter to Robertson summing up the position:

My dear Robertson,

In order to put the situation before the C-in-C I propose to enter into a certain amount of detail. You will remember I told Montgomery [General Staff, GHQ] the night before last, after seeing General Putz's orders, that as he was only putting in a small proportion of his troops (and those at different points) to the actual attack, I did not anticipate, any great results. You know what happened—the French right instead of gaining ground, lost it, and the left of the Lahore Division did the same, but the British regiment on the right of the Lahore Divison, the Manchesters, did very well and took some enemy trenches and held them for a considerable time.

The Northumberland Brigade to their right made a very fine attack on St. Julien and got into it, but were unable to remain there.

Away to the right between St. Julien and our old trenches there was a good deal of fighting, but with fairly satisfactory results, the Germans eventually retiring.

The enemy's losses are very heavy. Artillery observing officers claim to have mown them down over and over again during the day. At times the fighting appears to have been heavy and our casualties are by no means slight.

I enclose on a separate paper a description of the line our troops are on at this moment. I saw General Putz last night about to-day's operation and he told me he intended to resume the offensive with very great vigour. I saw his orders, in which he claimed to have captured Het Sas, but on my asking him what he meant he said the houses of that place which are to the West of the Canal. He told me also that the success at Lizerne had been practically nil—in fact the Germans were still in possession of the village, or were last night.

From General Putz's orders of to-day he is sending one Brigade to cross the river east of Brielen to carry forward the troops on the East of the Canal in the direction of Pilckem, and he assured me that this Brigade was going to be pushed with great vigour.

It was not till afterwards that I noticed that, to form his own reserve, he is withdrawing two battalions from the east of the Canal and another two battalions from the front line in the same spot, to be used as a reserve on the bank of the river, so the net result of his orders is to send over six fresh battalions to the fighting line and to withdraw four which had already been employed.

I have lately received General Joppé's orders. He is the General commanding the attack towards Pilckem on the East of the Canal, and I was horrified to see that he, instead of using the whole of this Brigade across the Canal for this offensive, is leaving one regiment back at Brielen, and only putting the other regiment across the Canal to attack—so the net result of these latter orders with regard to the strength of the troops on the east of the Canal for the fresh offensive is the net addition of one battalion.

I need hardly say that I at once represented the matter pretty strongly to General Putz, but I want the Chief to know this as I do not think he must expect that the French are going to do anything very great—in fact although I have ordered the Lahore Division to co-operate when the French attack at 1.15 p.m., I am pretty sure that our line to-night will not be in advance of where it is at the present moment.

I fear the Lahore Division have had heavy casualties and so, they tell me, have the Northumbrians, and I am doubtful whether it is worth losing any more men to regain this French ground unless the French do something really big.

Now, if you look at the map, you will find the line the French and ourselves are now on allows the Germans to approach so close with their guns that the area East of Ypres will be very difficult to hold, chiefly because the roads approaching it from the west are swept by shell-fire, and were all yesterday and are being to-day.

If the French are not going to make a big push, the only line we can hold permanently and have a fair chance of keeping supplied would be the GHQ line passing just East of Wieljie and Potijze, to join our present line about 1,000 yards North East of Hill 60.

This, of course, means the surrendering of a great deal of trench line, but any intermediate line, short of that, will be extremely difficult to hold, owing to the loss of the ridge to the East of Zonnebeke, which any withdrawal must entail.

I think it right to put these views before the Chief, but at the same time to make it clear that, although I am preparing for the worst, I do not think we have arrived at the time when it is necessary to adopt these measures. In any case, a withdrawal to that line in one fell swoop would be almost impossible, on account of the enormous amount of guns and paraphernalia which will have to be withdrawn first; and therefore if withdrawal becomes necessary it must start gradually from the left. I intend to-night, if nothing special happens, to re-organize the new front and to withdraw superfluous troops west of Ypres.

I always have to contemplate the possibility of the Germans gaining ground west of Lizerne, and this, of course, would make the situation more impossible—in fact, it all comes down to this, that unless the French do something really vigorous the situation might become such as to make it impossible for us to hold any line east of Ypres.

It is very difficult to put a subject such as this in a letter without appearing pessimistic—I am not in the least—but as an Army Commander I have, of course, to provide for every eventuality, and I think it right to let the Chief know what is running in my mind.

More British troops of course could restore the situation—but this I consider would be out of the question as it would interfere with a big offensive elsewhere which is after all the crux of the situation and will do more to relieve this situation than anything else.

Since writing above our cavalry report that the French actually took the whole of Lizerne last night capturing 120 Germans, and are now attacking the bridgehead covering the bridge leading over the Canal to Steenstraat. General Putz has answered my protest and has ordered General Joppé to put in the whole of the fresh brigade and not to leave one Regiment of it in reserve at Brielen. The attack is to commence at 1.15 p.m. and we are to assist with heavy artillery fire and the Lahore Division is only to advance if they see the French troops getting on. Our Cavalry is where it was last night, one Division west of Lizerne, one dismounted in reserve holding GHQ trenches east of Ypres, one dismounted in huts at Vlamertinghe. I am still at my advanced HQ in Poperinghe. Whether I remain here to-night again I do not know, my main advantage in being here is my close touch with General Putz and my being able to impress my views upon him.

This, on any view of the matter, is a thoroughly competent, professional assessment of some very hard facts. Only the good fortune that the Germans did not know of the utter havoc they had wrought amongst the French with the gas had saved the city. They were going to have no more massed infantry attacks and for them the artillery was going to resume its position as queen of the battlefield. Every counsel of common sense demanded that the Allies give up Ypres altogether, for a less defensible position than the Salient would be hard to devise. But Ypres was like Verdun, a name charged with sentiment and it must therefore not be given up, cost what it might. And it was not given up—but at what a cost.

Sir John on reading the letter took umbrage. He was angry enough to write in his diary on the 27th: "Smith-Dorrien has, since the commencement of these operations, failed to get a real grip of the situation. He has been very unwise and tactless in his dealings with General Putz. He has acted quite against the instructions I had given him (1) by sending the Cavalry into the area east of Ypres without any reason and (2) by arranging his attack in a manner independent of and in front of the French. His messages are all wordy and unintelligible. His pessimistic attitude has the worst effect on his commanders and their troops and to-day he wrote a letter to Robertson which was full of contradictions and altogether bewildering. I have therefore been obliged to take the command of and the direction of the Ypres operations out of his hands." We shall answer these accusations before recounting what Sir John did.

Sir Horace had issued no order to send cavalry east of Ypres. He had placed the 2nd Cavalry Division at Plumer's disposal and by him they were sent, dismounted, to occupy the GHQ Line. If Sir John had grasped the situation he would probably have approved but any stick which came to his hand would do if he could beat Sir Horace with it. The second charge is equally absurd for, as the letter shows, Sir Horace was in the closest possible touch with Putz who clearly needed watching. As to Sir John's accusation of pessimism hear what Ballard says:

> As one of Sir Horace's Brigadiers I have a right to protest emphatically against this statement. . . . I know what the Second Army thought of its Commander: he had won the confidence of all ranks chiefly because they trusted his sincerity and straightforwardness. Other Commanders had sought to encourage their men by promises of immediate and glorious success but when the results were not glorious faith began to grow weak. And after the process had been repeated more than once the troops came to the conclusion that senior officers at the rear knew nothing about what was going on. Sir Horace did not indulge in golden prophecies: he had sufficient strength of mind to look at a black situation without dismay; he made preparation for every possible change that might occur. And this was the frame of mind that he wanted to see in his subordinates. They regarded it not as pessimism but as foresight and far from having a bad effect it cheered them to know that their Army Commander realized what they were up against. The worst effect was caused not by the attitude of Sir Horace but by his removal. . . . [He] had been the Chief who helped and cheered everybody in the weary Retreat from Mons; he had spent the whole winter in trying to overcome the discomforts of his men; he was tireless in visiting troops; he knew most of the senior officers well and many of the juniors; he looked upon all ranks as his friends.

From the lower reaches of the commissioned ranks Major Corbett-Smith, a middle-aged special reservist who was also a member of the Bar, wrote a widely-read book giving a worm's-eye view of the retreat which he dedicated to a much-loved chief. The Official Historian himself, Brigadier-General J. E. Edmonds who had been at the time a staff officer with the 4th Division, took up the cudgels about "the altogether bewildering letter writing in the *Daily Telegraph* of 5th February 1931 that, "Those who are interested in the matter can judge for themselves whether the Field Marshal's entry is justified. I imagine that most of them

26 *The Victors of 1914: with Marshal Joffre at Oporto 1921.*

27 *The Man Who Won the War visits Gibraltar.*

28 The Old Harrovian and the New Harrovian

29 Early days of the British Legion, Nottingham 1922.

who read it will consider it a clear, complete and soldierly statement of the situation; as such it was thought worthy to be included in the History." Sir John must stand convicted on all counts.

His response to the letter was swift and brutal. At 1600 he sent to Sir Horace a Staff Officer with a paper saying "the Chief thought I was taking a pessimistic view of the situation", simultaneously dispatching Maurice direct to Plumer with orders to consolidate his present line and to prepare a position east of Ypres for occupation if and when a withdrawal became necessary. The following courteous telegram was sent in clear to Advanced and Permanent HQ of Second Army, repeated to Vth Corps: "Chief directs you to hand over forthwith to General Plumer the command of all troops engaged in the present operations around Ypres. You should lend General Plumer your Br.-General, General Staff and such other officers of the various Branches of your Staff as he may require. General Plumer should send all reports to GHQ from which he will receive his orders." As will have been realized, Sir John is now ordering Plumer to carry out the very thing which Sir Horace had suggested.

Sir Horace returned with a heavy heart to his Headquarters, shorn of all his staff, all authority except over a fragment of II Corps and, as he thought, discredited by his chief in the eyes of all who had seen or knew of the telegram. It was a villainous thing Sir John had done. Within a few days heavy fighting was going on around Hill Sixty but he was powerless to influence events and remained a spectator. His friend Plumer was shocked and indignant but could do no other than obey his orders. His diary entry for 30th April makes his feelings plain: "The position is very uncomfortable and is likely to remain so unless the French make a real effort. Things have not been made better by Sir John French slighting Sir Horace and taking all my force away from him and leaving me almost independent of him. It is the last thing I wanted. It is not fair because Smith-Dorrien and I were in absolute agreement as to what should be done. I am only doing exactly what I should have been doing had I remained under Smith-Dorrien. He feels it very much of course and came to me yesterday and we had a long talk." Second Army was in good hands.

On 6th May Smith-Dorrien was summoned to a meeting of Army Commanders at the C-in-C's house to discuss a forthcoming offensive by the First Army—the battle of Aubers Ridge. He then decided that "the only patriotic step for me to take was to sacrifice myself" and wrote this letter:

6th May 1915

My dear Field Marshal,

I have just received an order for Army Commanders to meet at your house at 9 a.m. tomorrow. I am still in ignorance of the action you intend to take regarding the papers, so important to me and the Army I command, I sent you on the 1st instant and it would make things easier for me were I to know your views before the meeting. Whatever may be the reason there can be no question that your attitude to me for some time past has been to show that you had, for some reason or other unknown to me, ceased to trust me.

Latterly I have been shorn first of one wing of my Army and then of the other, on the latter occasion the announcement being made in such a way and in such terms as to leave no doubt in the minds of many in the 2nd Army that their Commander was no longer believed in by their Chief.

My position as Army Commander has become impossible and I regard my remaining in command, with a cloud hanging over me ready to burst at any moment, as a positive danger to the cause for which we are fighting. Plenty of complicated situations have arisen in the last few months and the difficulty of dealing with them has been greatly enhanced by the knowledge that unless I was successful I and the 2nd Army would be blamed—in fact I have had more to fear from the rear than from the front.

We have got to win this war and to do so there must be no weak links in the chain. Your attitude to me constitutes a very seriously weak link and I feel sure that, trying as that attitude has been to me, you have not wished to carry it quite so far as to appoint someone else to command the 2nd Army in my place.

This step is, however, to my mind the only one that will strengthen up the chain again, and it is to render it more easy for you to take it without delay that I am writing this letter.

Please do not let any false considerations for me personally stand in the way, for the War Office will doubtless find some place for me where I can still do useful work towards helping our Army fighting in France.

The papers to which he refers to are set out *in extenso* in Appendix II.

The "wild beast" disdained to reply. At 1930 on the evening of 6th May Sir Horace received this official message addressed to him by name over the signature of Macready, the Adjutant General. "The C-in-C directs me to inform you that the Secretary of State for War wishes to see you and he requests that you will proceed to England to-morrow—7th May—Lieut. General Sir H. Plumer has been instructed to assume command of the II Army and informed that you will communicate direct with him as to when you leave for England. Kindly arrange this together with any information you may consider it necessary to give him. Please acknowledge receipt of this memo."

CHAPTER TWENTY-TWO

O<small>N</small> the 8th May Sir John was pleased to write to him in these terms:

My dear Smith-Dorrien,

The action I have taken has resulted from the firm conviction I have that you need rest after the terrible trial and strains to which you have been subjected since August last.

I write this short line to express the deep regret I feel personally and to ask you to accept my heartfelt gratitude for the help you have given me.

Yours always sincerely,
J. D. P. French

For the moment the wild beast was a tearful crocodile.

The end came in a manner which lowered the temperature from high tragedy to low comedy. Robertson, seeing that he would never prevail on his captious chief to alter his decision tried to persuade him that he should at least see Smith-Dorrien as Joffre had done with Lanrezac. As Sir John flatly refused this elementary courtesy Robertson went alone to see his old chief for whom he had lost none of his respect and affection to strike the blow with such gruff kindliness as he could muster. Colonel Lord Malise Graham, Fergusson's ADC, was present to bear witness to the scene which is part of the Army's folk lore. "We were standing talking somewhere in front of the Ypres salient, when Wully drove up in his car, pulled Smith-Dorrien aside and remarked, loud enough for us all to hear, "'Orace, you're for 'ome'."

And home he went. Everyone to whom Smith-Dorrien was a living man and not merely a name in a book (to say nothing of the many many who have heard it from their fathers) knows this anecdote. It was an incongruous end to the long fighting career of a Victorian general but the end it was. General Sir Horace Smith-Dorrien had fought his last battle. Immediately on his return to England Sir Horace presented himself to Kitchener "Who was surprised to see a robust individual as he had been informed from France that my health had broken down", and was also graciously received by the King. He made it his business to write swiftly to Kitchener explaining what he had done:

> Red Lion Hotel
> Henley-on-Thames.
> 14.5.15.

My dear Lord Kitchener,

I think on the whole I had better send you a copy of the ONLY communication I have had from Sir J. French—with reference to my resignation as it makes the memorandum I prepared for you on the subject quite complete. Sir J's letter was written after the memorandum and received by me in England on the 10th May.

It is evident from the tone of his letter that he imputes no blame to me, that his wish is to suppress the fact that I resigned, while implying that the campaign had affected my nerves and health so seriously as to make rest imperative. I conclude that the latter is the explanation he will allow to get about of my disappearance from the Field Army. Any comments on my part are unnecessary, for it is obvious that he cannot have chosen this course in my interests. Unfortunately, I am the only General in high command since the commencement of the Campaign who has not received public recognition from the hands of His Majesty— for instance Sir J. himself received an O.M., Haig was promoted etc. etc. and I am told that the conclusion then drawn was that French's glowing mention of me in his first dispatch was not accepted at its face value and as since then, whilst the Commander of the 1st Army has been constantly lauded whilst no reference has been made to myself, people are getting confirmed in the view that I am more or less a failure. Luckily, for my peace of mind, I know what HM and you think and that is all that concerns me.

He wrote too to Wully, who answered with commendable promptitude: "I certainly will do anything I can to prevent the spreading of rumours that you have broken down in health but I have never heard a whisper this side. Why should I? No one thinks so. It is a London yarn. I heard from there the other day you were in a nursing home."

His complaint that his services had not been marked may cause the raising of an eyebrow but Sir Horace is making no selfish claim. He was so closely identified with his Corps that he saw it as a lack of recognition of all they had done (for the British Army knows no form of collective decoration equivalent to the French Fourragère or the American Presidential Unit Citation). It is, however, difficult to see what could be done. The only promotion left was to Field Marshal which obviously was not practicable. If Smith-Dorrien had been given a step in his existing order, it could only be the order of St Michael and St George for he was already GCB, and it could be seen as preferring the victor of Le Cateau to the victor of First Ypres. The award of the Order of Merit to Sir John shows an imagination worthy of Caligula.

For Sir John himself it had been a near thing and since the Dunkirk conference on 1st November he knew well that he was on probation. Foch deals exactly with him, for he knew his man by now. When Huguet mentioned earlier that Sir John was displeased with him Foch replied "Bah! It is of no importance; you have only to tell him that he has just saved England; that will put him in a good humour again." When Huguet passed on the operative part of the message he received the perfectly serious if monumentally complacent answer "But, my dear fellow, I know it only too well. I knew it from the beginning."

Smith-Dorrien returned to England much cast down, not entirely on his own account, but because of his well-grounded apprehension as to what might become of the Army. His personal future was also a matter of concern for as we know he was far from being a rich man; the boys were growing up and before very long the school bills would be coming in from Harrow. Hamilton, formerly commanding in the UK, had now been packed off to the Dardanelles, relieving Sir John of his most formidable competitor and, apart from De Wet's re-appearance in German South West Africa where he was being rounded up by his old comrade Louis Botha, there was no other front which demanded the presence of a full General. One further blow awaited Sir Horace for he had been promised by Kitchener the revived office of Inspector-General in the UK (implicitly with the reversion of the chief command at home) at present held by his old friend Sir Leslie Rundle, at a salary of £4,000 a year. This would at least have taken care of his financial problems but the appointment was snatched from him by Asquith without any reason being given In fact, as we now know, Sir John French was being given one more chance, and Rundle was merely keeping the seat warm for him until after the battle of Loos, the mis-handling of which finally brought Sir John down. Quite apart from any personal considerations, it was a bad day for the Army when it was for so base a reason deprived of the services of its most experienced general. If the training of the New Armies had been confided to the man most fitted to give it, the ghastly casualty list of 1st July 1916 would have been greatly shortened. Sir Horace would never for one moment have permitted a situation in which men were taught to advance in long waves over open country, doing no more than present perfect targets for the waiting German machine gunners. Balfourier's poilus showed how with superior tactics far more could be gained at a much lower cost and Sir Horace would have been no less aware of the suicidal nature of the British methods. It was a crime against the Army that all his talents and recent experience were rejected and false doctrines were allowed to be preached by men who, militarily speaking, were not fit to black his boots.

From June to November 1915, while great battles were raging in France and in the Gallipoli peninsula, Smith-Dorrien commanded a so-called Army from the agreeable headquarters of

Caius College, Cambridge. "There was something peculiarly grand, silent and peaceful living in such beautiful surroundings, especially after the hideous noises of the past ten months and nothing could exceed the kindness and cordiality shown to us by Mr H. K. Anderson, the Master of Caius College and all the Dons and also by the Venerable Master of Trinity, Dr Montagu Butler, in whose house I had been a boy when at Harrow." There could have been no better place for meditation, and for the gradual healing of the unmerited hurt he had suffered. He was still only fifty-seven, quite young as generals went then, and still in hard condition. Surely in what was now plainly to be a long war there was work somewhere for him to do. While he was here he received his GCMG, much to his satisfaction.

The last chance came in November 1915 in the shape of an offer first from Bonar Law, the Colonial Secretary, and then from Asquith himself of the command of an expedition against German East Africa. Though privately disapproving of this dispersal of effort Smith-Dorrien accepted the chance. He encountered, however, the formidable obstacle of Kitchener who was having trouble in finding enough men, guns, and war material for French and also for Hamilton at Gallipoli. Not one man, gun or aeroplane would the great war lord detach from his slender store for this sideshow and although Sir Horace as a man had the greatest sympathy with the Secretary of State and kept his demands to an irreducible minimum, he got nowhere with him. In the end the matter was referred to the arbitration of Asquith himself and Sir Horace's demands were met. The bulk of the troops were to come from the Union of South Africa and he felt it essential to see what was being provided as no details were known in London as to their state of training, their numbers, arrangements for replacements and reinforcements, or, indeed, anything else. For this reason he insisted on going by way of the Cape to see things for himself (this was just as well for the P and O steamer *Persia* which had been set aside for his voyage to Mombasa was torpedoed soon after leaving Marseilles).

Before leaving London he had assimilated the available information the War Office had in its possession; von Lettow-Vorbeck, an outstanding commander, had repulsed a half-hearted attempt to take the port of Tanga with an infantry brigade from India and was now usefully reinforced by the crew of the cruiser *Königsberg*, sunk by monitors of the Royal Navy in the Rufiji River, with ten excellent 4·1 guns taken from the ship and equipped with land carriages made in the railway workshops. He was known to be occupying the strong Taveta position under Mount Kilimanjaro and Sir Horace was working on an enveloping plan in the Roberts's style. The troops already there were one British brigade, a brigade of the King's African Rifles, 9,000 Indian troops reputed to be in poor shape, eight fifteen-pounders, and two mountain guns. It was not much of a force with which to carry on a campaign in waterless country plagued by the Tsetse fly, but coming to its aid was another British Brigade, a South African brigade, a couple of Indian battalions and two of the old five inch cowguns plus twenty thirteen-pounders. On top of this Sir Horace was to have a command of 2,000 mounted Boers which he would have loved to lead. Von Lettow was said to have about 2,000 Europeans and 25,000 Askaris under his hand. Sir Horace planned to hold von Lettow in front until the rains were over (he knew more about African rains than most men) and then to move against Taveta from the west with the help of a column from the Belgian Congo and another from Rhodesia, the Royal Navy being charged with clearing the enemy shipping from Lake Tanganyika. As soon as all their forces were in play he would land at Dar-es-Salaam under the guns of the four cruisers he had extracted from Asquith and arrive like a bolt from the blue on Von Lettow's left, neatly rolling him up. He was absolutely insistent that the campaign should not open until everything was ready, diplomatically reminding Kitchener that this had been the way he conducted his own Nile campaign back in 1898. The plan was sound and imaginative, making full use of the two elements of surprise and economy of force. As he finished it, Murray, who had become CIGS, almost a sinecure in the shadow of Kitchener, gave place to the forceful Wully, whose relations with his political chief were to be of a very different kind. To his old friend Smith-Dorrien wrote a long letter deprecating the entire expedition but reminding him that there had already been quite enough failures. He refused flatly to start the campaign in March (as the War Office wished) insisting on the principle of "more haste, less speed". Events proved him to have been absolutely right.

Troubles, however, are said to come in threes and the third blow was about to fall. He sailed from Plymouth in the liner *Saxon* and was hardly out of sight of the Hoe when he was struck down by pneumonia. Such was the severity of his illness that Dr Stevens of the ship's staff and Dr Wollaston, a naval surgeon who happened to be on board despaired of his life. Thanks to their devoted attention, however, he saw Table Mountain again and in the kindlier climate of the Cape made good progress towards recovery. As soon as he began work again he suffered a relapse and underwent two lung operations at Groot Schuur Hospital. Again he recovered, fighting desperately by telegraph from his bed against the South African politicians' insistence that (for reasons of a non-military kind but which seemed good to them) the campaign be opened in March, before the rains came. This effort put paid to his last faint chance of taking command for his condition again deteriorated. To his bedside came his old enemies, though now affectionate friends—Louis Botha and Jan Smuts—together with a figure from the past "Doctor Jim" himself. But it was no good and Sir Horace sailed for home again. On the voyage he nearly met his death for yet another emergency operation had to be carried out, this time by a Mr Riviere who happened to be a fellow passenger and but for whom he would never have seen England again. Jan Smuts assumed his command and obedient to his political chiefs, made his attack during the rains with the results that everybody knows; Von Lettow was still in the field and very much operational when the Armistice came.

Sir Horace went home to Berkhampstead and hung up his sword. He did not like the England he found after his convalescence, though there was now less of the shameful persecution of all who by any stretch of a warped imagination might be thought to have some tenuous connection with the enemy. This had done mischief enough in forcing the resignation of the First Sea Lord, Prince Louis of Battenberg, because he had committed the mortal sin of being born with a German sounding name. Haldane also had been brought down in a spate of rumours of staggering ingenuity the maddest being that he was an illegitimate half-brother to the Kaiser and that he was secretly married to a German wife. Dachshunds could again walk openly in the streets without fear of insult and worse at the hands (or feet) of total strangers but the atmosphere was not that of a country dedicated to the determined prosecution of a war to the death. In 1916 there was no Dunkirk spirit amongst the factory workers for the trade unions were not ready to lay their hard-won privileges on the altar of sacrifice though many of their members had offered and given their lives. The low moral tone of London shocked the puritan in Sir Horace; he waged war against the authorities of the Alhambra theatre which packed in crowds to see George Robey, amongst them many women of doubtful morals. He assisted his wife in her work with the Hospital Bag Fund and the Blue Cross, both of which call for a word of explanation. The former was instigated by a Miss Scudamore-Smith, a nursing sister at a Casualty Clearing Station in France, who had written to Lady Smith-Dorrien to explain that when a man was admitted with wounds no provision was made for his personal belongings. If he were in a fit state to do it he might, if lucky, find an odd piece of paper into which he could put his letters, watch, pipe, knife, money, lighter, and other small things until he was moved. If he was unlucky or his wounds were so grievous as to render him unable to look after them in this way his possessions usually disappeared. In January 1915, while he was still commanding Second Army, Lady Smith-Dorrien wrote on the subject and asked him to consult his DDMS, Surgeon-General Porter, to see whether use could be made of the few hundred linen bags complete with strong double draw strings and labels which she and her friends had made. The result was a demand for 50,000 of them. An appeal for funds was successfully launched and dedicated ladies stitched all round the clock. Long before the 50,000 were finished the Director-General of Medical Services, that same Sir Alfred Keogh who had recruited the doctors for the Territorial Force, wrote to Lady Smith-Dorrien asking whether she and her friends could supply the entire British Army in all theatres. By Armistice day they had turned out just under six million bags, including fulfilling a standing order from the Red Cross of

50,000 a month. There were no less than 40,000 contributors, each carefully card indexed, from all over the empire, for dominion troops were of course included, and even many from the USA.

The Blue Cross—not to be confused with either the Red Cross or Green Cross (a particularly odious gas produced by German scientists)—was an organization to provide comforts for the vast numbers of animals pressed into service by Christian men to suffer in their cause. It provided sick lines for countless horses and mules, French as well as British, and the 18,000 *chiens de guerre* which carried out tasks varying from the useful, like rat-catching and guarding prisoners, to the bizarre like tracking down spies. The most important single task was the provision of baths and heated stables for horses suffering from mange. This seemed to have been overlooked by the Army veterinary authorities for mange was both prevalent and difficult to eradicate in that the only effective treatment was by total immersion in a bath of powerful chemicals. Lady Smith-Dorrien gave a lecture at that never failing source of money for patriotic causes, Guildhall, and £3,500 was subscribed at once. With it the bath was established at Meaux on the Marne and many thousands of animals which might otherwise have been cast out were cured and returned to duty.

The French Government showed its appreciation by the award to Lady Smith-Dorrien of the Gold Order of the Reconnaissance Française and the King bestowed on her the award of the DBE. While by no means unappreciative of the honour the recipient observed to her Sovereign, whom she knew well, that she had no wish to be addressed as Dame at the age of thirty-eight. The King, much amused, took the point and so things were arranged; until her death in 1951, the new Dame remained Lady Smith-Dorrien.

In these useful if unspectacular tasks was engaged the man who had a good claim to being Britain's finest general. While the east wind brought to the fields of Kent the distant thunder of the guns in Flanders and when on 7th June 1917 London shook to the explosion of the nineteen great mines at Messines Smith-Dorrien remained with time on his hands. At the end of 1915 his old enemy, the wild beast, at last got his quietus but Sir Horace did not rejoice. He was relieved that the Chief Command was now in the best possible hands but was disgusted by the downfall of his old friend Hamilton, the rancorous inquest of the Dardanelles Committee, and by the persecution of a fine but ill-served general by the sedentary Nicholson. He heard with shock of the end of his old Chief Lord Kitchener, choking to death in the icy waters of the North Sea when the cruiser *Hampshire* carrying him to Russia was sunk by a mine. Smith-Dorrien's name, even, was passing into oblivion as the long roll of battles in which he was not engaged mounted and as new men came into high command. For a brief moment, however, his name and the doings of his IInd Corps came into prominence again. As has been seen, Sir Horace had interested himself in raising the tone of public entertainment to which the fighting men were attracted when on leave. In this he found an unexpected ally, for the editor of the *Weekly Despatch* was exercising his mind on the same subject. In February 1917, he telephoned Sir Horace enquiring whether he had read an attack on his handling of II Corps at Le Cateau which had appeared in another paper. Sir Horace, over the telephone, replied to the editor's question as to where the truth lay. Sir Horace gave him a straightforward account of what had occurred, knowing that the facts would be presented in the paper but quite unconscious of the fact that the forthcoming article would be ascribed to him. It appeared, however, in the issue of 18th February 1917 under the heading "How The Old British Army Died. General Sir Horace Smith-Dorrien interviewed on the historic retreat from Mons." The account that follows is fair and factual, giving merited praise to his men enumerating them regiment by regiment and containing no criticism of anyone. There does, however, appear this passage: "Meanwhile I had received orders from Sir John French not to make a stand at Le Cateau but to continue retiring. These orders I could not see my way to obey, for I feared, with the men tired as they were, further retirement might end in a rout, and I also considered that to show our teeth was the only way of stopping the enemy. I therefore informed the Commander-in-Chief by telephone of my decision. I said that before I could retire I must fight and that in order to avoid defeat a hard blow must be dealt the Germans. In reply I was informed that I was risking a Sedan. I said I was prepared to take that risk and it was suggested to me that Sir John might be willing to come and take over the command. But I was anxious not to avoid the responsibility. I thought that if there was going to be a Sedan that, for the sake of the cause of the Allies, Sir John should be able to return to England and organize a New Army. Personally I had fears that there might be a Sedan but I could not see what other course I could take to save my force." The new Viscount had friends in Fleet Street for he had allied himself both with Repington and the Harmsworth press during his curious attempt to go behind Kitchener and the cabinet over what became known as the Shell Scandal. Whether he instigated it or whether he was guiltless will never be known but the reply was swift in coming and it was to the *Weekly Despatch* article (the publication of which as attributed to his own pen Sir Horace would never have permitted) that he assigns the violence and intemperance of the attacks made by Lord French, as we must now learn to call him, in *1914*.

Mr Lovat Fraser was a war correspondent, not a former soldier, but by no means a military ignoramus. Now he emerged from obscurity with an article entitled "Should General Smith-Dorrien have disobeyed Lord French's orders?" He begins, disarmingly enough, by describing himself as "a layman who makes no pretence of being a military expert" and he leans heavily on Mr Frederic Coleman, a splendid American who was amongst those members of the RAC who put themselves and their cars at the disposal of the Army at the outbreak of War and did most valuable work with it. In an effort to play down the exhaustion of the corps at nightfall on 25th August, Mr Lovat Fraser extracts this quotation: "The Second Army Corps was well in place by evening. Some of the brigades were in the towns, some in camp by the fields, the rest going into position along the roads as fast as they arrived. The first battalions were divided into working parties, and while the trenches were being dug kettles were singing merrily over roadside fires." There is no need to call in question Mr Coleman's sincerity, for General Ballard agrees that the description could be that of his own leading battalion which was the first to arrive. General Snow, however, puts it more pithily. "Lovat Frazer's balderdash made me very angry with his "Kettles singing merrily over roadside fires." I do not think any of my division got anything to eat except what they had in their haversacks from the time they left Briastre about 8 p.m. on the 25th until their arrival at about 11 p.m. on the 26th at their halting place near Epehy." Lovat Fraser warms to his works, inferring that the 4th Division had no business to be tired at all "It had advanced northward very early on the 25th to cover the retreat of the Second Corps but was back on its battle position in good time on that day." To score a quick point he says that "General Smith-Dorrien appears to imply that he assumed control of the 4th Division without orders in an emergency. This is obviously not the case. Lord French's despatch says 'The 4th Division was placed under the command of the GOC IInd Army Corps. Why General Smith-Dorrien is so constantly anxious to reveal himself as acting without orders, or in violation of orders, passes the lay understanding'." We have already seen what happened. Snow, who certainly had no such orders, contents himself with saying "All I remember is that about 9 a.m. on the 26th Edmonds saying 'We are now under Smith-Dorrien' and I said, 'Naturally'." This particularly lay understanding might have been relieved of some errors by a reading of Field Service Regulations. Like Lord French, Mr Lovat Fraser magnifies the casualties and permits himself the comment, "I have still to learn of any soldier of eminence who approves of General Smith-Dorrien's decision to give battle at Le Cateau or his strange repudiation of the behests of his Commander-in-Chief." Of course in 1917 one "soldier of eminence" named Alexander von Kluck was not available for comment. So the dismal farrago goes on. The German failure to pursue was due to "the fierce attacks of General Sordet's cavalry" but Sordet never attacked anybody at all. His contribution, valuable though it was, consisted entirely of artillery fire and he certainly never made any other claim. Mr Coleman continues, though Lovat Fraser found it unnecessary to quote these paragraphs: "Standing near the bridge close to the station I saw General Smith-

Dorrien a few feet distant. He turned to a passing officer. I hardly remember his words. Something like plenty more of the same command being down the road a bit, I think. It was good to see Smith-Dorrien's face and hear his voice. I had heard much of him during those days and never was he spoken of save in terms of affection. As he looked at me he smiled, with the sort of smile that everyone within range takes to himself as his own property. It was of inestimable value that morning in St Quentin—Smith-Dorrien's smile. It put heart into many a man." Sir Horace did not deign to reply: he preferred as, he says, the dignity of silence and the verdict of History. However, some of the mud must have stuck for while amongst those competent to form an opinion there were few, if any, dissidents, Lloyd George, now firmly in the Prime Minister's chair, held most generals in contempt, his particular hatred being, as everyone knows, for Haig. The acuity of his assessment of their professional abilities can be judged from a passage in a Foreword he wrote many years later to a biography of Lord French written by Sir John's eldest son: "I knew Lord French well. I valued him highly as a soldier and an administrator. I frequently sought his advice and esteemed his council [sic]. In my judgment he was a bigger man than his successor. Lord Haig had many admirable qualities. He was efficient, courageous, and within the measure of his abilities a thoroughly competent General. But he had not that breadth and instinct or military vision which Lord French possessed." So, by definition, any subordinate who had found himself under the necessity of disagreeing with Sir John must have fallen into error if not something worse and obloquy should be his portion. His was the advice upon which the Sovereign must constitutionally act in the bestowal or withholding of honours and so in the golden shower which eventually descended on the victorious leaders, Sir Horace remained in the dry. There can be little doubt that Lloyd George had read the article which reinforced his existing opinion and some years were to pass before his singular attitude to the principles governing the gifts of Royal approbation were to become known in the wake of scandals which led to a change in the law. The King's private feelings will naturally never be known but it is

30 Colonel of the Sherwood Foresters.

31 Lieutenant Grenville Smith-Dorrien, K.R.R.C.

licit to suppose that so pointed a neglect would not have represented his wishes.

Like Cincinnatus, he watched the war go on, seeing his old jockey Hubert Gough take the same, sad road after the March Retreat of 1918. Money was becoming a serious problem for school bills were now beginning to make themselves felt, were soon going to get worse and he could see no prospect of further employment at sixty. He worked hard at the Hospital Bag Fund and the Blue Cross but it brought in not a penny and served only to keep him occupied. However, he was not entirely forgotten and in September 1918, with the last phase of open warfare beginning, he was delighted with the offer of the Governorship of Gibraltar.

CHAPTER TWENTY-THREE

THOUGH he had not been there for years, he knew the Rock well and he was about to enter into one of his happiest duties. The family loved it, the talents of Lady Smith-Dorrien and himself for both entertaining and gardening had every possible scope. He started, characteristically, by forming an elected City Council to replace the previous autocratic rule, by closing some of the lower grade brothels, and by building a squash court. Out again with the Calpe hounds with memories of those fine gallops back in the eighties, racing again after a lapse of years and swimming with the children were balm to his soul. His old friend Fortescue was a frequent visitor, observing with affectionate severity that "I never saw a house with fewer books than Government House. Anyone would have thought that he gave no thought to anything but games and racing." Anyone but Fortescue, that is; he knew him better than that. Sir Horace knew a great deal about the Rock and its history and took Fortescue to see two tombs there which were threatened with destruction. "He rejoiced when I told him that one of them was probably that of Sir Robert Boyd, Elliott's second in command, who had wished to be buried in the King's Bastion." No one could have dreamed that this cheerful and genial man, so youthful in manners and appearance was a man with a grievance, a very real grievance such as would have soured the hearts and embittered the lives of nine men out of ten. Littleness was not to be found in Horace Smith-Dorrien.

The war ended. Honours and rewards were deservedly heaped

on the leaders, peerages, parliamentary grants of money, freedoms of cities. Sir John when created a peer in 1915 after his dismissal had taken the title Viscount French of Ypres. Of this Huguet says, "Bowing to the surprise caused by such pretension, even in England, he discontinued it for some time. But when, after the war he was made with Sir Douglas Haig, an Earl, he resumed the title he felt he had so well earned and was henceforward known as Field Marshal the Earl of Ypres." Plumer, the warden of the Salient for three long years, had to be content with the Viscounty of Messines. Sir Horace received nothing. In the Victory Parade he was not present: the French at least remembered to invite Joffre (because Foch chivalrously refused to take part without the old chief riding at his side) who rode in his ungainly way along the Champs Elysée, still in his 1914 dark blue uniform—no *bleu d'horizon* for "Le Grandpère". Too much blood had been spilt, too many telegrams delivered since 1914 for many to remember those early days. Unperturbed, Sir Horace cultivated his garden. He was getting to be rather good at it.

The Smith-Dorriens entertained vastly. The Prince of Wales on his world tour, the Crown Prince of Japan, who conferred on him a rather flashy-looking decoration, the Crown Prince of Denmark, and the wonderful old Empress Eugenie. As the beautiful Eugenie de Montijo, the Empress had become the affianced wife of the future Emperor Napoleon III while a guest at the same palace of Compiègne which Sir Horace had last seen festooned with wire as the RE hammered away in the galleries to provide the communications for Sir John's GHQ. As a young Empress she had seen St Arnauds's army off to the Crimea, and from the Tuileries she had fled from the mob in disguise under the protection of an American dentist to be spirited away from Cherbourg in the yacht of Sir John Burgoyne through a terrible Channel gale knowing nothing of the fate of her husband after Sedan. It was 1920 and she was coming home at last to die. Colonel Willoughby Verner, a great naturalist and authority on birds of prey with whom Sir Horace, his wife, and the two elder boys had been on some hair-raising expeditions after an eagle's nest (Lady Smith-Dorrien and Gren had both insisted on following his example by being lowered over the edge of a sheer cliff 200 feet high on the end of a rope held by the apprehensive Sir Horace, to get a better look at it) was waiting to recieve her. He had been on calling terms with her for twenty-five years but had only got to know her well during the war when a wing of Farnborough Hill had been turned into a hospital for officers. "She would discuss matters," he said, "some of them of the highest importance—with a first-class knowledge of the facts and with incisiveness and brilliance." As they motored through the spring weather she refused dark glasses saying "The sun of Andalusia is my friend" and talking delightedly of the *romero*, the wild rosemary of Spain, and of her joy at feeling again the beauty, warmth, and wildness of the land from which she had been so long an exile. The meeting with Sir Horace, white of hair and moustache now, but still the young subaltern who had brought the news of the death of her son, brought back the tears, her biographer tells us. The next day her nephew, the Duke of Alba, came to drive her to Madrid. "No young girl," said Verner, "could have shown more vivacity and charm than the Empress as she bade us farewell." As a girl she was a devotee of the bullring, an *aficionada en extrema* who wrote with starry eyes to her sister Paca from Seville that she had actually met and talked to the famous Andalusian *torero*, Jose Redondo, universally worshipped as El Chiclanero. What a pity that O'Hara, the Matador Ingles, came a little too late for her to have seen him, though no doubt Sir Horace told her all about him. She had of course known Bazaine and his pretty little Mexican wife, Pepita, had been hostess to Queen Victoria during her State visit in 1855 and was well acquainted with the son of Marie Walewska. Sir Horace found her "sparkling with wit", largely at the expense of what she called "the undressed modern young woman", her mind having been stirred by the sight of many of her young Spanish relations, who had come on board to see her with low necks, short sleeves, and shorter skirts. "In the middle of her scathing criticisms it suddenly dawned on her that she had not noticed my wife's clothes and that she might be wearing offending garments, and she stopped and, scrutinizing her closely through her glasses, explained what had struck her, remarking that 'she need have had no qualms'." Certainly the carefully preserved photographs exhibit nothing but the utmost decorum. When the Princess died in Madrid four months later an era ended.

One visitor ceased to be invited to Government House when Lady Smith-Dorrien discovered that she was covering her expenses (and better) by buying cheap tea-gowns in London and selling them to local ladies at enhanced prices. But of course the best fun of all was provided by the Royal Navy. In the days when we had a great fleet, Gibraltar was an invariable source of hospitality to ship after ship. The mischievous boy of the 1870s always had a soft spot for the young and many were the parties organized by and for the Governor's young people; naturally this brings one to the story of the monkey. Remember that the Smith-Dorriens had adopted the two Power-Palmer girls. One of them owned a monkey. In his study Sir Horace always kept a camp bed to which it was his habit to retire on occasions when he was working late in order not to disturb the household. One day on entering the room he found it in chaos. The floor was strewn with torn letters and papers, pens, pencils, sealing wax, red tape, and matches. He not unnaturally exploded with rage and cursed the monkey in a voice which could be heard all over the house, not sparing the monkey's owner who ran downstairs trembling to see what had happened. "She gazed round the devastated room until her eyes reached the camp bed where they stopped spellbound. There lay the monkey, his whiskers stained blue-black lying between the sheets his head buried in the pillow, fast asleep. On the bed itself lay the empty ink bottle surrounded by a huge stain of drying ink. Clasped in the monkey's right paw was Horace's own particular bottle of aspirin the contents of which had been consumed to the very last tablet. Horace's eyes followed the girl's to the bed and she quaked before the outburst she feared must inevitably come. He was quivering but speechless and in a moment collapsed in uncontrollable laughter. The monkey was banished. Sir John, who was having a thoroughly disagreeable time as Viceroy of Ireland, would have had it court-martialled. There came too a most welcome visitor from the past, his old friend, jockey, and companion in misfortune, Hubert Gough, on his way back from an improbable civilian assignment to the Russian Black Sea port of Baku, where he had been sent to carry out an inspection on behalf of the share-holders in the Waterworks Company of that unrewarding place. The two generals must have had a lot to say to each other for they had not met for years and Gough would have been eloquent on the subject of the iniquities of the CIGS, Henry Wilson, at whose door he firmly laid the blame for all the injustices he had suffered.

As at Quetta and at Aldershot, Sir Horace left Gibraltar a pleasanter place than he found it. More playing fields, the abrogation of the rule going back to the 18th century which forbade games on Sundays, and the introduction of the game of football to the civil population were amongst his benefactions. In return a road was re-named in his honour. In 1921 he had a week in Lisbon after the ceremonial burial of no less than two Portuguese Unknown Warriors, a time of national rejoicing once the obsequies were over. To his delight Joffre, for some years now a Marshal of France, was there representing the French Army. They spent most of the week together and "we had some most interesting talks, when he told me of the difficulties he had had in the 1914 retreat. I can't repeat what he told me—I wish I could for it would clear up many doudy points." How one wishes to have been a fly on the wall. They were both made Doctors of Science of the University of Coimbra; did anyone remember that it was the students of that ancient seat of learning who of their own initiative seized the old fort at the mouth of the Mondego river in August 1808, to make the landing of Sir Arthur Wellesley's troops possible? It is a matter of great regret that amongst the many photographs still extant of the two old soldiers during their mild spree, none seems to exist of 'Le Grandpère' in blue silk hood and cap. The famous Port firm of Graham & Co. set aside three *tonels* (each holds 20,000 bottles) to be christened by the three warriors, for General Diaz was there on behalf of the Italian Army. Sad to relate the three gentlemen had retired to bed only a few hours before the christening ceremony was to take place and only Sir Horace was equal to the feat of rising in time. The firm gave him a handsome reward in the form of several dozen of their admirable beverage.

His time was now nearly up and in September 1923 the five year tour came to an end and with it Sir Horace's life in the public service. He had been in the Army for forty-seven and three quarter years, half of the time as a General officer. He ends his own book with the words "having had far more good luck in it [the Army] than I deserved." This represented, in spite of all the sad events recounted, his true feelings for mock-modesty and humbug were unknown to him.

Now the question of ways and means pressed very hard for he had virtually nothing beyond his retired pay; to maintain a family of seven in the style which would be expected of him at home was simply out of the question. He had for years had a liking for living in the sun which after all his lung operations was almost a necessity. So he bought a house at Biarritz, when he had taken his last farewell of the dying King Edward, and moved his furniture into it. He then bought another house in Biarritz but abruptly sold them both. (Almost certainly at a loss, his son David observes.) His reasons for doing this are now lost but in the end he decided to settle in Dinard where in the 1920s there was a noticeable population of retired British officers eking out their inadequate pensions and unable to live, for purely financial reasons, in the land they had fought to save. There he bought a charming house called Les Bocages with a large garden which was a source of great joy to him. He kept his friendships in repair, regularly attending the reunion dinners of one kind and another that came the way of all officers of long service and being a conscientious Colonel of the Regiment to his Foresters.

In 1919 there appeared in print Lord French's *magnum opus* which he called *1914*. Many people, including that doyen of military historians Sir John Fortescue turned eagerly to it in the hope of learning the truth of many arcane things. Men recoiled on reading it for it made no pretence to being a work of history but consisted almost entirely of an attack on Smith-Dorrien of such malevolence as to pose seriously the question of its author's sanity. Sir Horace was now in a very difficult position. His standing in the eyes of the Army and of those who had recently left it was unassailable, but there were many to whom the truth was not known. The Official History was unlikely to see the light of day for a long time and with every passing year the number of those who realized the contents of French's book to be pelting nonsense would grow less. Could he, for the sake of his own honour and that of II Corps allow his defence to go by default? One did not need to be a lawyer to realize that here was an indefensible libel and that if Sir Horace were to sue, the damages must be very large indeed—and money was still a pressing matter to him. There is no reason to think that he ever gave a second thought to such a course though there must have been those who would have urged it on him. To him it would have been unthinkable that two very senior officers should go to law, publicly wash the Army's linen, and leave the decision to a jury of a dozen civilians. He did the next best thing and applied, still being on the Active List, to the Army Council for permission to publish his own defence. The Army Council, new Pharaohs who knew not Joseph, were not anxious for more adverse publicity. In the immediate post-war world the tide was running against generals; the myth that all the men who had commanded the great armies which in the end had broken the armed might of Germany and her Allies were in reality homicidal imbeciles was being sedulously propagated. The boat, unsteady enough, needed no more rocking and the most the Army Council would permit was that Sir Horace should prepare and submit his own statement to be published only after a long lapse of time. It is a scrupulously fair and accurate document, and naturally is much quoted in this book. Sir Horace wrote copious letters to those officers who had personal knowledge of the truth and who could authoritatively deny some of the statements and actions attributed to him; Allenby, Murray, Snow, Forestier-Walker, and Vaughan with one voice scouted the charges of depression and despair. In the meantime a number of private accounts of the early battles had appeared in print, amongst them Sir Henry Newbolt's, *Tales of the Great War* (the accuracy of which Sir Horace approved, though he considered himself over-praised), Corbett-Smith's, *Retreat from Mons* and Major A. F. Becke's *The Royal Artillery at Le Cateau*; all give the fullest credit to the General in command. If Sir Horace had brought an action for defamation (and there were those who urged such a course on him) it is hard to see how the Earl of Ypres could have shown his face in public again. Within a few years all those chiefly concerned were dead, including Wilson who, as CIGS, had refused any enquiry both to Sir Horace and to Hubert Gough (who places the blame for his own downfall squarely on the shoulders of Wilson—this man whom General Spears has described to the author as "the evil genius of the Army"). An enquiry into the actions of 1914 might not have been to Wilson's taste for there was much of his own part in the matter that would have had to be called in question.

Sir Horace did live to see his vindication in the Official History (edited by that same Edmonds who had been on General Snow's staff during the battle) but not to know that when it was re-fought as an exercise in 1933 his action received the stamp of official approval. The saddest thing is that if he had lived for only another six months he would almost certainly have been promoted to fill a vacancy in the rank of Field Marshal. This he would have cherished above Earldoms for it would have been the outward visible sign of his Sovereign's approval and confidence as was Gough's belated GBE in 1937. No officer or man who served under him in those grim days thought of him but as a cheerful, practical and utterly unshakeable commander, a view which was shared by Generals von Kluck and von Fabeck.

His career of nearly half a century links the older Army and the new. As a young man he had served under Evelyn Wood (who in his own youth during the Crimean War was commanded by men who had known Wellington). In his maturity there served in the same Army in France a young Guards officer named Gort who in the fulness of time was to undergo trials not so very dissimilar and with equal lack of appreciation. He had been, at Isandhlwana, with the last Army to fight in red coats, carrying their colours as at Blenheim, and he had known of the first battles fought by the tank.

If one must search for comparisons in the rich store of British military commanders it is to Sir John Moore whom he bears the greatest likeness. Each saw action in every grade of commissioned rank, each was upright, honourable and greatly loved; each found himself unexpectedly engaged in a terrible retreat facing impossible odds and snapped fiercely back at his pursuers when all experience showed this to be impossible. For the benefit of his sons he spent much time on his own apologia, published in 1925 under the name of *Memories of Forty Eight Years Service*. It must ruefully be admitted that the book is rather heavy going. Sir Horace had no gift for words but writes a simple straightforward account of his doings over this long period, sometimes prolix and at others excessively curt (part of the reason also is that Lady Smith-Dorrien was heavy-handed with her blue pencil over the original draft and the laudable intention of sparing the feelings of living people and the relatives of those recently dead has robbed the book of much of the greatest interest).

In 1919, only a matter of months after he had taken up his appointment at Gibraltar, the old wound so nearly healed, was re-opened by the publication of Lord French's book *1914*. The two men had not met since Sir Horace's resignation and at the time the book came out French was heavily involved in troubles with the Sinn Feiners. It is reasonable to assume that he composed it during the latter years of the War when his military employment must have left him with time on his hands and although his feud with Haig was far more recent it was upon the unfortunate Smith-Dorrien and all his works that the vials of his wrath were poured. It is not necessary to quote extensively from this lamentable work, riddled as it is with inaccuracies and now and then plain falsehoods. Many men shared the feelings of Sir John Fortescue who, buying a copy in quest of enlightenment, put it down with horror concluding that the author must have taken leave of his senses. Lord French, whose last public utterance on the subject of the battle of Le Cateau had been the official dispatches in which he paid a well-deserved tribute to the victor, seemed to have come to the conclusion on mature consideration that everything that had gone wrong was the fault of one man and the entire work is devoted not to a factual account of the campaign for the benefit of those who would come after but to a deliberate vilification of the Commander of II Corps. To any reader with some knowledge of the course of the campaign, and in 1919 these were legion, it must have been apparent that the book contains lie upon lie.

In 1925 Sir John French died at Deal Castle. Sir Horace, at something more than mere personal inconvenience, hurried across France to be one of his pall bearers. Sir John's son in his biography of his father expresses appreciation of this act of magnanimity but Sir Horace probably did not see it in that light at all. It was a parade and death pays all scores. Three years later Haig died also, and in 1930 on 12th August, death came unexpectedly to Sir Horace. On a brief visit from Dinard, staying with friends in Wiltshire, he was a passenger in their motor car which emerging from a side road became involved in a collision. He received severe injuries and died in hospital the same day. At the service, again at St Peters, Eaton Square, his pall bearers were Sir Bruce Hamilton, former Brigadier of 21 Brigade in South Africa, Sir Charles Fergusson, Sir Walter Cowan (whom we last met so long ago at Fashoda) and Sir Robert Whigham, once a Company Commander in his XIIIth Sudanese at Omdurman. *The Times* accorded him an obituary of two and one half columns quoting the Official Historian likening him to Ulysses Grant and Von Kuhl (Von Kluck's Chief-of-Staff) who observed in an obvious context "One Corps stands to fight, the other marches away. Where was GHQ that day?" They buried him at Berkhampstead where he had been born 72 years before and where he had so often returned in triumph. At Dinard they held a memorial service with the Maire suitably engirthed with his tricoleur sash of office.

Fortescue imagines him being welcomed in another life by Moore and Abercrombie. Is it too fanciful to imagine that in some celestial mess he was dined in, a worthy new member, by John, First Duke of Marlborough, Arthur, First Duke of Wellington, Douglas, First Earl Haig, with Cadogan, Ligonier, Heathfield, Hill, and his old Chiefs Roberts and Kitchener waiting to welcome him?

APPENDIX I

Text of letter from Lieut. H. L. Smith-Dorrien to his father after Isandhlwana.

25th January 1879.

Rorke's Drift,
Buffalo River.
January 25

Since I wrote the first part of my letter a dreadful disaster has happened to us. It seems to me a pure miracle that I am alive to tell you about it. On the 21st January an order came to me, then stationed at Rorke's Drift, to go out to advanced camp to escort a convoy of twenty-five waggons from there to Rorke's Drift and bring them back loaded with supplies. Accordingly I slept in camp. At about 3 a.m. on the morning of the 22nd the General sent for me and told me not to take the wagons, but to convey a dispatch to Colonel Durnford, who was at Rorke's Drift with about 500 mounted black fellows, as a battle was expected. He (Colonel Durnford) accordingly started off with his men to join the camp. I did not return with him, but came out an hour afterwards by myself. When I arrived in camp I found the greater part of the column gone out with the General to meet the Zulu force, so that there was really only a caretaking force left in the camp—viz. five companies of the 1st Battalion of the 24th, two guns, about 600 Native Contingent, and a few servants looking after the tents; the Army Hospital Corps (thirteen men), and the sick in the hospital tents. The first Zulu force appeared about six o'clock in the morning. Two companies of the 24th were sent out after them. The Zulus seemed to retire and there was firing kept up at long ranges. At about 10.30 the Zulus were seen coming over the hills in thousands. They were in most perfect order, and seemed to be in about twenty rows of skirmishers one behind the other. They were in a semi-circle round our two flanks and in front of us and must have covered several miles of ground. Nobody knows how many there were of them, but the general idea is at least 20,000. Well, to cut the account short, in half an hour they were right up to the camp. I was out with the front companies of the 24th handing them spare ammunition. Bullets were flying all over the place, but I never seemed to notice them. The Zulus nearly all had firearms of some kind and lots of ammunition. Before we knew where we were they came right into the camp, assegaing everybody right and left. Everybody then who had a horse turned to fly. The enemy were going at a kind of very fast half-walk and half-run. On looking round we saw that we were completely surrounded and that the road to Rorke's Drift was cut off. The place where they seemed thinnest was where we all made for. Everybody went pell-mell over ground covered with huge boulders and rocks until we got to a deep spruit or gulley. How the horses got over I have no idea. I was riding a broken-kneed old crock which did not belong to me, and which I expected to go on its head every minute. We had to go bang through them at the spruit. Lots of our men were killed there. I had lots of marvellous escapes, and was firing away at them with my revolver as I galloped along. The ground there down to the river was so broken that the Zulus went as fast as the horses, and kept killing all the way. There were very few white men; they were nearly all mounted niggers of ours flying. This lasted till we came to a kind of precipice down to the River Buffalo. I jumped off and led my horse down. There was a poor fellow of the mounted infantry (a private) struck through the arm, who said as I passed that if I could bind up his arm and stop the bleeding he would be all right. I accordingly took out my handkerchief and tied up his arm. Just as I had done it, Major Smith of the Artillery came down by me wounded, saying "for God's sake, get on, man; the Zulus are on top of us." I had done all I could for the wounded man and so turned to jump on my horse. Just as I was doing so the horse went with a bound to the bottom of the precipice, being struck with an assegai. I gave up all hope, as the Zulus were all round me, finishing off the wounded, the man I had helped and Major Smith among the number. However, with the strong hope everybody clings to that some accident would turn up, I rushed off on foot and plunged into the river, which was little better than a roaring torrent. I was being carried down the stream at a tremendous pace, when a loose horse came by me and I got hold of his tail and he landed me safely on the other bank; but I was too tired to stick to him and get on his back. I got up again and rushed on and was several times knocked over by our mounted niggers, who would not get out of my way, then up a tremendous hill, with my wet clothes and boots full of water. About 20 Zulus got over the water and followed us up the hill, but, I am thankful to say, they had not their firearms. Crossing the river, however, the Zulus on the opposite side kept firing at us as we went up the hill and killed several of the niggers round me. I was the only white man to be seen until I came to one who had been kicked by his horse, and could not mount. I put him on his horse and lent him my knife. He said he would catch me a horse. Directly he was up he went clean away. A few Zulus followed us for about three miles across the river, but they had no guns, and I had a revolver, which I kept letting them know. Also the mounted niggers stopped a little and kept firing at them. They did not come in close and finally stopped altogether.

Well, to cut it short, I struggled into Helpmakaar, about twenty miles off, at nightfall, to find a few men who had escaped, about ten or twenty, with others who had been intrenched in a wagon laager. We sat up all night, momentarily expecting attack. The next day, there was a dense fog all day, nearly as bad as night, and we could not make out what had happened to everybody. I was dead beat, of course, but on the 24th I struggled down to Rorke's Drift, my former headquarters, which had been gallantly defended for a whole night against the Zulus by a single company, to find that the General and remainder of the column had arrived all right. I am there now in a laager. We keep a tremendous look-out, and sit up all night expecting attack. It has been raining for the last three hours and did so all night. The men have no coats or anything, all being taken by the Zulus. We shall have another dreadful night of it tonight, I expect, lying on the wet ground. I have just had to drop this for a minute for one of our numerous alarms. I have no time for more now. What are we to do for transport I have not the faintest idea, the Zulus having captured 107 wagons and about 2,000 oxen, mules, horses, etc. However, we must begin to work again to get fresh transport together. I thank God I am alive and well, having a few bruises. God bless you.

P.S. We are expecting pestilence to break out here, to add to our enemies, what with the rain and the air tainted with dead bodies, as there are about 350 Zulus killed here and some are buried in the ruins.

APPENDIX II

30th April, 1915

My dear Field Marshal,

It has been due to my wish to avoid troubling you on a personal matter whilst your mind was so occupied by this disappointing upset to your plans by the retirement of the French, that I have waited to write this letter to you.

You have always given me credit for loyally trying to carry out your plans, whether in S. Africa or elsewhere, and it is a great blow to me to feel that you no longer do so, and I cannot help thinking that when you know the facts, you will not only have your confidence in me restored, but will give me credit for the way I handled what I think you will admit was a by no means easy situation.

On the evening of the 25th at ST. OMER you gave me your views and instructions which were generally as follows:

"You did not want to surrender any ground if it could possibly be avoided, but unless the French regained the ground they had lost, or a great deal of it, you realized that it might become impossible to retain our present very salient position in front of YPRES. It was essential, though, that the situation should be cleared up, and the area quieted down as soon as possible, even if I had to withdraw to a more retired line, so that you might be able to continue your offensive elsewhere. You felt sure I should not take a retired line until all hope of the French recovering ground had vanished. You did not wish me to have many more heavy casualties, as you thought the French had got us into the difficulty and ought to pull us out of it.

"You mentioned that in any combined attack I was to be careful to see that our troops did not get ahead of the French."*

I will not trouble you with more details than I can help to explain my actions.

The disaster to the French occurred on the evening of the 22nd, by dawn on the 23rd a sort of a line of our troops had been formed across the gap made by our Allies' withdrawal. This on the curve they took up from the point where the French originally joined the Canadians to the canal bank south of BOESINGHE was about 8,000 yards. It was late in the morning before I could ascertain where the Germans were and directly I did, realizing the importance of a second counter-attack before the Germans could make strong defences, I placed all the troops I could lay my hands on under General Plumer for the purpose, i.e. my own Army Reserve consisting of a Canadian Brigade and the 13th Brigade, and I told him to use the only other available troops, namely, 7 Battalions, 27th and 28th Divisions, which were Divisional reserves.

Plumer said he could not withdraw all the latter from their proper role, but I told him he must and I made him happy later on by saying you had given me the use of the Northumbrian Division, which would be up in time to provide reserves for elsewhere.

It naturally took time to collect these troops and organize this attack, but by 4 p.m. he was able to move forward on both sides of the YPRES-PILCKEM road and took the front line of German trenches, but the French, who were to have moved forward in co-operation, did not budge.

I will not enter into the story of the next few days, but suffice it to say I was personally in close touch with the French, frequently seeing General Putz and urging him to more vigorous offensive, and on the morning of the 27th I at last came to the conclusion that any chance of the French wresting back lost ground was very remote indeed.

Accordingly, I wrote to Robertson a statement of the situation for your information.

I have gathered from Robertson that the view you took of my letter was that I had no confidence in being able to carry

---

* This last instruction was also conveyed to me written at 10 a.m. on 26th from CGS as follows: "Attack same time as French. Secretly keep in mind not to attack before them."

out my plans, and that you had come to the conclusion through one unfortunate phrase which appears to have given a totally different impression to what was intended.

The phrase reads:

"I intend to-night if nothing special happens to reorganize the new front and to withdraw superfluous troops west of YPRES."

The new front I referred to was the one our advanced troops were fighting on when I wrote, where the units were rather mixed. By 'superfluous troops' I referred chiefly to exhausted units. I had, as a matter of fact, too many troops east of YPRES, except for weighty offence and as units were getting exhausted and I had arranged to co-operate with the French in a fresh attack that afternoon (the 27th) I knew they would be more exhausted still, and that rest in the fire-swept area east of YPRES being impossible, the only thing to do was to withdraw them west.

The attack was to be made by the weakened Lahore Division next to the French, with the 10th Brigade on their right, Plumer's Corps Reserve of four battalions supporting the former, and the 13th and Northumberland Brigades the latter.

On ST. JULIEN itself, and to the east of it, I did not think it advisable to ADVANCE to the attack, for until the ground had been gained towards the line PILCKEM-FORTUIN an advance on that front would merely accentuate the salient and entail loss without any advantage.

Robertson told me that your interpretation of the phrase was that I was already starting that night, thinning out my advanced troops with a view to retirement as in a rearguard action. Directly he pointed this out to me, I saw that such a meaning could perfectly well be understood from it, but I can assure you that nothing was further from my mind than any thought of retirement, and this is borne out by a sentence a few lines previous in that same letter, which reads:

"I think it right to put these views before the Chief, but make it clear that although I am preparing for the worst I do not think we have arrived at the time when it is necessary to adopt these measures."

With regard to pessimism I cannot detect any in that letter with regard to OUR troops. I see I talk of "heavy fighting with fairly satisfactory results and very heavy losses to the enemy."

The letter, however, is full of justifiable pessimism regarding the chances of the French gaining ground.

Remember—you had impressed on me that unless they gained sufficient ground I must be prepared to relinquish some of ours, and there they were, the 5th morning after the disaster, frittering away their troops in small futile attacks, in which they had certainly never gained a yard, and from the orders for their fresh attack that afternoon I was convinced that nothing further would result that day.

With regard to there being any doubt in my mind as to my ability to carry out my plans, I submit that my letter showed that I was prepared for any eventuality and it was to set your mind at rest that I entered into particulars.

Except from the impressions you got from my badly-expressed letter to Robertson that I was actually commencing to retire, I submit you were generally in accord with what I did.

For instance—the use of the cavalry to watch in case the Germans broke through north of the French. Directly I heard you were sending the cavalry, I asked that a Division might be sent there and when you put the Corps under my orders I at once requested Byng to take that as his principal role, and when the French said it was unnecessary I persuaded Putz it was necessary, and to get my way placed Byng under Putz for the purpose until such time as sufficient French reinforcements arrived to safeguard that flank. I subsequently received a note from Robertson that you thought the cavalry should be employed there.

Then, with regard to my plan in case of retirement, I gather if such becomes necessary, Plumer is adopting my plan more or less, and that you have approved of it and so it can only have been that wretchedly-expressed phrase which gave you the impression that I was actually off and which decided you to take no risks.

In a war such as this, there is no room for taking risks, but I trust now I have explained matters, you will send for me and tell me that so far from deserving blame I did not handle the situation too badly after all.

Yours sincerely,

(Sd.) H. L. SMITH-DORRIEN

1st May, 1915.

My dear Field Marshal,

There is nothing in the least urgent in these papers but will you as an old friend of many years find five minutes in the next day or two to read them through. The telegram removing me from the command of the operations round YPRES was sent "in clear" to Advanced 2nd Army at HAZEBROUCK, so many in the 2nd Army are aware that you are not satisfied with their Commander and I owe it to my Army to explain matters with a view to regaining your confidence.

I have put it in writing as I thought it would take less of your time to read my explanation, than if I gave it personally.

Yours sincerely,
(Sd.) H. L. SMITH-DORRIEN.

BIBLIOGRAPHY

GENERAL:

Memoirs of Forty-Eight Years Service. Gen. Sir H. L. Smith-Dorrien, John Murray, 1925.
Smith-Dorrien. Brigadier-General C. Ballard, Constable, 1931.
The Scilly Isles. C. C. Vyvyan, Robert Hale, 1954.
The Education of an Army. Jay Luvaas, Cassell, 1965.
The Kaiser. Virginia Cowles, Collins, 1963.
The Weapons of the British Soldier. Col. H. C. B. Rogers, Seeley Service, 1960.
Military History. Sir John Fortescue, Cambridge University Press, 1914.
The Royal George. Giles St Aubin, Constable, 1963.
The Development of the British Army 1900–1914. Colonel J. K. Dunlop, Methuen, 1938.
Following the Drum. Sir John Fortescue, Blackwoods, 1931.

THE ZULU WAR:

Zulu Battle Piece—Isandhlwana. Sir Reginald Coupland, Collins, 1948.
The Last Zulu King—Cetewayo. C. R. Binns, Longmans, 1963.
The Washing of the Spears. D. R. Morris, Jonathan Cape. 1964.
The Empress Eugenie. Harold Kurtz, Hamish Hamilton, 1964.

EGYPT, 1882:

From Midshipman to Field Marshal. Sir Evelyn Wood, Methuen, 1906.

Winnowed Memories. Sir Evelyn Wood, VC, Cassell, 1917.
All Sir Garnet. Joseph Lehmann, Jonathan Cape, 1964.
Memoirs of Lord Grenfell. Hodder-Stoughton, 1921.
Queens Regulations, 1886.

INDIA, 1888 *et seq.*

The Romance of The Indian Frontier. Sir George Macmun, Jonathan Cape, 1939.
Frontiers and Wars. Sir W. S. Churchill, Cassell, 1966.
Forty-One Years in India. F.-M. Lord Roberts, VC, etc., Richard Bentley, 1897.
Small Wars of The Empire. Blackwoods, 1933.

THE SUDAN CAMPAIGN:

The River War. W. S. Churchill, Eyre & Spottiswoode, 1899.
Send a Gunboat. Preston & Mayo, Longmans Green, 1967.
The Life and Letters of Sir David Beatty. Rear Admiral W. S. Chalmers, Hodder & Stoughton, 1951.
Toll for the Brave. John Montgomery, Max Parrish, 1963.
Kitchener. Sir Philip Magnus, John Murray, 1958.
Fire and Sword in the Sudan. Rudolf Slatin, Edward Arnold, 1896.

THE SOUTH AFRICAN WAR:

The Official History of the War in South Africa. Major General Sir F. Maurice, Hurst & Blackett, 1906.
'The Times' History of The War in South Africa. L. S. Amery, Samson Low, 1900.
The German Official Account of the South African War. John Murray, 1904.
Rhodes. J. G. Lockhart & C. M. Woodhouse, Hodder & Stoughton, 1963.
The Life of Lord Roberts. David James, Hollis & Carter, 1954.
Jan Christiaan Smuts by his son. Cassell, 1952.
The Three Years War. C. R. De Wet, Constable, 1902.
Bullers Campaigns. E. B. Knox, R. Brimley Johnson, 1902.
Bullers Campaigns. Julian Symonds, The Cresset Press, 1963.
The Story of The 9th Division. Maj.-Gen. Colvile, Constable, 1901.
Kekewich in Kimberley. O'Meara, Medici Society, 1926.

On the Heels of De Wet. "The Intelligence Officer" (Lionel James) Blackwoods, 1902.
War Impressions. Mortimer Mempes, Charles Black, 1901.
The Life of Sir Arthur Conan Doyle. John Dickson Carr, John Murray, 1949.
Thoughts and Adventures. Sir Arthur Conan Doyle, Hodder & Stoughton, 1924.
Ian Hamilton's March. W. S. Churchill, Cassell, 1900.
Ian Hamilton by his nephew. Cassell, 1968.
Mafeking—A Victorian Legend. Brian Gardiner, Cassell, 1966.
Goodbye, Dolly Gray. Rayne Kruger, Cassell, 1959.
Infantry Drill, 1896. HMSO, 1896.
With General French and the Cavalry in South Africa. C. S. Goldman, MacMillan, 1902.

THE GREAT WAR:

The Official History of The Great War. Brig. J. E. Edmonds, Vol. I, 1926.
August 1914. Barbara Tuchman, Constable, 1962.
Britain and The War. General Huguet, Cassell, 1928.
Liaison 1914. Maj.-Gen. Sir Edward Spears, Cassell, 1931.
Richard Burdon Haldane (autobiography), Hodder & Stoughton, 1929.
The Tragedy of Lord Kitchener. Lord Esher, John Murray, 1921.
The Vanished Army. Tim Carew, William Kimber, 1964.
The Retreat from Mons. Major A. Corbett-Smith, Cassell, 1917.
The First Seven Divisions. E. W. Hamilton, Hurst & Blackett, 1916.
Forty Days in 1914. Maj.-Gen. Sir F. Maurice, Constable, 1919.
F. M. Earl Haig. Brig-Gen. J. Charteris, Cassell, 1929.
Douglas Haig. John Terraine, Cassell, 1963.
Plumer of Messines. Gen. Sir Charles Harington, John Murray, 1935.
Allenby. Brian Gardner, Cassell, 1965.
Great Contemporaries. W. S. Churchill, Odhams Press, 1947.
Soldier True (Sir William Robertson), Victor Bonham Carter, Frederick Muller, 1963.
Soldiering On. Gen. Sir Hubert Gough, Arthur Barker, 1954.

The Lost Dictator (Sir Henry Wilson) Bernard Ash, Cassell, 1968.
M.I.5. John Bullock, Arthur Barker, 1963.
1914. F. M. Viscount French, Constable, 1919.
Following The Drum. Sir John Fortescue, Blackwoods, 1931.
British Museum Add. Mss. 52776 & 52777.
The First World War. Capt. Cyril Falls, Longmans, 1960.
Sir John French by his son. Cassell, 1931.
The Royal Corps of Signals. Maj.-Gen. R. F. H. Nalder, Royal Signals Institution, 1958.
The Memoirs of Marshal Joffre. Vol I. Geoffrey Bles, 1932.

LATER:

Gibraltar. The Keystone. J. D. Stewart, John Murray, 1967.

INDEX

Abu Klea, 92, 96.
Aisne River, 208, 212, 228-9.
Albert I, H.M. King, 154.
Aldershot, 93, 128.
Aldworth, Colonel, 63.
Alexandra, H.M. Queen, 133.
Alexandria, 20, 22.
Alexandrie (S.A.), 78.
Allenby, F.M. Viscount, 89, 119, 157, 171, 185, 186, 189, 190, 191, 208, 211.
Ali-Wad-Helu, Emir, 34, 40.
Amade, General Paul d', 167, 179, 190, 202.
America Siding (S.A.), 83.
Ansell, Colonel, 190.
Apthorp, Colonel 'Kitty', 26.
Arabi, Ahmed, 20.
Arnold-Forster, H. O., 115, 118.
Asquith, Rt. Hon. H. H., 157, 246, 264.
Athlone, 13.
Audencourt, 194.
Azrak, Emir Osman, 33, 40.

Bailly, 213.
Baker, Col. Valentine, 23, 72.
Balfour, Rt. Hon. A. J., 118, 120.
Balin, Herr, 148.
Ballard, Brig. Gen., 256.
Bareilly, 27.
Bartlett, Ashmead, 114.
Bavai, 179, 181.
Bazaine, Marshal A., 179, 276.
Beatty, Admiral-of-the-Fleet, Earl, 36.
Becke, Major A. F., 199.

Belfast (S.A.), 88.
Belgium, 150, 151.
Belgrade, 149.
Belin, General, 209.
Benedek, General, 149.
Berchtold, Count, 148.
Berthelot, General, 155, 209.
Bertry, 183, 192.
Bethlehem (S.A.), 76.
Bethune, 237.
Bethmann-Hollweg, 152.
Biarritz, 279.
Bikaner, 104.
Binche, 171.
Bismarck, Prince, 148.
Bloemfontein, 54, 75.
Blue Cross, 268.
Boesman's Kop, 67.
Boileau, Colonel, 178.
Bonar Law, 264.
Botha, General Louis, 79, 87, 89, 266.
Botha, Philip, 75.
Brandwater Basin, 83.
Brabazon, Colonel, 72.
Brabant's Colonial Horse, 54, 77.
Briastre, 187.
Bridges, General Sir Tom, 204.
Broadwood, General, 34, 35, 67, 68.
Brodrick, Rt. Hon. St. J., 110, 118.
Bromhead, Captain Gonville, 14.
Buffalo River, 14, 16.
Buller, General Sir Redvers, V.C., 46, 75, 76, 86, 91, 92, 94, 106, 114.
Bullock, Colonel, 88.
Bulow, General von, 175.
Burns, John, 118.
Byng, F.M. Viscount, 108.

297

Caledon River, 83.
Cambrai, 190, 194.
Cambon, Paul, 143, 150.
Cambridge, F.M. H.R.H. The Duke of, 101.
Campbell, General Sir Colin, 119, 217.
Campbell-Bannerman, Rt. Hon. Sir. Henry, 115.
Canterbury, 93.
Cape Town, 13, 266.
Capper, Maj.-Gen. Sir Thomas, 29, 37, 235.
Carey, Lieut., 18.
Castlenau, General de, 155.
Caudry, 187, 194.
Cecil, Lord Edward, 43.
Cetewayo, 14.
Chamberlain, Sir Neville, 96.
Charasia, 95.
Charleroi, 173.
Chelmsford, Lord, 13, 14.
Chemin des Dames, 229, 233.
Chetwode, F.M. Lord, 171.
Chitral, 27.
Chotek, Countess Sophie, 148.
Churchill, Lady Randolph, 13.
Churchill, Sir Winston, 33, 103, 147, 152, 232.
C.I.V., 53.
Clarendon, Earl of, 151.
Clements, Maj.-Gen., 87.
Cody, Mr., 135.
Coghill, Lieut., 16.
Colenso, 47.
Colesberg, 54.
Coleman, Frederic, 270.
Colvile, Maj.-Gen. Sir Henry, 47, 48, 59, 63, 64, 67, 69, 70, 71, 191.
Compiegne, 206, 211, 275.
Corbett-Smith, Major, 256.
Coulommiers, 221, 226.
Cork, 12.
Cowan, Lieut. Sir Walter, 44, 283.
Crichton, Capt. M. M., 196.
Cronge, General Piet, 55, 56, 58, 60, 64, 65.
Curzon, Marquess, 101, 102.

Dalmanutha, 88.
Dammartin, 213.
Dargai, 96.
Davis, Jefferson, 118.
Deal Castle, 145.
De Kiel's Drift, 55.

Delagoa Bay, 74, 86.
Dewetsdorp, 75.
De L'Isle, General Sir B., 178, 208.
Diamond Hill, 110.
Dinard, 279.
Dingaan, 76.
Disraeli, Benjamin, 13.
Doornkop, 110.
Douglas, General Sir Charles, 117, 145, 157.
Doyle, Sir Arthur Conan, 66, 73.
Dublin, 13.
Dundee (S.A.), 17.
Durban, 14, 46.
D'Urbal, General, 235.
Duruy, Colonel, 212.
Du Toit, Commandant, 58.

Early, Gen. Jubal, 82.
East Africa, 265.
Edwards, Brig.-Gen. Sir J. E., 281.
Edward VII, H.M. King, 138.
Elandslaagte, 93, 97.
Elgin Committee, 107, 114.
Elkington, Colonel, 204.
Elles, Maj.-Gen., 102.
Ellison, Maj.-Gen., 117.
Esher Committee, 114.
Esnes, 188, 192.
Eugene, Prince, 169.
Eugenie, H.M. Empress, 18, 135, 275.
Ewart, General Sir Spencer, 117, 141.

Fabeck, General von, 241.
Falkenhayn, General von, 233.
Fashoda, 42 *et seq.*
Fergusson, General Sir Charles, 29, 172, 192, 238, 283.
Ferreira, Commandant, 58, 64, 65.
Fisher, Admiral-of-the-Fleet Lord, 118, 140, 147.
Foch, Marshal, 142, 221, 225, 275.
Forestier-Walker, Maj.-Gen. Sir George, 173, 176, 189, 237, 245.
Fortescue, Sir John, 12, 113, 274, 283.
Frameries, 170, 175.
Franchet D'Esperey, Marshal, 159, 167, 209, 220, 221, 223, 225.
Franz Ferdinand, Archduke, 148.
Frazer, Lovat, 114, 270, 271.

French, F.M. Sir John D. P., 24, 54-60, 64, 88, 91, 93, 97, 106, 114, 128, 132, 157, 158, 164, 168, 173, 175-9, 183, 192, 204, 207, 209-14, 218, 221, 224, 246, 259, 262, 275, 279, 283.
Froneman, Commandant, 83.
Fugitive's Drift, 16.

Gallieni, General, 155, 221, 222.
Gaselee, General, 134.
Gatacre, General Sir W., 46, 70, 76, 87.
Geddes, Colonel, 251.
George V, H.M. King, 104, 112, 153.
George, Rt. Hon. David Lloyd, 78, 113, 118.
Gibraltar, 20, 273, 278.
Gilbert, Captain W. S., 108.
Ginniss, attack on, 24.
Girouard, Sir Percy, 74.
Gladstone, Rt. Hon. W. E., 113.
Gleichen, Count (General Sir Edward Gleichen), 72.
Givenchy, 241.
Givet, 156, 159, 167.
Givry, 169.
Gordon, General Sir Charles, 23, 113.
Gort, F.M. Viscount, 281.
Gochen, Sir Edward, 152.
Gough, General Sir Hubert, 26, 148, 173, 208, 273, 277.
Graham, Colonel Lord Malise, 260.
Grandmaison, Colonel, 155.
Grand Morin, 221, 226.
Grant, General U.S., 74, 283.
Grenfell, F.M. Sir Francis, 23, 45, 85.
Grey, Sir Edward, 139, 140, 150, 152.
Grierson, General Sir James, 130, 140, 141, 143, 157, 159.
Grobler, Commandant Piet, 75.
Gronau, General von, 200.
Guest, Captain F. E., 246.

Haig, F.M. Earl, 57, 93, 104, 116, 127, 157, 165, 175, 177, 180, 208, 211, 213, 240, 283.
Haking, Brig.-Gen. R., 175.
Haldane of Sloan, Viscount, 111, 115, 116, 118, 120, 127.

Ham, 206, 207.
Hamilton, Maj.-Gen. H. H., 61, 170, 172, 176, 189, 190, 236.
Hamilton, General Sir Ian, 73, 78, 79, 85, 91, 95, 108, 111, 114, 123, 157.
Hamer, Commissary, 17.
Hamley, General Sir E. B. 25, 134.
Hannay, Colonel, (MI), 60, 62.
Harnham Cliff, 144.
Harrismith, 83.
Haucourt, 187, 193.
Hausen, General von, 225.
Hazebrouck, 244.
Heilbron (S.A.), 88.
Helpmakaar, 17.
Helvetia (S.A.), 87.
Henderson, Colonel, 53, 106.
Hicks, Colonel, 24.
Hickman, Major, 38.
Hodson, Herbert (   ), 100.
Hollebeke, 234.
Hooge, 234.
Hood, Lieut., R.M.L.I., 53.
Horne, Colonel, 57, 130.
Hospital Bag Fund, 267.
Hotzendorf, Marshal Conrad von, 149.
Houtnek, 78.
Huguet, General, 140-43, 149, 158, 168, 174, 203, 213, 218, 222, 262, 275.
Hunter, General Sir A., 75, 83.
Hunter-Weston, General Sir Aylmer, 188, 197, 206.
Huy, 168.

Isandhlwana, 14-16.
Israel's Poort, 73.
Inchy, 194.

Jackson, Colonel A., 42.
Johannesburg, 74.
Jellicoe, Admiral of the Fleet Lord, 183.
Joffre, Marshal J. C., 114, 155, 159, 179, 208, 219, 220, 221, 223, 275, 278.

Kabul, 95.
Kandahar, 95.
Kekewich, Colonel, 57.

Kell, Colonel (M 15), 147.
Kelly-Kenny, General Sir T., 47, 59, 61, 108, 114.
Kemmel Hill, 244.
Kentish, Captain R. J., 129.
Keogh, Sir Alfred, 124, 267.
Keppel, Captain, 198.
Kerrerri Ridge, 30.
Khalifa, the, 29 et seq.
Khartoum, 30 et seq.
Kimberley, 48, 54, 57.
Kipling, Rudyard, 50.
Kirbekan, 96.
Kitchener, F.M. Earl, 24, 29, 40-2, 43, 59, 62, 64, 71, 83, 87, 91, 101, 104, 113, 157, 158, 160, 215, 216-18, 261, 269.
Kluck, General Alexander von, 146, 172, 185, 192, 214.
Koedesberg, 48.
Komati Poort, 74, 86.
Korn Spruit, 67.
Kroonstadt, 79.
Kruger, President Paul, 86.

Ladybrand, 76.
Ladysmith, 17, 46, 54, 75.
La Fere, 203.
Lahore Division, 241, 251.
Landrecies, 179.
Lanrezac, General, 154, 159, 166-8, 175, 190, 192, 202, 220, 224.
La Rochelle, 213.
Leeuwsspruit, 83.
Lee, Robert E. 205.
Le Cateau, 156, 164, 179, 181, 182, 183, 185-7, 192, 193.
Le Mans, 213.
Lewis, Colonel, 37-40.
Lichnowsky, Prince, 152.
Liege, 159, 167, 173.
Ligny, 188.
Limoges, 167.
Lincoln, President A., 118.
Lindley, 71, 83.
Lobell, Colonel van, 106.
Lockhart, General Sir W., 101.
Longman, Lieut., 198.
Lucknow, 22.
Luxemburg, 150, 151, 167.
Lyttleton, General, 37, 98.

McCracken, Brig.-Gen., 185, 196.

MacDonald, Maj.-Gen. Hector, 29, 36, 40, 47, 55, 60, 67, 83, 95.
MacDonogh, General, 158, 174.
McInnes, Colonel, 203.
Macready, General CFN, 208, 259.
Machadodorp, 87, 88.
McKenzie, General, 238.
Mafeking, 80.
Magersfontein, 49, 55.
Maguire, Mr., 134.
Mahon, General B., 80.
Majuba, 95.
Malplaquet, 169.
Malta, 44-5.
Mantes, 212.
Manchuria, 97.
Mandalay, 96.
Mangin, General, 44.
Marchand, Commandant, 42-4.
Marlborough, 1st Duke of, 50, 82, 88, 169, 172, 232.
Marlborough, 8th Duke of, 13.
Marne River, 224, 225.
Maroilles, 179.
Martyr, Colonel (M.I.) 67.
Marwitz, General von der, 190, 196, 200, 222.
Massey, General 'Redan', 95.
Maubeuge, 156, 179, 182.
Mauchberg, 87.
Maunoury, General, 203, 221, 223, 225.
Maurice, General Sir Frederick, 111.
Maurice, Maj.-Gen. F., 189.
Maurois, 187, 194.
Maxwell, Colonel, 36, 41.
Meaux, 213.
Melun, 222, 223.
Melville, Lieut., 16.
Mempes, Mortimer, 82.
Menin, 234, 251.
Menin Gate, 235.
Messines, 242, 268.
Methuen, General Lord, 46.
Michel, General, 155.
Midleton, Earl of, see Broderick, St. J.
Militia, 107 et seq, 120.
Milne, F.M. Sir George, 245.
Modder River, 48.
Moltke (the elder), 91, 97, 117.
Moltke (the younger), 153, 156, 233.
Monro, General Sir C., 145.
Mons, 169, 170, 172.
Mons-Condé Canal, 165.
Montgomery, Lieut. B. L., 187.

Moore, General Sir John, 224, 282.
Morland, General Sir T., 238.
Morley, Rt. Hon. John, 118.
Mormal, Forest of, 179, 184, 190.
Motienling, 98.
Mottistone, Lord, see Seeley, J. E. B.
Murdoch, R., 114.
Murray, General Sir Archibald, 158, 165, 176, 180, 185, 211, 222, 246, 248.

Namur, 159, 167, 173.
Nancy, 225.
Napoleon, III, 206.
Napoleon, Prince Imperial, 18.
Nery, 222.
Neuve Chapelle, 241.
Newbolt, Sir Henry, 220.
Nicholson, John, 100.
Nicholson, F.M. Sir William, 26, 97, 98, 116, 269.
Nimy, 173.
Nogi, General, 97, 131.
Norfolk, Duke of, 114, 120.
Nouvelles, 177.
Noyon, 192, 202, 204.

Obourg, 173, 174.
Officers' Training Corps, 126.
O'Hara (El Ingles), 12.
Oissel, Colonel Hely d', 166, 168.
Olivier, Commandant, 75.
Olifant's Nek, 85.
Omdurman, 30 et seq.
Orange River, 48, 54.
Otter, Colonel (Royal Canadians), 61, 74.

Paardeberg, 60, 74, 76.
Palmer, General Sir A. Power, 101, 102, 132.
Penn-Symons, General, 27, 96.
Pétain, Marshal, 148, 209.
Pietretief, 89.
Pilckem, 253.
Plumer, F.M. Viscount, 160, 244.
Poincaré, President Raynard, 153.
Poissy, 212.
Pole-Carew, Maj.-Gen., 73, 75.
Pommeroeul, 169.
Poplar Grove, 76.
Porter, Brig.-Gen., 69.
Potsdam, 105.
Pretoria, 74, 81, 82.
Prinsloo, Martinus, 83.

Pulteney, General Sir W., 208, 226.
Punch, Mr., 65.
Putz, General, 252.

Quetta, 104, 105.
Quiévrain, 171.

Rawlinson, F.M. Viscount, 29, 73, 130-3, 234.
Reddersberg, 70, 80.
Reitz, Denys, 95.
Rendsberg, 54.
Rennenkampf, General, 156.
Reumont, 187, 193.
Rey, de la, Commandant, 77.
Repington, Col. C. à Court, 139, 141, 143, 149, 270.
Rhenoster Spruit, 82.
Rhodes, C. J., 57.
Richtofen, General von, 213, 214.
Ridley, Colonel, (M.I.), 60.
Riet River, 56.
Robb, Maj.-Gen., 208.
Roberts, F.M. Earl, V.C., 47, 49, 53, 59, 65, 69, 74, 76, 79, 82, 85, 87, 95, 157.
Robertson, F.M. Sir William ('Wully'), 112, 131, 132, 207, 222, 248, 260, 261, 262.
Rommel, General Erwin, 77.
Roodewal, 82.
Roon, General Albrecht von, 91.
Ron'arch, Admiral, 221.
Rorke's Drift, 14.
Rouen, 156.
Roux, Commandant, 83.
Rouvier, M., 141.
Ruffy, General, 167.
Ryan, Colonel, 180.
Rundle, General Sir Leslie, 44, 73, 263.

St. Ghislain, 172.
St. Quentin, 183, 186, 202, 204, 205.
Salisbury, 144.
Samsonov, General, 206.
Sannah's Post, 67, 78, 80.
Sarrail, General, 220.
Sars-la-Bruyère, 169, 170.
Schlieffen, Graf von, 141.
Schneider, Miss O. (Lady Smith-Dorrien), 104, 128, 133, 135, 144, 249, 267, 268, 274, 275, 276, 282.

Schreiner, Olive, 104.
Scott, Admiral Sir Percy, 52.
Scudamore-Smith, Miss, 167.
Seeley, Colonel J. E. B., 145.
Seydlitz, General, 114.
Seymour, Admiral Sir B., 21.
Shaw, Brig.-Gen. F. C., 176.
Sievier, Robert, 128.
Slabber's Nek, 83.
Slatin, Rudolf, 29.
Smith, Augustus, 11.
Smith, Major, R. A., 16.
Smith, Field Cornet, 82.
Smith-Dorrien, Colonel, R.A. (Sir Horace's father), 11.
Smith-Dorrien, Mrs. M. A. (Sir Horace's mother), 11, 136.
Smith-Dorrien, Admiral H. T., Royal Navy, 22.
Smith-Dorrien, T. A., 11.
Smith-Dorrien, Edward, 48, 245.
Smith-Dorrien, General Sir Horace Lockwood, Birth at Berkhampstead, Harrow R.M.C., Commissioned 95th Foot (2nd Sherwood Forresters), 11-12; Zulu War, recommended for Victoria Cross, 13-19; Egypt 1882, promoted Captain, 22-22; meets General Gordon, 23; D.S.O. for services at Ginniss, 24; Staff College (1887), 25; Staff appointment in India and Tirah Valley campaign, 26-8; Commands XIII Sudanese at Omdurman, 29-40; at Fashoda, 41-45; Brevet Colonel, 44; to Durban in command of Sherwood Foresters, 46; local Maj.-Gen. commanding 19th Brigade, 47; South Africa War, 55-90; Adjutant-General India, 89; Curzon's hatred of Army, 102. Inaugurates Staff College, Quetta, 105; G.O.C. Aldershot Command, 112; reforms there, 128, 133; declines South Africa Command, 136-59; chosen by Kitchener to succeed Grierson in command of 2nd Corps B.E.F., 160; relations with Sir John French, 160, 165; situation of 2nd Corps at Mons, 170; Battle of Mons, 173-8; orders from G.H.Q. to continue retreat, 183; visit from Allenby confirmed this impossible. Decides to fight at Le Cateau, 189-91; Battle of Le Cateau, 192-200; 'Dump Kits' order, 206; quarrel with French, 206; Battle of the Marne, 225; the Aisne, 229-33; 2nd Corps moves to Ypres Salient, 234; French accuses him of despondency. First Battle of Ypres, 239-44; Given command of Second Army, 244; relations with French deteriorate, 247-50; Resigns command, 258; Accepts Command in East Africa but prevented by severe illness, 265; unemployed at home. Newspaper articles appear regarding Le Cateau, 269-72. Governor of Gibraltar, 274-8; settles at Dinard, 279; Lord French's book *1914*, attacks 2nd corps. Army Council refuses leave to publish reply, 279-80; death in car accident, 283.
Smith-Dorien, Grenfell (son of Sir Horace), 104, 133, 275.
Smith-Dorien, Peter (son of Sir Horace), 104, 133, 274.
Smith-Dorien, David (son of Sir Horace), 104, 274, 279.
Smuts, F.M. J. C., 87, 90, 266.
Snow, General Sir D'Oyly, 181, 187, 271.
Sobieski, John, 114, 148.
Solesmes, 179, 181, 185, 193.
Sordet, General, 179, 181, 190, 200, 202.
Spears, Maj.-Gen. Sir E. L., 148, 168, 173, 174, 212, 213, 223, 248.
Spitzkop, 86.
Spragge, Colonel, 71.
Stamfordham, Lord, 112.
Starkey, Captain Barber, 198.
Steyn, President, 75, 80.
Stephenson, Colonel (M.I.), 60, 62.
Stephens, Colonel (R.A.), 198.
Stewart, Sir Donald, 104
Stopford, Maj.-Gen., 106.
Stomberg Junction, 49, 76.
Stuart-Wortley, Major, 30.
Sullivan, Sir Arthur, 108.
Surgham, Jebel, 32 *et seq.*
Swaziland, 88.

Tel-el-Kebir, 22, 92.
Territorial Force, 120, 156.
Tewfik, Khedive, 20.
Thaba'nchu, 73, 78.

Thebus, 48.
Theron, Danie, 83.
Thoba Mountain, 78.
Tirah Valley, 27, 96.
Tournai, 179.
Townsend, Maj.-Gen. Charles, 30.
Troisvilles, 192.
Tucker, Maj.-Gen., 47, 75.
Tyrwhitt-Drake, Mrs., 136.

Ulundi, 19.
Umballa, 27.

Vailly, 232.
Valabregue, General, 179.
Vaughan, Maj.-Gen. John, 173, 189.
Vauxbuin, 213.
Venizel, 213.
Vendutie Drift, 60.
Verdun, 225.
Vereeniging, 90.
Verner, Sir Willoughby, 275.
Viesly, 187.
Viljoen, Commandant Ben, 87.
Villiers, de, Commandant, 77, 79.
Vincent, Colonel, M.P., 109.
Volunteers, 109 et seq.

Wales, H.R.H. George, Prince of, see King George V.
Walmer Castle, 91.
Walters spade, 50.
Warnelle Ravine, 196.
Waterval Drift, 56, 57.
Wauchope, Maj.-Gen. A., 37.
Wavell, Maj.-Gen. A., 56.
Wellington, 1st Duke of, 91, 146, 278.

Weilbach, Commandant, 77.
Wepener, 75.
Wet, de Piet, 75, 84.
Wet, de, General Christiaan, 55, 56, 62, 64-8, 70, 71, 75, 78, 81, 82, 84, 85, 263.
Whigham, General Sir Robert, 29, 37, 283.
White, Gen. Sir George, V.C., 46, 76, 95, 96.
Wilhelm II, H.I.M. Kaiser, 118, 174, 175, 177, 183.
Wilhelm, Crown Prince, 225.
Willcocks, General Sir James, 241.
Wilkinson, Spencer, 111, 120, 140.
Wilson, Brig.-Gen., 188, 193.
Wilson, F.M. Sir Henry, 108, 123, 132, 133, 140, 141, 146, 147, 157, 165, 168, 192, 207, 208, 222, 248.
Wing, Maj.-Gen., 231.
Winter Hoek, 55.
Wolseley, F.M. Viscount, 21, 91.
Wonderfontein, 88.
Wood, F.M. Sir Evelyn, V.C., 18, 21, 22, 23, 92, 135.
Woodville, Caton, 114.
Wright, Professor, 66.
Wurtemburg, Duke Albrecht of, 225.

Yakub, Emir, 34-40.
Yate, Major, 198.
Ypres, 235, 240, 241, 251, 255.
Ypres, Earl of, see French Sir John.

Zand River, 78.
Zulus, 14-19.

Soc
DA
68.32
S5
S6